Second Edition

PHILOSOPHICAL FOUNDATIONS OF ADULT EDUCATION

Second Edition

PHILOSOPHICAL FOUNDATIONS OF ADULT EDUCATION

by

John L. Elias

and

Sharan B. Merriam

with Foreword by

Malcolm S. Knowles

KRIEGER PUBLISHING COMPANY
MALABAR, FLORIDA
1995

Original Edition 1980
Second Edition 1995

Printed and Published by
KRIEGER PUBLISHING COMPANY
KRIEGER DRIVE
MALABAR, FLORIDA 32950

Elias, John L., 1993–
    Philosophical foundations of adult education / by John L. Elias
and Sharan Merrriam : with foreword by Malcolm S. Knowles, — 2nd ed.
    p.   cm.
    Includes bibliographical references and index.
    ISBN 0-89464-918-3 (acid-free paper)
    1. Adult education—Philosophy.   I. Merriam, Sharan B.
II. Title   94-33663
    LC5291.E46   1995   CIP
                        10 9 8 7 6 5 4 3 2

CONTENTS

PREFACE TO THE SECOND EDITION

Over 15 years ago we completed the manuscript for *Philosophical Foundations of Adult Education.* We have been surprised and pleased by the continued interest in this book and the apparent value it has had for both academicians and practitioners in adult and continuing education. Readers have told us that *Philosophical Foundations* has given them the means to think about their practice, to reflect upon the origins and reasons behind the way they do things, and to bring some clarity and purpose to their everyday activities. Readers have also commented that with greater familiarity with philosophical material the somewhat artificial division of philosophies into schools or systems begins to break down. This shortcoming we recognized in the introduction to the first edition. But we also stand by our original thinking that this approach is helpful especially to new adult educators who appreciate some systematic organization of a rather diverse and widespread body of information. It is with this understanding in mind that we updated *Philosophical Foundations* with a bibliographic essay.

The enduring quality of *Philosophical Foundations* has much to do with the historical grounding of each of the six schools of philosophy we chose for organizing the original book—liberal, progressive, humanist, behaviorist, radical, and analytical. The origins and basic principles that characterize each of these approaches have remained unchanged. The bibliographic essay is thus organized by the original six schools of philosophy. For each school we present a discussion of developments of the past 15 years, referencing major contributors and issues from the larger arena of education, as well as focusing on work published by adult educators.

We are aware that at least three areas of philosophical writing that have had an impact on adult education since 1980—phenomenology, critical theory, and feminist theory—could be considered as separate schools or systems of philosophy. However, we felt that each of these also shared much with two schools in our preexisting framework. Thus, we have included a discussion of phenomenology under humanistic adult education, and critical theory and feminist theory under radical adult education.

We hope you as readers of the second edition will find it as helpful to your understanding of the field and to your practice of adult education as the first edition has apparently been. We encourage you to consult any of the numerous works we review for an even greater appreciation of the philosophical orientations that underlie our field of adult education. We would like to point out that while we have added this preface at the front and the bibliographic essay at the end, the original chapters remain unchanged. We were thus unable to incorporate nonsexist language into the original chapters; for that we apologize to our readers.

Finally, we would like to acknowledge two people who have assisted us in our updating efforts. Nancy Carmack and Vivian Mott, Ph.D. candidates at the University of Georgia, helped in the location of sources, in writing sections on phenomenology, critical theory, and feminist theory, and in copy editing the manuscript. Thank you both!

FOREWORD

During the entire time I have been in the field of adult education, which is almost a half a century, I have heard it being criticized for not having a philosophical foundation. I can remember reading many articles in the *Journal of Adult Education* published by the American Association for Adult Education between 1929 and 1948, and in its successors, *Adult Education* and *Adult Leadership*, published by the Adult Education Association of the U.S.A., flailing the adult education movement in this country for not having a unified sense of purpose, a cohesive set of aims, a coherent framework of beliefs and, therefore, a significant impact on society. I remember attending numerous conferences sponsored by the two national organizations and by the Center for the Study of Liberal Education (between 1951 and 1961) in which eloquent speakers left me with an even stronger sense of guilt for not doing something about bringing some intellectual order into our field.

I remember feeling uneasy about this kind of pressure being exerted on me, and for several reasons. For one thing, I thought that the pressurizers were not perceiving the nature and function of philosophy in the same way, and so they were not helping me think through how I might get help from it or contribute to it. For another thing, I resisted the idea of uniformity—of our having (or even aspiring) to agree on a single set of aims, purposes, and beliefs. I attributed much of my own personal growth to having been exposed to a variety of systems of thought, often conflicting systems of thought, which forced me to think more critically and deeply about the issues they were examining. Finally, I didn't see how I could do much about the situation, since philosophy was not my discipline.

Our field has attracted a few professional philosophers into its fold, and I read their writings avidly and talked with several of them eagerly to try to get help in clarifying the meaning of philosophy for our field. Eduard Lindeman, John Walker Powel,

Kenneth Benne, Paul Bergevin, and Jerrold Apps were my philosophical consultants. I got many useful ideas from them, and can see a good deal of influence from them on my way of thinking about adult education. But I didn't get the one thing I wanted most, a broad overview of the philosophical foundations of our field, since each of them was a proponent for a particular philosophical position.

So when Robert Krieger called me to inform me that John Elias and Sharan Merriam had written a book on the philosophical foundations of adult education, and would like me to write a foreword, my hopes soared. I waited for the manuscript to arrive with a mixture of anticipation and wariness. Would it be the usual punishing flailing of our field's philosophical backwardness? Would it exude ideological passion for one position? Would it be written in dull, strange (to me) philosophical jargon?

I started reading the page proofs the minute they arrived, and had a hard time putting them down to tend to other things that had to be done. It is clear, exciting reading. It presents the nature and function of philosophy as a discipline—but also as a tool for the practitioner to use—in a way that I found completely understandable. It describes the various philosophical approaches appreciatively and respectfully, but with a careful analysis of their strengths and weaknesses as applied to our field. It makes it legitimate for me to take ideas from each approach that make sense to me and to incorporate them into a personal philosophical position. It made me feel more comfortable with philosophy and more secure about philosophizing.

I hope it will do the same for you.

Malcolm S. Knowles
Professor Emeritus
North Carolina State University

CHAPTER I

INTRODUCTION

PHILOSOPHY OF
ADULT EDUCATION

While the roots of philosophical inquiry can be traced back to ancient Greek philosophy, it has only been in the past two centuries that education has received rigorous treatment by philosophers. In the 19th century, Kant and Hegel directed attention to philosophic issues involved in education. Philosophy of education as a separate discipline of study developed, however, in the 20th century largely as a result of the writings of John Dewey. His philosophical approach to education provided a critique of traditional education and gave rise to the development of various approaches to a philosophy of education.

It has been traditional to discuss educational philosophy in terms of various schools or systems such as realism, idealism, and pragmatism. More recent approaches include reconstructionism, existentialism, behaviorism, and analytic philosophy. The problems of classifying different philosophers into schools have long been recognized. Nevertheless, the systematization of the discipline continues and schools of thought develop because similiarities and affinities do exist among theorists. Also, the practical necessity of introducing new students to the field warrants some shorthand method of presenting the educational thought and philosophy of numerous theorists.

Although education in general has been systematically analyzed from philosophical perspectives, there has been no extended attempt to explore the various philosophical approaches to adult education. Articles and monographs have appeared in which adult educators have taken positions on questions of a philosophical nature or have espoused personal philosophies of adult education. Merriam (1977), in a review of the philosophic work in adult

1

education, concluded that much still needed to be done in terms of disciplined philosophical analysis of major issues and problems in adult education. What also needs to be done, and what this book does, is to systematically analyze the positions of a number of influential adult educators. This effort will add clarity to the enterprise of adult education and enable adult educators to become more consciously purposeful in their educational efforts.

Philosophy

For many people the connotation of the word philosophy is negative. It is thought to be a vague and abstruse subject. It implies a body of abstractions which has little bearing on real life. It deals with theories that are considered abstract, vague, general, and perhaps useless. Most cultures tend to place greater value on the practical and the useful. What is philosophical or theoretical is viewed by many as irrelevant to human life and its problems.

Some of these objections to philosophy have justification. Philosophers have at times succumbed to the temptation to think too much about thinking and too little about life's problems. Philosophers also have often made too many mental distinctions that have little correspondence with reality. They have often been more interested in the tools of thought – logic and reasoning – than they have been with the objects of thought – the understanding and changing of human existence.

Though negative in its connotation to some, philosophy can be a fruitful and exciting human endeavor. Philosophy etymologically signifies the love of wisdom. For the ancient Greeks, who coined the word, it was the search for what is truly real in a world of appearances. It was the quest for the beautiful in a garish world. It was separating the good from the evil. It was searching for unity among the fragmented elements of life.

Philosophers deal in theories, a word of Greek origin suggesting a beholding, a spectacle. For the ancient Greeks to theorize was to look at, to behold, to have a vision. For Aristotle, theorizing was the highest power of the human mind. It was the activity of persons that made them most like the gods. The theories of the philosophers are attempts to understand the world and everything in it in an active and constructive manner. Scheffler indicates this explanatory function of philosophy when he explains that:

> philosophy seeks general perspective, on a rational basis. Historically, those called "philosophers" have concerned themselves with such subjects as the nature of the physical universe, mind, causality, life, virtue, law, good, history, and community. . . . The philosopher wants to see things in perspective and he wants to see things sharp and clear. He strives for a maximum of vision and a minimum of mystery. [Scheffler, 1960, p. 5]

While theory and philosophy are intellectual efforts, they are more fundamentally efforts of feeling and imagination. The philosopher first wonders at a work of nature or a human work, then follows the effort to imaginatively understand it in some meaningful manner. Before he analyzed knowledge philosophically, Plato first pictured it as the ascent from the dark shadows of the cave to the world brightly illuminated by the sun.

Philosophy is interested in the general principles of any phenomenon, object, process, or subject matter. Principles are general if they apply to a large number of phenomena. The philosopher of education considers the general principles that apply to the educational process. Principles are the foundations or basic structures by which phenomena, events, and realities are understood. The philosopher of education is interested in certain general principles that are involved in education: aims and objectives of education, curriculum or subject matter, general methodological principles, analysis of the teaching-learning process, and the relationship between education and the society in which education takes place.

Philosophy as a discipline has traditionally been divided into a number of subdisciplines. Logic is concerned with the rules for correct reasoning and thinking and the various forms of argumentation. Epistemology investigates the rules for determining whether we have arrived at truth, opinion, or falsehood. Metaphysics searches out the most general principles of reality. Many contemporary emphases in philosophy question the possibility of metaphysical knowledge, i.e., knowledge about reality in the most general sense that is applicable to all reality. An important branch of philosophy is ethics, an investigation of rules or principles of moral reasoning and conduct.

Philosophy, like most disciplines, has many divergent viewpoints or systems. Competing schools of thought have developed approaches to basic questions about man, knowledge, ethical good, reality, and other issues. Many philosophical answers to questions about basic issues are often contradictory. In the examination of philosophies of adult education, some of these differences between conflicting schools of thought will become apparent. Though some philosophers of education approach these distinctions in an eclectic manner and attempt to resolve them, it appears preferable to allow these differences to surface for they often involve fundamental issues that cannot be submerged.

Philosophy and Action: Theory and Practice

A major dispute among philosophers concerns the relationship between philosophy and action or between theory and practice. Some see philosophy and action as mutually exclusive concepts belonging to different realms. Others view one's practice and action as being logically derived from one's theory and philosophy. Still another approach is to attempt to synthesize the two into one view. There appears to be an emerging consensus among philosophers that both are necessary in the life of men and women. Theory without practice leads to an empty idealism, and action without philosophical reflection leads to a mindless activism. In the early 1970's, Charles Silberman lamented the lack of philosophical interest in educational practice:

> If teachers make a botch of it, and an uncomfortably large number do, it is because it never simply occurs to more than a handful to ask *why* they are doing what they are doing, to think seriously or deeply about the purposes or consequences of education.
> This mindlessness—the failure to think seriously about educational purpose, the reluctance to question established practice—is not the monopoly of the public school; it is diffused remarkably throughout the entire educational system, and indeed the entire society.
> If mindlessness is the central problem, the solution must lie in infusing the various educating instructions with purpose, more important, with thought about purpose, and about the ways in which technique, content, and organization fulfill or alter purpose. [Silberman, 1970, p. 11]

Silberman's indictment of mindlessness in the educational enterprise is a valid one. Many current debates in educational policy and practice would be conducted more rationally if some clarity were achieved on basic philosophic differences. The point of philosophical inquiry is to clarify issues so that decisions can be made on proper grounds. Arguments over means in education are fundamentally reduced to differences in ends or purposes to be achieved. For example, the current debate over "back to the basics" revolves around what types of persons we expect our educational system to produce. And the arguments between the proponents of liberal arts and vocational education stem from basic philosophic issues related to the purposes of a free society.

There is a sense in which it can be said that anyone who acts is guided by some theory or some philosophy. We act for reasons, good and/or bad, and generally have some understanding of what we are doing, why we are doing it in the way we do, and the consequences of our actions. What we have here in the ordinary course of human activity is common sense which, though related to philosophy, can be distinguished from it. Ancient philosophers raised questions about common opinions and practices and demonstrated that the common sense view of things could not always be trusted.

Philosophy is a more reflective and systematic activity than common sense. Philosophy raises questions about what we do and why we do it, and goes beyond individual cases and phenomena to treat questions of a general nature. When considering the interrelationship of philosophy and activity, it is clear that philosophy inspires one's activities, and gives direction to practice. The power of philosophy lies in its ability to enable individuals to better understand and appreciate the activities of everyday life.

Adult Education

While the concept of education has been analyzed extensively in recent philosophical literature, the concept of adult education has not been so clearly delineated. Even an attempt to define adult education presupposes philosophical questions. As K. H. Lawson states:

> Such a wide range of agencies engaging in such diverse fields of activity raises questions about the criteria which entitle us

to bring them together in one portmanteau category. What is it about them which makes them examples of 'the education of adults.' [Lawson, 1975, p. 14]

Adulthood is another term which further confounds the defining of adult education. Age, psychological maturity, and social roles appear to be the essential variables in such a definition, but the priority of these variables often depends upon the context of the discussion. There is also the important question of whether adult education is to be distinguished from education in general. The argument between Malcolm Knowles and Cyril Houle over whether there is a distinct art and science of teaching adults to be termed andragogy is an important definitional problem.

Contrary to what many philosophers have stated, the problem of definition is not answered at the beginning of philosophical inquiry. Arriving at accurate and clear definitions is at the heart of philosophical inquiry and is often reached in the later parts of investigation. Also the conclusions and definitions for one philosopher often provide the starting points and problems for the next philosopher. Thus it will be demonstrated in the course of this work that there are major differences among the various schools of thought on these important issues of definition. Liberal adult education will view education differently than progressive educators. Radical adult educators will find inadequate a definition of adult education that does not include raising peoples' consciousness of the social and political contradictions in their culture.

Though definitions related to adult education are crucial philosophical issues, there are many other important questions that will surface in the treatment of various philosophers in this book. Adult educators, for example, differ in their handling of needs and interests of adult learners. As a result, there also exists among these educators contrasting approaches to content and method in instructional settings. Likewise, there is a varying emphasis upon the social and individual aims of education.

Since a great deal of adult education takes place in institutions and organizations, analysis of these is important. Again in this area we can expect to find significant differences. Radicals take one view towards institutions; behaviorists take another; still another view is held by those who favor a personal growth or humanistic model of adult education.

Related to the question of the place of institutions in adult education is the issue of social change. All philosophies include social and political dimensions. The adult educator looks beyond the institution within which he or she works and sees larger social goals. In recent years, adult educators have been seriously challenged in this area by the revolutionary pedagogy of Paulo Freire. Whether one agrees with Freire's approach or not, one must concede that he has raised the social relevance issue rather dramatically.

Any number of issues in adult education might also be considered in terms of the increasingly important concept of adult development. Extensive psycho-social research is being done in this area and, it is clear that the concept of adult development and its connection with education need to be explored. Most philosophical schools have not taken sufficient notice of this research and its implications for analyzing and presenting normative statements in adult education. An attempt has been made in this text to incorporate adult development into appropriate philosophical paradigms.

Finally, the curriculum of adult education usually takes the form of programs. The development of programs can be improved if there are clear philosophical discussions of the various elements of programs and their logical and psychological development. The development of program objectives and the distinction among the various types of programs is basically a philosophic inquiry, though certainly not detached from pragmatic considerations. The debate in adult education over the appropriateness of using behavioral objectives is fundamentally a philosophic difference among various theorists of adult education. Philosophic issues are also involved in the logical design of curricula and the evaluation of program outcomes.

Thus, within this text, issues salient to the field of adult education are explored from the perspective of various philosophical schools of thought. Needs and interests of adult learners, method and content in adult education, adult development, curriculum,

institutions, and the questions of social change are better understood and appreciated by the adult educator when analyzed in
light of differing philosophical approaches.

Philosophy of Adult Education for Adult Educators

As for all educators, the appealing adult education courses are
usually those concerned with program planning and methods of
instruction. The educator is generally more interested in skills
than in principles, in means than in ends, in details than in the
whole picture. The philosophy of adult education does not equip a
person with knowledge about *what* to teach, *how* to teach, or how
to organize a program. It is more concerned with the *why* of education and with the logical analysis of the various elements of the
educational process. Philosophies of education are interpretative
theories, not applicatory theories. This study supplies the educator
with ideas and attitudes that one teaches *with*, not to students.

While emphasizing the theoretical nature of the discipline of
philosophy of education, it is our purpose to show how each
philosophy expresses itself in a concrete type of program. The
close relationship between theory and practice that we have
already described in this chapter will become manifest in the
investigations of educational programs. The encounter group as
an educational experience, for example, expresses the philosophy
of humanism. The Great Books Program captures the philosophical emphasis of liberal adult education. And Freire's literary
program for adults shows clearly the radical adult educator's
interest in social change.

In our presentation and analysis of these concrete educational
programs that embody an educational philosophy, we believe
that we add a significant dimension to the study of philosophy of
education, particularly the philosophy of adult education. The
philosophy will be clarified by the practice; the practice will be
illuminated by the theory. In this way the particular value of
educational philosophy will be enhanced for the adult educator.
In doing this it is not our purpose to give the reader a philosophy
of education, though this may happen. It is rather to encourage
adult educators to ask important questions about the whole educational process. The value of a study of educational philosophy,

we believe, is more in the importance of the questions asked than in the certitude of the answers given.

In writing this book it is our belief that it is the knowledge of philosophy of education that distinguishes a professional educator from a para-professional or a beginning teacher. True professionals know not only what they are to do, but are also aware of the principles and the reasons for so acting. Experience alone does not make a person a professional adult educator. The person must also be able to reflect deeply upon the experience he or she has had. In this manner the professional adult educator is more like the person of art who creatively combines experience and theory in the activity of teaching.

Overview of Philosophies of Adult Education

Philosophies of adult education, like all thought systems, originate within particular socio-cultural contexts. Though individual philosophers are responsible for developing a philosophical approach to adult education, the development of their thought is greatly influenced by the particular problems, issues, and challenges that existed in their culture. To understand adequately a philosophy of education then, it must be analyzed within the context in which it originated and developed. This does not mean that the particular theory cannot be adapted to other cultural situations with some degree of success. But there are problems with these attempts at application in differing cultural contexts, as will become clear in the course of this book.

Liberal Adult Education has its historical origins in the philosophical theories of the classical Greek philosophers, Socrates, Plato, and Aristotle. This liberal education tradition was adopted and adapted in the Christian schools in early, medieval, and modern times. It became the predominant educational theory in the Western world and is still a strong force in educational thought today. The emphasis in this tradition is upon liberal learning, organized knowledge, and the development of the intellectual powers of the mind. Contemporary philosophers who espouse this viewpoint include Mortimer Adler, Robert Hutchins, Jacques Maritain, and Mark Van Doren. An educational program that is inspired by this orientation is the Great Books Program.

Progressive Adult Education has its historical origins in the progressive movement in politics, social change, and education. This approach to educational philosophy emphasizes such concepts as the relationship between education and society, experience-centered education, vocational education, and democratic education. Leading progressive educators include James, Dewey, and William Kilpatrick. Philosophers of adult education with the progressive orientation include Lindeman, Bergevin, Benne and Blakely. Various educational practices in adult education are inspired by this philosophical orientation: Americanization education, English as a Second Language, and the Community School movement. Since the beginnings of the Adult Education movement in this country were in the progressive period of history, this movement has been greatly influenced by this particular philosophy of education.

Behaviorist Adult Education has its roots in modern philosophic and scientific movements. Behaviorism in adult education emphasizes such concepts as control, behavioral modification, learning through reinforcement, and management by objectives. Early behaviorists include Thorndike, Pavlov and Watson. The most prominent behaviorist philosophy is that of B. F. Skinner. His ideas have permeated many disciplines and fields of study and practice. Various adult education practices are inspired by this philosophic view: programmed learning, behavioral objectives, and competency-based teacher education.

Humanistic Adult Education is related in its development to existential philosophy and humanistic psychology. The key concepts that are emphasized in this approach are freedom and autonomy, trust, active cooperation and participation, and self-directed learning. Philosophical roots are found in such writers as Heidegger, Sartre, Camus, Marcqel, and Buber. The Third Force psychologists have been equally responsible for the development of this particular approach to education: Maslow, Rogers, May, Allport, and Fromm. Among adult educators Malcolm Knowles is prominent in espousing this orientation in his needs-meeting and student-centered andragogical approach to adult learning. This philosophic orientation also permeates the research efforts of Allen Tough and his associates. There are numerous adult education practices connected with this philosophical approach: group dynamics, group relations training, group processes, sensitivity workshops, encounter groups, and self-directed learning.

Radical Adult Education has its historical roots in the various radical movements that have emerged in the past three centuries: anarchism, Marxism, socialism and left-wing Freudianism. The radicals in education propose education as a force for achieving radical social change. Education in this viewpoint is closely connected with social, political, and economic understanding of cultures, and with the development of methods to bring people to an awareness of responsible social action. Radical educators include George Counts and Theodore Brameld in the 1930's. This philosophic orientation was revived during the 1960's in the efforts of Jonathan Kozol, John Holt, Paul Goodman and Ivan Illich. A prominent adult educator of this philosophic position is Paulo Freire who has proposed radical conscientization as the true function of education among the oppressed. Educational practices inspired by this philosophy include the Freedom Schools in the South during the 1960's, free schools, and Freire's radical approach to adult literacy education.

Analytic Philosophy of Adult Education is the most recent approach to the philosophy of adult education. Its historic origins lie in such movements as logical positivism, scientific positivism, and British analytic philosophy. This approach to philosophy emphasizes the need for clarifying concepts, arguments, and policy statements used in adult education. Philosophers of education in this tradition include Israel Scheffler, R. S. Peters, and Thomas Green. Lawson and Patterson are two British philosophers of adult education who have pioneered this approach to the philosophy of adult education. This philosophical approach finds its practical application not in any particular educational practice or program, but rather in its attempt to establish a sound philosophic basis for the field of adult education.

Summary

Adult education has advanced to the point where a more systematic investigation of philosophies of adult education is both possible and necessary. Philosophies of adult education are concerned with the most general principles of the educational process. All philosophies of adult education grapple with the important problem of the relationship between theory and practice. Philosophic issues in the field of adult education include the definition of adult education, the place of the needs and interests of adults, contrasting views of method and content, the concept and relevance of adult development, programs and objectives, the teaching-learning process, and education for social change. The value of a knowledge of philosophic theories of adult education for adult educators lies in attitudes and understandings that the educator will bring to his task. Finally, all philosophies of adult education originate and develop in a particular historical and sociocultural context. Six philosophies are analyzed in this book: liberal adult education, progressive adult education, behaviorist adult education, humanistic adult education, radical adult education, and analytic philosophy of adult education.

REFERENCES

Lawson, K. H. *Philosophical Concepts and Values in Adult Education.* Nottingham, England: Barnes and Humby, Ltd., 1975.

Merriam, Sharan, "Philosophical Perspectives on Adult Education: A Critical Review of the Literature," *Adult Education*, 1977, 27, 195-208.

Scheffler, Israel. *The Language of Education.* Boston: Allyn and Bacon, 1960.

Silberman, Charles. *Crisis in the Classroom.* New York: Random House, 1970.

CHAPTER II

LIBERAL ADULT EDUCATION

The oldest and most enduring philosophy of education in the Western world is the liberal arts approach to education. This philosophy goes by a number of names such as classical humanism, perennialism, rational humanism, liberal education, and general education. A religious version called neo-Thomism was named after the Catholic philosopher and theologian Thomas Aquinas. Although over a long period of time various approaches have developed, all versions emphasize liberal learning, organized knowledge, and the development of the intellectual powers of the mind.

The earliest efforts in adult education in the Western world developed under the influence of this philosophy of education. From the Academy of Plato to the Great Books programs in contemporary America, the tradition of liberal learning among adults has persisted as an important thrust in the learning that adults engage in individually or in groups. Though liberal arts education is closely associated in the minds of many with high school and college education, it will be seen how this theory has in the past manifested itself in the education of adults, and still persists in various forms in contemporary society.

This chapter will first present the historical development of the philosophy of liberal adult education. An analysis of this philosophy will clarify its various components: a particular view of man and society, a theory of reality, a view of knowledge, a theory of values, and an attitude toward social change. Then the educational principles of this theory will be developed, concentrating upon the aims and objectives of education, the proposed curriculum of education, and the view of the teaching-learning process. In keeping with the plan of the book to show how theories

13

manifest themselves in practice, programs that embody this philosophy in adult education will be examined. Finally, an assessment will be made of the status of this view of education at present and the role it might play in the movement toward lifelong education.

Historical Development of Liberal Adult Education

The origins of the liberal education tradition can be seen in the contrast between the educational theory of the Sophists and the classical approaches of Socrates, Plato, and Aristotle. The goal of the Sophists was to train statesmen and politicians through a utilitarian education. These men were the first professional teachers. They proposed to produce the trained orator and politician. The means to this end were in the study of rhetoric, skill in argument, and a knowledge of the audience that was to be persuaded. Education was thus seen as the acquiring of skills and the storing of facts. Skills were to be in public speaking, legal case pleading, and cultural information. Educators in this tradition include Protagoras, Isocrates, and Hippias in Greece. In Rome, this tradition was continued by Cicero and Quintilian (Broudy and Palmer, 1964, pp. 15-30).

This utilitarian approach to education was strongly opposed by the three men who stand at the beginning of the liberal arts tradition, Socrates, Plato, and Aristotle. These men proposed an intellectual education for statesmen and politicians. The aim of education was to produce the good and virtuous man. In the case of Plato, the highest ideal was the philosopher-king who knew what was true and of value and who could govern according to these principles. The aim of education was to be met through a rigorous intellectual training that began with a knowledge of grammar and rhetoric, extended to the natural sciences, history and literature, and was completed with a study of logic and philosophy.

Socrates' chief contribution to this tradition was in his method of exhorting his disciples to question all assumptions and to become knowledgeable, for the person who knows the truth will also do the truth. Plato's contribution lay in his portrayal of the process of learning as an individual's radical encounter with a truth that existed outside of himself. Learning was the painful process of freeing the mind of prejudices and accepting the responsibility to help others to achieve this goal. Aristotle brought to this tradition a careful investigation of the components of a moral education through the formation of habits, and an intellectual education through the development of practical wisdom (art, prudence) and theoretical wisdom (knowledge of science, intelligence, and wisdom). For Aristotle, wisdom, the contemplation of truths, constituted the ideal life; it equaled happiness. It was an activity that was performed as an end in itself and not as a means to another end. This happiness was to be found in leisure and not in the conduct of the affairs of life. Man was capable of the life of contemplation because he had an element of the divine within him (Marrou, 1956, ch. 6).

Before passing on to other contributions to this liberal tradition, it must be pointed out that this educational theory is conditioned by the culture in which it originated. Socrates, Plato, and Aristotle proposed an education for the leadership class of a society in which work was done by a servile class. Their negativism toward vocational and utilitarian education was criticized by Dewey for its class bias (1914, pp. 252-254). Throughout its history, liberal education has suffered from this elitist bias. Contemporary liberal philosophers of education have still been accused of it, despite efforts to shed these ancient prejudices.

The liberal arts tradition in education became enriched through its encounter with the early and medieval Christian church. The meeting of Christian faith, espousing the Bible as the revelation of God, with classical Greek learning produced a struggle between competing views of life and education—the one being based upon religious faith and the other upon rational inquiry. It was the particular achievement of Augustine of Hippo to accomplish the union of ascetical and moral education in the religious tradition with the intellectual education of the Greeks. Augustine accepted liberal learning as an important component in Christian education. In his view, though, the ultimate aim of education was to prepare man for life after death through an understanding and practice of the Christian virtues of faith, hope, charity, and humility. This aim could be advanced through the development of the intellect in classical learning (Marrou, 1954, ch. 9).

With Augustine's endorsement, the classical liberal arts tradition became an essential part of the curriculum of all schools of Christendom. The curriculum of these schools included the trivium (grammar, rhetoric, and logic) and the quadrivium (arithmetic, geometry, music and astronomy). Though for many these liberal arts were taught in a mechanical fashion and subordinated to the aims of providing skills for reading and understanding the Bible, there is ample evidence that a love of learning was nicely balanced with a love of God (LeClerq, 1961).

The intellectual high point of medieval Christian thought is found in the theological and philosophical system of Thomas Aquinas. Though in his educational theory Thomas did not rely heavily on the classical literature (excepting his strong dependence on the philosophical writings of Aristotle), he did carry on and extend the decidedly intellectual approach to education found in the classical liberal tradition. Following Aristotle, Thomas argued that:

> happiness is what men strive for. It is achieved in the attainment of complete truth by the intelligence and supreme good by the will. Only in the possession of the truth and the good does man attain his full liberation. Nothing less gives him complete and permanent satisfaction. [Beck, 1964, p. 117]

Intellectual contemplation was for Thomas the highest good because it enabled a person to gain a measure of knowledge about his destiny and his nature.

The wedding of Christian thought and liberal learning is a phenomenon that has continued to this day. Later in this chapter we will examine the religious or neo-Thomist version of liberal education that influences education both in Christian schools and in adult religious education.

The liberal arts tradition was an essential component of the classical humanistic philosophy of education which prevailed in the West from 1450 to 1850. The aim of this educational theory, as found in the writings of such humanists as Erasmus, Thomas More, and Ignatius Loyola, was to produce the gentleman scholar, the cultured gentleman, fit for the demands of citizenship in the new world of commerce and the worldly court. This ideal also included training for service in the church. The Greek literary classics and the Latin poets and orators became the new masters, replacing the dominance and authority of Aristotle. Though education in religion for a life hereafter was stressed, an equally strong emphasis was placed on human life and nature. Renaissance humanism advocated a sensitivity to nature, all living things, and a deep appreciation of the arts and culture, including painting, poetry, literature, and architecture. In the educational theory of Ignatius was laid the foundation for Jesuit education which greatly influenced both secular and religious education in Europe and America.

Liberal arts education also found expression in some important Enlightenment thinkers who wrote on educational theory. Though romantics like Rousseau and empiricists like Bacon were not favorably disposed to liberal learning, such rationalist Enlightenment figures as Kant and Hegel saw great value in the study of liberal subjects. Their goals of developing the rational powers of the human person through mathematics and philosophy corresponded to the intellectual emphasis of the liberal tradition.

The educational theories of the humanists and rationalists contained a number of ambivalences which have constantly plagued liberal education. The study of the liberal arts may be conducted in a formalistic, non-liberating manner. This was often an education for an elitist class, the leaders and the aristocracy. With the development of the natural sciences, the weaknesses of this liberal learning became clearer to such thinkers and writers as Bacon, Spencer, and John Dewey. Modern efforts to promote liberal learning have taken into consideration scientific and technological knowledge that has accumulated since 1850.

Developments in European thought and practice, especially in England and France, influenced educational theory and practice in the Colonial period of United States history. It was in the Colonial colleges that the liberal tradition of learning was transplanted to this country. The curriculum at Harvard at this time included the traditional trivium and quadrivium, the three philosophies (natural, moral, and mental), the ancient languages (biblical and classical), and the fine arts and religion (Cremin, 1970, p. 102). All colleges imitated Harvard in providing a strong emphasis on liberal studies for the education of the future leaders for the church and the country. Those who were being prepared for the professions were expected to devote themselves to this form of learning.

The Colonial period of education witnessed a struggle between two philosophies of education. There were those involved in collegiate education who were committed to an elitist-classical education and others like Franklin who pressed for a more utilitarian, democratic-vocational preparation (Bridenbaugh and Bridenbaugh, 1962, ch. 2). The argument has characterized American educational history at all levels. The advocates of liberal education have stressed the training of minds over the demands of preparing people for jobs and careers.

It is interesting to note, however, that even such a utilitarian as Franklin could appreciate the value of a liberal education for adults. This "founder of American adult education" established the Junto, which in his words:

> required that every member in his turn produce one or more queries on any point of morals, politics or natural philosophy to be discussed by the company, and once in three months produce and read an essay of his own writing on any subject he pleased. [Franklin, 1964 edition, pp. 116-117]

This particular club had ups and downs in its history and finally merged with the American Philosophical Society (Merriam, 1979). Franklin's interest in liberal adult learning also led to his encouraging the founding of libraries (Knowles, 1977, p. 8).

In the period after the Revolution a debate ensued in the new nation over the relationship between education and government. In the 1790's, the American Philosophical Society sponsored an essay contest on "a system of Liberal Education and Literary Instruction adapted to the genius of government" (Perkinson, 1977, p. 7). Jefferson emerged as the most outstanding figure in this national debate. Jefferson stressed the importance of an educated citizenry in order to prevent the abuses of government. He argued for the widespread diffusion of knowledge, the importance of self education, and the need for education to prepare leaders for the new nation. He wanted the leaders of the country to be trained through a liberal education. In the Preamble of the Bill for the More General Diffusion of Knowledge he recommended that

> those whom nature hath endowed with genius and virtue should be rendered by a liberal education worthy to receive, and able to guard the sacred deposit of the rights and liberties

of their fellow citizens, and that they should be called to that charge regardless of wealth, birth, or other accidental condition or circumstance. [Jefferson, quoted in Cremin, 1970, p. 439]

Benjamin Rush joined Jefferson in describing the liberal or learned education in a republic. Languages, including the classical languages, were to be learned. He also advocated a study of religion, eloquence, history, chronology, commerce, chemistry, and other liberal subjects. Rush was also concerned with the education of women in the new republic. They too should be instructed in the principles of liberty, government, and patriotism (Rush, 1786, pp. 119-121).

In the period before the Civil War, colleges and academies fostered the liberal emphasis in education. Several adult education enterprises also promoted liberal education. Institutes such as Lowell in Boston and Cooper Union in New York sponsored lectures and courses in philosophy, natural history, and the arts. The popularity of lyceums further reflected adults' interest in learning. Begun by Josiah Holbrook in 1826, the Lyceum Movement, using a national network of study groups, brought liberal learning to many American towns and cities. The movement introduced countless adults to the liberal ideas of Emerson, Thoreau, Holmes, and others (Knowles, 1977, pp. 16-17). Strong between 1820 and 1840, the Lyceum Movement eventually died out after directing its efforts toward the promotion of public schools.

With the emergence of science and the growth of the new industrial society after the Civil War, the debate between the defenders of liberal education and the advocates of a more progressive and pragmatic education grew more intense. Secondary education became more vocationally oriented as the curriculum was expanded to include vocational and life-related subjects. At the same time, progressive education began to dominate the national scene.

The most noteworthy movement to emerge at this time was Chautauqua. This program which entailed the careful, systematic, guided reading of books and other materials, mixed a strong religious orientation with liberal education. The movement, founded by John Vincent, was based upon the following assumptions: all of life is educational but the true basis of education is Christian faith; all knowledge becomes sacred by its relationship to God; those who receive no cultural education early in life desire it more avidly later in life; the intellect is to be developed through reading, reflection, and production; the intellectual powers of adults need direction, assistance, and encouragement; teachers could enter the process by direct contact or through correspondence; education could occur in voluntary associations, local circles, contact with resident scholars, lectures, and in summer schools and assemblies (Vincent, 1959, pp. 72-74).

For Vincent, intellectual education could continue throughout one's life. He envisioned education as being mental, social, moral and religious. His plan, in fact, sounds like a precursor to the Great Books Program:

> Let them read the same books, think along the same lines, observe the same sacred days. . . . Let the course of pre-scribed reading be broad and comprehensive; limited in its first general survey of the wide world of knowledge; opening out into special courses, according to the reader's develop-ment, taste, and opportunity. [Vincent, 1959, p. 67]

Church movements such as Chautauqua were not the only forms of adult education developed in the period after the Civil War. In 1898, Thomas Davidson, a Scottish Socialist, established a Bread Winner's College in New York City to bring a knowledge of liberal learning to working men and women. The course of studies involved philosophy, religion, science, literature and economics. Davidson's educational ideal was to combine a strong vocational education with a broad cultural education. His experi-ment floundered after his death (Davidson, 1959, pp. 84-101).

Adult liberal education also developed in this period as part of the extension programs introduced at colleges and universities. In the 1890's university extensions were established at the Univ-ersity of Wisconsin and the University of Chicago. The extension program at Wisconsin included both vocational and liberal educa-tion (Knowles, 1977, p. 48).

A resurgence of interest in the liberal arts tradition after World War I in American education began as a reaction against the pragmatic philosophy of the progressive education movement. From the late 1920's to the present time, literary and philosophic scholars in colleges and universities have called for a redirection of educational efforts toward the liberal tradition. a tradition that had been reduced in influence because of the rise of the teaching of science and other utilitarian subjects.

Pratte (1971, p. 176) has classified the resurgent liberal tradition into two philosophical groups, neo-rationalist and neo-Thomist. so called because it was based on the religious philosophy of man and on education that will foster this development. Major theorists in this group included Robert Hutchins (1936, 1953, 1968), Mortimer Adler (1937, 1940), Gilbert Highet (1950), and Mark Van Doren (1943).

The second wing of the liberal arts tradition was the neo-Thomist so called because it was based on the religious philosophy of Thomas Aquinas. Most members of this wing were Catholic philosophers and educators. The most important work to appear in this tradition was Jacques Maritain's *Education at the Cross-roads* (1943). Other theorists in this area included McGuchen (1942), Beck (1964), and Henle (1965).

The principles expounded by the above philosophers, though they were not expressly concerned with adult education, provided the basis for a philosophy of liberal adult education. A number of books and articles have appeared in the past half century that have treated liberal adult education explicitly. but these have not had the philosophical rigor of the above mentioned theorists. In 1926, for example, Everett Dean Martin argued for the continued education of a liberally educated adult (1926). His view was apparently elitist when he contended that only a few could attain this goal. Martin included members of the working class as possible persons to aspire to this type of education. His lectures were in fact given on Friday nights to working people at the Peoples Institute in New York City where he was a director. Stubblefield's characterization (1979) of Martin's work points out one of the enduring problems with liberal education:

> Martin, in his efforts to ground adult education in liberal education, viewed the popularizing of knowledge with disdain and elevated individual development over social improvement. [p. 5]

Stubblefield goes on to note that the adult liberal tradition has continued in the Great Books Program, study-discussion groups, foreign affairs associations, and other culturally oriented programs.

Beyond the general educational works by Adler, Hutchins, Maritain, and others mentioned previously, little writing since Martin's book in 1926 has appeared that bears directly on liberal adult education. In the 1950's and 1960's, essays on the topic were published by Houle (1955), Houle and Nelson (1956), Freidenburg (1958), and Whipple (1960).

Perhaps the strongest impetus for the study of liberal education of adults in this country came from the Center for the Study of Liberal Education for Adults. The CSLEA was established in 1951 in Chicago and was funded by the Ford Foundation. The Center had three main areas of interest: the improvement of liberal education for adults in university programs, the development of improved methods of teaching and instruction, and support for programs in adult liberal education. Important publications emanated from the CSLEA including the Notes and Essays series which examined purposes and philosophy, Reports on methods and practices in the field, Research Reports, monographs, and journal reprints. With the closing of the CSLEA in 1961, a strong force for the liberal education of adults was lost in the United States (Knowles, 1977, pp. 162-163).

In the 1970's the movement for the liberal education of adults received renewed interest both at the practical level and at the philosophical level. At the level of practice, the increase in adult programs brought an increase in programs for the liberal education of adults. Many of these programs existed at the college level and were programs to reach the non-traditional student. The motivation behind these programs was partly to attract new students to colleges and universities and partly to meet the needs of adults in middle and later years.

At the philosophical level, liberal adult education has received strong philosophical support from the work of two British analytic philosophers of education. Both Lawson (1975) and Paterson (1978) have argued for liberal adult education as the only form of education that can fit the rigid canons of educational activity that are presented in the analytic tradition of philosophy. The views of these philosophers will be examined in a later chapter.

Liberal Education and the Educated Person

The purpose of a liberal education is derived from a particular conception of the human person. No matter what the changes of time and culture have produced, the human person has remained essentially the same throughout the history of the world. In describing this view of human nature, Hutchins wrote:

> A sound philosophy in general suggests that men are rational, moral, and spiritual beings, and that the improvement of men means the fullest development of their rational, moral, and spiritual powers. All men have these powers, and all men should develop them to the fullest extent. . . . [1953, p. 68]

A liberal education is, first of all, a *rational* or *intellectual* education. An intellectual education attempts to lead persons from information to knowledge, to wisdom. Educated persons must have information and know the fundamentals of reading, writing, and computation. They possess basic information about the world in which they live. The mere knowledge of facts, however, does not make one intellectually educated. A person must move to the second phase, knowledge. For the liberal educator, knowledge is the systematic grasp of a subject matter, a discipline, or an area of study. True knowledge also entails the ability to communicate what one knows to others. Knowledge differs from information in that the person who possesses it can go beyond the facts to grasp the principles or assumptions, analyze a situation, and develop ordered synthesis.

Though information and knowledge are necessary for a person to be educated, it is only in the possession of wisdom that one truly becomes educated. Wisdom is of two types—practical, and theoretical or speculative. Practical wisdom refers to the ability to apply information and knowledge to the activities of daily life. It is the wisdom that makes a person a good parent, citizen, and worker. Practical wisdom is characterized by seeing the moderate position among the extremes. This wisdom cannot be directly taught for it demands direct experience. Theoretical wisdom is the contemplation of the deepest principles of a subject matter and the reorganization of the connection and relationship to other areas. Theoretical wisdom is the search for truth about the human situation and the world. It calls for study and reflection and a certain amount of leisure and freedom. It is the result of a life dedicated to learning for the sake of learning. Speculative wisdom is the wisdom of the scientist, the artist, the philosopher, and the poet.

In the liberal arts tradition it is recognized that a certain tension exists between these two types of wisdom. This tension goes back to Plato and Aristotle. Aristotle considered speculative wisdom the highest achievement of man. Plato put great emphasis on this form of wisdom but he also wanted his philosophers to engage in governing. The liberal tradition recognizes that every society must have its persons of practical wisdom and its persons of speculative wisdom. Persons of action and persons of thought are needed. What is distinctive about the liberal tradition is that it sees the training even of the person of action as accomplished through a strong intellectual education. Gray's attempt to resolve this tension between the two wisdoms is clear and succinct:

> The educated man is one who is either practically or theoretically wise. If such a one is not to descend the ladder, he must keep constantly educating and re-educating himself. Education is a search and not a state of being. And though wisdom is inevitably dual in nature, a new necessity is upon us. Though we cannot unite the two kinds of wisdom, they must learn to support and to supplement each other. [Gray, 1968, p. 29]

To the intellectual education that has been proposed, liberal educators add a second form of education, *moral education.* All educators in the liberal tradition have stressed that an intellectual education must form the basis of a moral education. According to Aristotle, the moral virtues in the liberal tradition were prudence, justice, temperance, and fortitude. Plato saw these four as parts of the one virtue of justice. To these virtues Augustine added the Christian virtues of faith, hope, love and humility.

Philosophers of liberal education have consistently held to one important truth in the area of moral education. This education is to be intellectually based, and not a direct education of the will, or an attempt at direct character formation. This intellectual basis for moral education was enunciated strongly in the face of Russian and Nazi Germany efforts at direct character formation which attempted to train wills and educate emotions to correct ways of action. Liberal educators today view with suspicion, efforts of behaviorists to modify behavior through reinforcement and punishment, as well as the efforts of some educators to use affective or emotional strategies to bring about value commitments.

For the liberal arts educator, values come about through a careful and close connection with great philosophy, literature and works of art. The formation of character is both an intellectual and a moral task. Modern proponents of this philosophy decry the way in which the so-called liberal arts subjects are taught in schools and colleges. For Murchland, liberal education should aim to make value issues central to the intellectual life. The ultimate value questions remain essentially unchanged: what is the good life and how are we to attain it? Murchland's program for moral education in a liberal arts perspective has the purpose of leading

> students into a thorough investigation of freedom, into the requirements of a democratic ethics, into what might be called the rituals of a democratic faith. . . . These would include attitudes of sympathy and cooperation, a sense of restraints and limits, a sensitivity to values and discipline, a desire for excellence, a respect for the common good and attention to duties and obligation as well as insistence on rights. [Murchland, 1979, p. 45]

Closely connected to the moral nature of the human person is the third dimension of liberal education, that of *spiritual or religious* education. Not all liberal educators emphasize the religious or spiritual dimension, but, as was mentioned earlier, a strong religious orientation is found in some writings. Maritain (1943) gave the strongest statement of this position when he founded his philosophy in the Greek, Christian, and Jewish view of man:

> Man as an animal endowed with reason, whose supreme dignity is in the intellect; and man as a free individual in personal relation with God, whose supreme righteousness consists in voluntarily obeying the law of God; and man as a sinful and wounded creature called to divine life and to the freedom of grace, whose supreme perfection consists of love. [Maritain, 1943, p. 7]

Consonant with this view of the human person, Maritain and other religious educators see as the highest goal or ideal of education the fostering of a knowledge of God and spiritual realities along with inculcation of Christian principles of life and a Christian view of the world.

In his classic statement of the religious liberal arts position, Maritain argued strenuously against the pragmatic or progressive view of education. Since for him the prime goal of education was the conquest of internal and spiritual freedom to be achieved in the individual person, he considered such goals as problem-solving, social adjustment, and social change to be subsidiary goals of education which should not impede the primary goal. In keeping with this view, Maritain argued that a truly liberal education must include both morality and religion.

The fourth and final broad ideal or aim of the liberal arts tradition, especially since the time of the Renaissance, is the development of the *aesthetic sense* in the human person. Even the ancient philosophers added the appreciation of beauty in nature and in art to the quest for the true, the good, and the holy. In the writings of such literary humanists as Van Doren, this dimension of liberal arts education gets a fuller treatment. For Van Doren, the Greek, Roman, and English literature classics are to be appreciated as is the beauty found in works in the humanities and fine arts. Van Doren contends that the humanities are necessary rather than nice:

> Poetry, story, and speculation are more than pleasant to encounter; they are indispensible if we would know ourselves as men. To live with Herodatus, Euripides, Aristotle, Lucretius, Dante, Shakespeare, Cervantes, Pascal, Swift, Balzac, Dickens, Tolstoy, to take only a few names at random, musicians, painters, sculptors—is to be wiser than experience can make us in those matters that have most closely to do with family, friends, rulers, and whatever gods there be. To live with them is indeed experience of the essential kind, since it takes us beyond the local and the accidental, at the same moment that it lets us know how uniquely valuable a place and a time can be. [Van Doren, 1943, p. 51]

In summary, the educated person possesses the four components of a liberal education: rational or intellectual education which involves wisdom, moral values, a spiritual or religious dimension, and an aesthetic sense.

The Broad Scope of Liberal Education

Liberal education produces a person who is literate in the broadest sense—intellectually, morally, spiritually and aesthetically.

When one reads the programs of study that liberal educators such as Hutchins, Maritain, and Van Doren propose, one is staggered by the amount of reading and study that a person must do in order to be liberally educated. The demands of these educators are broad, and they clearly envisage a life of continued learning or a "learning society," in the terms of Robert Hutchins. With the increase of leisure and the rapidity of change, liberal educators see the necessity of this form of education as even more urgent today. In fact, it is argued that the full scope of liberal education can best be grasped only by adults who have the life experiences and leisure to appreciate the wisdom found in our cultural heritage.

Liberal educators have devoted most of their attention to the content of education. They have been severely critical of the utilitarian and vocational direction that education has taken in this country since the advent of progressive education. Education of the schools should be devoted to developing ability in language and mathematics at the earlier stages. At the secondary stages, literature, languages, science, history, and other liberal studies should be pursued. The ideal college presented by these educators is one that places strongest emphasis on learning the arts of investigation, criticism, and communication through an intimate acquaintance with the Great Books.

A distinctive feature of the liberal arts philosophy of education is its treatment of the role of science in the curriculum. It is clear that philosophy, religion, and the humanities are superior to science at all points. Liberal education emerged as a separate American philosophy of education between the two World Wars when science and technology played (in the liberal educator's mind) a decidedly destructive role. The liberal tradition supplies the values by which science and technology are to be criticized. In the mind of Maritain and Hutchins, if science is taught at universities, it should be taught at special institutes and not viewed as part of liberal or general education (Maritain, 1943; Hutchins, 1936).

More recent expositions of the liberal tradition in education seem to have recognized the place of science in the curriculum. Hutchins (1968) agrees that science and mathematics are essential to the education the world needs, for they are the basis of the technology that has been developed. But the questions about the uses to which science can and should be placed are philosophic questions which demand a broader education than a scientific education can provide (pp. 121-123).

Given the broad nature of the components of the liberal education, the question arises regarding who should receive this type of education. Many liberal educators agree with Hutchins that the democracy in which we live entails that all be permitted to pursue liberal studies, but that "democracy does not require that the higher learning should be open to anybody except those who have the interest and ability that independent intellectual work demands" (Hutchins, 1936, pp. 19-20). In this view, those who would not profit by all the components of a liberal education should receive technical training around the time of adolescence. This view is close to the concept of education that Jefferson proposed. It contends that people should be taught as long as possible in terms of the equal abilities they possess, and that when differences emerge, the highest training, the liberal training, should be offered only for those that intellectually deserve it.

The position of other liberal educators, such as Van Doren, is different. He contends that a liberal education is worthy of every person's study and thus tries to avoid an elitist stance. Exposure to liberal education is demanded for all in a truly democratic society. Society needs all of its citizens to be developed to the limit of their capacities—intellectually, morally, spiritually, and aesthetically. Van Doren's sentiments on this issue are strongly expressed:

> What was once for a few must now be for the many. There is no escape from this—least of all through the sacrifice of quality to quantity. The necessity is not to produce a handful of masters; it is to produce as many masters as possible, even though this be millions. . . . Liberal education in the modern world must aim at the generosity of nature, must work to make the aristocrat, the man of grace, the person, as numerous as fate allows. [Van Doren, 1943, p. 31]

In these words of Van Doren, the sentiments of the Jacksonian democrat are again expressed—that is, the equality principle should be applied as far as it will go in educational policy and practice.

Gilbert Highet (1950) takes a view similar to Van Doren's. The liberal curriculum for him is made up of the classics, religion, politics, art, history, sociology, and the sciences, in addition to reading, writing, and manual arts. Everyone, according to Highet, should have an equal opportunity for such study. No differentiation should be made between rich and poor. Though vocational education is included in his curriculum, the main emphasis is on the classics. In Highet's view, persons must be liberally educated, for all persons in all walks of life are teachers, in their speech, their counsel to friends, and in dealing with others (Highet, 1950, pp. 227-229).

It is clear then that the scope of liberal education is as broad as the scope of human life itself. Central emphasis is to be given to the classics in literature and social and intellectual history. Though a number of liberal educators have conceded that science and manual training might be included in one's education, they do not usually consider these a part of liberal education. The emphasis is upon studies of an intellectual nature, and if the religious point of view is taken, then studies in religion and theology should also to be included.

The Process of Liberal Education

The process of liberal education is oriented toward conceptual and theoretical understanding rather than mere transmission and absorption of factual knowledge or development of technical skill. For Plato, the best way to achieve this theoretical understanding is through the dialectic. In dialogues, one clarifies the real meaning of concepts and can thus build syntheses of knowledge. This dialectic approach was also used among the medieval scholastic educators when they were involved in disputations or debates on important issues.

Another process that liberal arts educators have stressed is intuition or contemplation. Augustine first placed emphasis on this intuitive approach to knowledge. Through inner contemplation of oneself or introspection, one arrives at a knowledge of many things about oneself and others. In many ways, this method is similar to some modern forms of therapy whereby persons come to a knowledge of their present situation by carefully reviewing their past life experiences. This intuitive or introspective process is also followed by religious persons who believe that in such contemplation of self, one arrives at a knowledge of God and higher reality.

The dialectic and intuitive processes of liberal education were supplemented in Renaissance humanism by the contemplation of nature and works of human art. For Comenius, the great Moravian educator of the 16th century, and for modern-day romanticists, the contemplation of nature and beauty brings one to a knowledge of self and of the world in which one lives. In its order, design, prodigality, assimilation of evil elements, and the changes through which it goes, nature holds many lessons for the learner.

An educational process that has been most appealing in the liberal arts tradition is the critical reading and discussion of classical writings. The educational program of the Great Books used in a number of colleges and among adult groups exemplifies this form of education. With experienced leadership, the reading of these books brings one to intellectual understanding and enables a person to relate the great ideas to present experience and problems. One searches for the universal ideas or truths in contemporary writings as well.

Within the processes of liberal education, a prominent place is given to the role of teacher. There are many things, liberal educators feel, that can best be taught directly by the teacher. The lecture method, if well organized and suited to the ability of the students, is recognized as an efficient instructional strategy. Learning through projects, insight, or discovery methods de-emphasize the directive role of the teacher and are not endorsed by liberal educators.

The fundamental process of liberal education is as old as the philosophical position of Aristotle; it is to promote theoretical thinking. It focuses upon the operations of the intellect and attempts to promote the grasp and comprehension of truth. In this perspective, technical skills are of less importance, though they are not to be ignored in education. The liberal educator contends that if the mind is educated, then the person can apply this knowledge to any number of areas. Skills are more easily learned through experience, and, when an intelligently formed mind gains experience, it can acquire the skills that it needs in particular situations.

The contention of the liberal philosopher of education is that liberal learning never becomes obsolete. Since the main thrust of liberal education is the education of the mind to a knowledge of theory, such theoretical knowledge can be applied to many different situations. The person is thus able to bridge gaps between knowns, deal flexibly with the novel situation, and is capable of moving into the unknown.

While the demands of liberal education upon the student are great, the same can be said of the demands upon the teacher. Teachers must be student-scholars of exceptionally wide and lively intellectual interests. Teachers must never assume that they know all they need to know about their subject. Characterized as Socrates was, by their love of wisdom, teachers derive their authority from their wisdom and their command over their subject matter. The ultimate goal of teachers is that students become original or creative. The education of teachers is an education in the liberal arts and not a training in particular skills and techniques. Liberal educators have thus been foremost in their critique of schools of education that take the narrow or competency approach to teacher education.

The Liberal Education of Adults

Most of the theorizing about liberal adult education, in fact, most of the theorizing about liberal education in general, has been concerned with the education of children and youth. Yet it should be clear from our treatment of liberal education that much of what is said has applicability in the education of adults. In fact, a persuasive case can be made that liberal education will play an increasingly important role. Arnold Toynbee looked to the affluent society of the future in which part-time adult education could be offered "to every man and woman at every stage of grown-up life" (Toynbee quoted in Gross, 1963, p. 135). In the Danish high schools for adults he saw an institution that might be a foretaste of the future. For Toynbee, the paradox of liberal education was that one gets it when one can least take advantage of it:

> The student has been surfeited with book learning at a stage
> of life at which he has not yet acquired the experience to
> take advantage of it, and he has been starved for book
> learning at a later stage in which, if he had been given the
> opportunity, he could have made much more of it in the
> light of his growing experience. [Toynbee quoted in Gross,
> 1963, pp. 134-135]

The increase in adult education at all levels in this country gives
some indication that Toynbee's view of the future might still be
realized.

Liberal education of adults is for Van Doren the highest level of
education, following elementary, secondary schools, and college.
Liberal education should be a constant study for responsible persons. The life of the mind takes on more meaning as we progress
in years. Van Doren realized that this ideal was far from realized
in his time, though he did recognize that a large part of adult
education was liberal education:

> Whatever the reason, adult education continues to be in large
> part liberal education; though when Thoreau wrote that
> "it is time villages were universities, and their elder inhabit-
> ants the fellows of universities, with leisure—if they indeed
> are so well off—to pursue liberal studies the rest of their
> lives," he described neither his own time nor this one. Adult
> education is so far from universal that millions of people are
> unaware that it exists. [Van Doren, 1943, p. 104]

One of Van Doren's proposals was to give workers sabbaticals in
which they could pursue studies, a suggestion which has come
up again in our time. Such sabbaticals could help bring about the
learning society that liberal humanists have spoken about in their
writings.

Concern with the worker is a theme that can also be found in
the philosophical writings of Horace Kallen (1962). In Kallen's
view, the aim of adult education is to liberate the mind, to bring
about a synthesis of what he called a person's daylife and nightlife. The daylife is one's role as a producer in society, a worker.
It is in the nightlife that one is able to enjoy the cultural benefits
for which the person has worked during the day. Education,

according to Kallen, should be a liberating experience. And the way to achieve this sense of liberation is through liberal studies (Kallen, 1962, p. 62).

That a liberal education has a distinct function for adults was argued persuasively by Edgar Friedenberg (1956) in his article "Liberal Education and the Fear of Failure." The first function for a liberal education in his view was to teach persons the value of freedom and help them become competent to use it. Freeing persons meant insuring that they had facts and the ability to deal with facts. Friedenberg wrote this article in the midst of the McCarthy hearings, thus giving his words a particular pointedness.

The second function of the liberal education of adults for Friedenberg was to help them to respond appropriately to the difference between the objective and the subjectives; between the events in which they participated and their feelings about them. A liberally educated adult was able to include feelings as the center of his or her relationship to reality. Friedenberg was critical of the scientific approach which attempted to achieve a value neutrality that excluded feelings in perceptions of truth.

Friedenberg's last purpose of a liberal education was that of increasing the range of human experience to which one could respond. In giving persons a knowledge of the past, one increased the range of experience with which they could handle problems. Persons are then better able to accept the experiences of others.

Friedenberg contended that liberal education for adults would also contribute to other goals such as improvement in the quality of citizenship and the use of leisure time, improvement of self-concept, and a feeling of greater human dignity. Friedenberg saw a particularly important function of liberal adult education to empower persons "to cherish dignity and not to consent to violations of it" (p. 54). Values or virtues such as friendliness, cooperativeness, fairness, practicality, and humility should be fostered in adult groups. Human dignity was defeated in individuals who had a fear of failure. This fear of failure could be removed through education:

> Liberal education does not eradicate fear of failure by reassurance. It does so by helping people study the most

significant records of human experience. This one cannot do without becoming more interested in the texture of experience itself than in how the story which one has impertinently interrupted, turns out. One forgets to wonder whether Destiny is going to award one some kind of a prize; whether one is going to get as rich as Mozart; as influential in the affairs of the state as Machiavelli; as honored by a grateful citizenry as Socrates. They raise so many more interesting questions. [Friedenberg, 1956, p. 54]

The treatment that Friedenberg gave to the liberal education of adults was a rather broad one, concerned mainly with ideals in a rather abstract sense. At the other end of the spectrum is an evaluation study of liberal adult education by Miller and McGuire (1961). Funded by the Center for the Study of Liberal Education for Adults, they attempted to develop behaviorally stated objectives in liberal education programs for adults at college campuses. While the appropriateness of using behavioral objectives to evaluate liberal education programs would be objected to by humanist scholars, the study did reveal the scope of liberal adult education.

In their empirical examination of liberal adult education at colleges and universities, Miller and McGuire developed four categories of study. Programs existed (at the time of their study) in ethical and moral values, appreciation of the arts, political and social problems, and community participation. In their view, these four categories represented a rough approximation of the college liberal arts program: social sciences, arts, and philosophy. In the programs investigated there was a notable absence of science. The authors were surprised by this finding because of their belief that the knowledge of science among people is necessary for the survival of human existence (Miller and McGuire, 1961).

Though this scope for liberal education appears broad, it would not meet the rigorous demands of a Hutchins, Maritain, or Van Doren. This curriculum is also inadequate when compared with the Core Curriculum in the liberal arts recently developed at Harvard. After two years of extensive study and debate, the Task Force on the Core Curriculum decided on a core that includes mathematics, natural science, literature, moral philosophy, foreign cultures, social analysis, expository writing, history, and a foreign language (Wilson, 1978). While this core might not satisfy strict classicists, it appears that it will gain increasing acceptance in colleges and adult programs for liberal education.

The Great Books Program

Probably the best known program for the liberal education of adults is the Great Books Program. This program has been offered by many proponents as an adequate basis for the liberal education of both college students and adults. It was developed largely at Columbia University, the University of Chicago, and at St. John's College, Annapolis, Maryland. In 1947, the Great Books Foundation was established as an independent, non-profit educational organization designed to provide liberal education for people of all ages. The program has been offered by many school systems, colleges and independent educational agencies such as public libraries. Besides Adler, Hutchins, Maritain, and Van Doren, its distinguished list of supporters includes John Erskine, Stringfellow Barr, Scott Buchanan, Alexander Meiklejohn and Norman Forester.

Van Doren's description of this program captures its broad scope and idealistic spirit. The purpose of the program is to inculcate

> the arts of investigation, discovery, criticism, and communication, and achieve at first-hand an acquaintance with the original books, the unkillable classics, in which these miracles happen. [Van Doren, 1943, p. 145]

At the college level, it is preferred that these works be read in the original and this is still done at such purist institutions as St. John's. Most programs, however, deal with the classics in translation.

For Van Doren, the Great Books embody liberal arts tradition. Selections include poets: Homer, Virgil, Shakespeare; philosophers: Plato, Aristotle, Descartes, Spinoza, Hume, and Kant; theologians: Thomas Aquinas, Augustine; scientists: Ptolemy, Galileo, Boyle, Darwin; novelists: Tolstoy, Dickens. On the list are also mathematicians, playwrights, historians, economists, political scientists, and psychologists. The curriculum is formidable, for in the view of Van Doren, education is formidable. The list does not remain static, for new books are added when they have achieved the status of classics.

For Great Books advocates there are right and wrong ways to approach the classics. The right reading of such books is not a passive but an intensely active affair. The art of discussion has to be learned before one can approach these books. But basically it is these books that are instructive; they are the real teachers in the program. Van Doren's description of the St. John's program shows the centrality of the books:

> The heart of the tradition is there with its essential champion, and it is kept working for all of the students all of the time. It is the end of every other activity in the college; languages are learned so that these books may be read, and among the languages are those of mathematics and the laboratory. There are no textbooks to which the great books are supplementary; the great books are the textbooks of this college, as in a sense they are its teachers. For the faculty reads them too, in preparation for seminars where they will be discussed. And since there are no departments or division, all of the faculty must do what all of the students do: read all of the books. [Van Doren, 1943, pp. 149-150]

Few colleges have followed the program developed at St. John's. Harvard's recent efforts in the direction of a core curriculum indicate that the need is felt at least for core areas of liberal studies that will provide a basic and unified education.

A study of Great Books participants by Davis (1961) indicated that adults who participated in such groups tended to be well educated, of high social status, predominantly female, and young. The study also pointed out that the groups needed group discussion skills. Unfortunately, little systematic study has been done on such groups since 1961 when the Center for the Study of Liberal Education disbanded.

The Great Books Foundation, based in Chicago, is currently very active in selecting and publishing soft-cover editions of the works to be discussed, providing promotional materials and organizational assistance to local leaders, and training volunteers and teachers to conduct discussion groups in their communities. As of this writing, more than 40,000 adults throughout the United States are participating in Great Books discussion groups sponsored by the Foundation.

The Great Books Program of liberal education has not been

without its detractors. Many have criticized the very concept that a core of common books could provide an adequate education in contemporary society. Such a program also does not appear to allow for social and individual differences among learners. Kenneth Hansen in a doctoral dissertation at the University of Minnesota (1949) criticized the underlying educational philosophy of the Great Books Program. Hansen contended that the Program prevented the development of a specialized or professional focus, opposed an elective system of course selection, and was presumptuous in assuming its participants could arrive at absolute, objective truth. For Hansen, the program attempted to return to a unity of knowledge through prescriptive reading, and promoted a supernatural view of the world.

In addition, Hansen considered the metaphysics of the program absolutistic, dualistic, and authoritarian. In his opinion, it placed too great emphasis on the rational mode of learning. It manifested an antiquated view of the psychology of the person, presuming that there were separate faculties of the mind to be cultivated. He criticized the notion that once these faculties were trained, knowledge and skills could be transferred from one area to another.

Many of the criticisms leveled against the Great Books Program have been points of difference between the progressive view of education and the liberal arts view of education. From the progressive viewpoint, the program does not take sufficient cognizance of the needs and interests of learners. It tends to dismiss present concerns in favor of past wisdom and tradition, and thus holds itself aloof from social affairs. Liberal education, which is centered on humanistic studies and intense intellectual activity and discussion, has been little accepted by progressives who emphasize problem-solving through scientific and experimental methods.

Though some of the criticisms that Hansen and others have made of the Great Books Program and the liberal philosophy of education that underlies it were justified, something can be said in defense of this program as it was presented by Hutchins, Van Doren, and others. This approach to college and adult education developed when many in society feared for the very continuance of Western civilization. In the face of World Wars, the uncontrolled development of science and technology, and a vacuum in values that would hold a civilization together, Hutchins saw the liberal curriculum as a countervailing educational influence. He and others did not exclude contemporary problems from consideration, but believed that the emphasis should be placed upon the unifying factors of a common cultural tradition.

Hansen's criticism that an acceptance of the Great Books program commits a person to a particular metaphysical or philosophic view does not appear correct. The program was intended as an introduction to the Western intellectual tradition with the ideal that persons would be better able to participate in self-government. The Great Books do not bring a person to transcendental truth, but rather enable persons to grapple more intelligently with present problems in light of the best thinking that has taken place on human problems and existence. The very diversity of the books' historical contexts and subject matter insure that persons are introduced to a broad republic of learning.

The underlying problem with Great Books programs is not that they commit one to a particular philosophical view of the world—whether it be realism, perennialism, or idealism. Rather, one may succumb to the danger of scholasticism or biblicism, holding too strongly to the particular views of classics and persons at the expense of examining present problems in present terms. Truths are found in the classics but often their expression and distance from present cultural patterns and concerns remove those classics from the understanding of persons today. Most of the values contained in the classics are also present in contemporary writers, who themselves are often immersed in this literature. Contemporary writers express these ideas in a contemporary idiom that speaks more to individuals of this time. What is needed is a balanced educational approach that utilizes the best of both views.

An Evaluation of Adult Liberal Education

The continuation of the Great Books Program and Harvard's return to a liberal curriculum indicate a continuing interest in this tradition in educational circles today. While it does not have the eloquent advocates that it had in the past, liberal adult education can be found in various forms and situations. Many persons engage in programs of self-education inspired by the liberal ideal. Colleges are enrolling more and more non-traditional students and are offering them liberal studies among other programs. In addition, liberal adult education can be found in programs sponsored by churches, labor unions, evening schools, businesses, and industries. In a recent report on a UCLA extension program with the Bank of America, Lenz (1979) notes:

> the humanities are not only alive and well, but have a significant role to play in business and industry. In fact, in today's social climate, the liberal arts studies, with their emphasis on values, may provide the most effective means for promoting healthy interpersonal relationships in the workplace. [Lenz, 1979, p. 11]

Perhaps more than other segments of the adult population, men and women over sixty are being offered opportunities to engage in liberal studies. Several writers have in fact argued that old age is a particularly appropriate time for taking up liberal studies. Moody (1976), for example, challenges educators to

> make available to older people the great ideas of the humanities and the social sciences that can nourish this psychological development in old age. In the fields of philosophy, religion, psychology, and literature there are elements that can *only* be grasped in all their depth and richness by individuals who bring a lifetime of personal experience to their study. [Moody, 1976, p. 11]

Colleges and universities across the United States are offering just such experiences. Programs like Fordham University's College at Sixty and Fairleigh Dickinson University's Education Program for Older Persons focus largely, if not entirely, upon liberal education. Another intriguing and highly successful program of liberal education for older persons is the Elderhostel. Inspired by youth hostels and folk schools of Europe, Elderhostel is a network of over 230 colleges and universities in 38 states which offer special low-cost, one-week summer residential academic programs for older adults. Courses are non-credit, have no exams, grades, or required homework. The main objective of an Elderhostel program is intellectual stimulation. Participants become involved in learning for its own sake.

Adults who are lifelong learners are often motivated by the liberal ideal. The learning efforts of two such men, Cornelius Hirschberg and Malcolm X, are described by Ronald Gross in *The Lifelong Learner* (1977). Hirschberg, a retired salesman, has spent at least 20,000 hours in getting a liberal education through his own efforts. He has read widely in philosophy and literature. In his memoirs *(The Priceless Gift*, Simon and Schuster, 1960), he beautifully expresses the values that his studies have had on his life:

> I am stuck in the city, that's all I have, I am stuck in business and routine and tedium. But I give up only as much as I must; for the rest I live my life at its best, with art, music, poetry, literature, science, philosophy, and thought. I shall know the keener people of this world, think the keener thoughts, and taste the keener pleasures, as long as I can and as much as I can. [Hirschberg, quoted in Gross, 1977, p. 27]

While Hirschberg found personal consolation and pleasure in his liberal studies, Malcolm X found in them a force that was truly revolutionary. In his *Autobiography* (1964), he reports the influence of great reading on his ideas. He read deeply in history, especially black history and became interested in philosophy both of the West and of the East. When asked about his alma mater, he could proudly say that books served as his college. His writings and his life manifested the power of ideas in forging a man and a movement.

Another powerful testimonial to the enduring value of liberal studies has come from Gus Tyler, assistant President of the International Ladies Garment Workers' Union, and a long-time advocate of labor education. From his perspective, labor education should view the worker as a worker, a consumer, economic being, political citizen, and human being. In describing the needs of workers as human beings he notes that

> as leisure is democratized, workers can turn to the onetime aristocratic pastimes of sports, art, music, dance, travel, rhetoric, philosophy, and reading. In pursuit of these many interests, workers cannot be limited by some archaic time mold, such as the kindergarten to twelfth grade pattern followed by four years here and four years there. Learning lasts for a lifetime, through the working years, during preretirement and into retirement. [Tyler, 1979]

Tyler expressed his hesitations about this new marriage between universities and labor unions. He feared that professors in the liberal arts might not be able to reach out to communicate to fellow workers. He also called for an education that would take a stand on the current political and economic situation.

While individuals have been inspired by liberal studies, the overall influence of liberal education in both general and adult education in the United States has been mitigated by two factors. The first is the movement toward career and vocational education. Since the 1960's, funds that the federal and state governments have allotted to education have gone primarily to skill development and job-oriented programs. The social programs of the past two decades have been practical and utilitarian in orientation. It has thus been difficult for adult liberal education to get a hearing in this context.

The second development that has also gone against the liberal educational philosophy is the strong behaviorist orientation of much of contemporary education theory and practice. Emphases on stating objectives behaviorally, measuring outcomes in quantifiable terms, and developing measurable competencies mitigate humanistic thrusts in education. Liberal aims and methods do not easily lend themselves to such statements, analyses, and evaluations. Behaviorist and progressive educational theory and practice thus characterize the American temperment and spirit more strongly today than does the liberal arts philosophy of education.

Nevertheless, the old and venerable tradition of liberal education is not dead. At this writing, the prospects for adult liberal education appear bright. Any strong movement for lifelong learning will necessarily need a philosophy of education that takes seriously the great accomplishments of civilization and the great teachers of the past. Shorn of a number of historical biases— elitism and antipathy toward vocationalism and specialization— this tradition can truly be a liberating force in the lives of individuals and society. A knowledge of past civilization and culture does not in itself *liberate* persons, but it can be an important step in any process of liberation. Though the world is constantly in a state of change, there are some things that do not change. People continue to search for truth, desire to develop their moral characters, strive for spiritual and religious visions, and seek the beautiful in life and nature. As long as the human person does these things, the liberal tradition in education will be a potent force.

REFERENCES

Adler, Mortimer. *The Revolution to Education.* Chicago: University of Chicago Press, 1937.

Adler, Mortimer. *How to Read a Book.* Chicago: University of Chicago Press, 1940.

Beck, George A. "Aims in Education: Neo-Thomism." In T. Hollins (ed.), *Aims in Education: The Philosophic Approach.* Manchester: Manchester University Press, 1964.

Bridenbaugh, C. and J. Bridenbaugh. *Rebels and Gentlemen* (2nd ed.). New York: Oxford University Press, 1962.

Broudy, Harry and John Palmer. *Exemplars of Teaching Method.* Chicago: Rand McNally, 1965.

Cremin, Lawrence. *American Education: The Colonial Experience, 1607-1783.* New York: Harper and Row, 1970.

Davidson, Thomas. "Education for All: Problem for the 20th Century." In C. Hartley Gratton (ed.), In *American Ideas about Adult Education, 1710-1951.* New York: Teachers College Press, 1959.

Davis, James. *Great Books and Small Groups.* New York: Free Press, 1961.

Dewey, John. *Democracy and Education.* New York: Macmillan, 1914.

Franklin, Benjamin, *The Autobiography of.* In Leonard Laboree (ed.), *The Writings of Benjamin Franklin.* New Haven: Yale, 1964.

Friedenberg, Edgar. "Liberal Education and the Fear of Failure." *Leader Digest,* Vol. 3, Washington: Adult Education Association, 1956, 51-54.

Friedenberg, Edgar. "The Purpose of Liberal Study versus the Purpose of Adult Students." *Adult Leadership.* May 1958.

Gray, J. Glenn. *The Promise of Wisdom: A Philosophical Theory of Education.* New York: Harper and Row, 1968.

Gross, Ronald. *The Lifelong Learner.* New York: Simon and Schuster, 1977.

Hansen, Kenneth. *The Educational Philosophy of the Great Books Program.* Unpublished doctoral dissertation, University of Missouri, 1949. A lengthy abstract appears in L. Little (ed.), *Toward Understanding Adults and Adult Education,* Department of Religious Education, University of Pittsburgh, 1963.

Henle, Robert. "A Roman Catholic View of Education." In Philip Phenix (ed.), *Philosophies of Education.* New York: Wiley, 1965.

Highet, Gilbert. *The Art of Teaching.* New York: Knopf, 1950.

Hirschberg, Cornelius. *The Priceless Gift.* New York: Simon and Schuster, 1960.

Houle, Cyril, "How Useful is a Liberal Education." *Adult Leadership.* January 1955.

Houle, Cyril and C. W. Nelson. *The University, The Citizen and World Affairs.* Washington: American Council on Education, 1956.

Hutchins, Robert. *The Higher Learning in America.* New Haven: Yale University Press, 1936.

Hutchins, Robert. *The Conflict in Education in a Democratic Society.* New York: Harper and Row, 1953.

Hutchins, Robert. *The Learning Society.* New York: Britannica Books, 1968.

Kallen, Horace. *Philosophical Issues in Adult Education.* Springfield, IL: Charles C. Thomas, 1962.

Knowles, Malcolm. *The Adult Education Movement in the United States.* New York: Robert E. Krieger Publishing Company, 1977.

Lawson, K. H. *Philosophical Concepts and Values in Adult Education.* Nottingham, England: Barnes and Humby, Ltd., 1975.

LeClerq, Jacques. *The Love of God and the Love of Learning.* New York: Fordham University Press, 1961.

Lenz, Elinor, "Values in Transition." *The Forum for Continuing Education,* 1979, *2,* 8, 11.

Malcolm X. *The Autobiography of Malcolm X.* New York: Grove Press, 1964.

Maritain, Jacques. *Education at the Crossroads.* New Haven: Yale University Press, 1943.

Maritain, Jacques. In Donald and Idella Gallagher (eds.), *The Education of Man.* New York: Doubleday, 1962.

Marrou, H. I. *A History of Education in Antiquity.* New York: Sheed and Ward, 1956.

Martin, Everett Dean. *The Meaning of a Liberal Education.* New York: Norton, 1926.

McGuchen, William, "The Philosophy of Catholic Education." In *Philosophies of Education.* National Society for the Study of Education, Forty First Yearbook, Part I. Chicago: University of Chicago Press, 1942.

Merriam, Sharan. "Ben Franklin's Junto Revisited," *Lifelong Learning: The Adult Years,* 1979, *2,* 18-19.

Miller, H. and G. McGuire. *Liberal Education: An Evaluative Study.* Chicago: Center for the Study of Liberal Education of Adults, 1961.

Moody, H. R. "Philosophical Presuppositions of Education for Old Age." *Educational Gerontology,* 1976, *1,* 1-16.

Murchland, Bernard, "Reviving the Connected View; Reforming the Liberal Arts," 1979, *106.*

Paterson, R. W. K. *Values, Education and the Adult.* Boston: Routledge and Kegan Paul, 1978.

Perkinson, Henry. *The Imperfect Panacea: American Faith in Education, 1865-1976* (2nd ed.). New York: Random House, 1977.

Pratte, Richard. *Contemporary Theories of Education.* Scranton: Intext, 1971.

Rush, Benjamin, "Thoughts Upon the Mode of Education Proper in a Republic," (1786), In S. Alexander Rippa (ed.), *Educational Ideas in America: A Documentary History.* New York: McKay, 1969.

Stubblefield, Harold. *The Aims of the American Education Movement in the Nineteen Twenties: A Historical Analysis.* Paper presented at the Adult Education Research Conference, Ann Arbor, Michigan, April 1979.

Toynbee, Arnold, "Education in the Perspective of History," (1960). In Ronald Gross (ed.), *The Teacher and the Taught.* New York: Dell, 1963.

Tyler, Gus, "The University and the Labor Union: Educating the Proletariat." *Change*, 1979, *2*, 32-37, 64.

Van Doren, Mark. *Liberal Education*. Boston: Beacon, 1943.

Vincent, John, "The Rationale of the Chatauqua Movement," (1886). In C. Hartley Grattan (ed.), *American Ideas about Adult Education, 1710-1951*. New York: Teachers College Press, 1959.

Whipple, James. *A Critical Balance*. Chicago: Center for the Study of Liberal Education for Adults, 1960.

Wilson, James Q., "Harvard's Core Curriculum: A View from the Inside," *Change*, 1978, *10*, 40-43.

CHAPTER III

PROGRESSIVE
ADULT EDUCATION

Progressivism has had a greater impact upon the adult education movement in the United States than any other single school of thought. The rapid growth of adult education occurred at a time when progressive education in varying forms was a predominant influence. In an attempt to deal with a society that was quickly becoming urbanized and industrialized, early adult education looked to the dynamic progressive movement as an inspiration in establishing theoretical positions and practical programs.

Elements of progressive thought are found in the writings of all major theorists in the field of adult education including Knowles, Rogers, Houle, Tyler, Lindeman, Bergevin, and Freire. Many forms of adult education were inspired by progressive ideals: adult vocational education, extension education, education of the foreign born and citizenship education, family and parent education, and education for social action. In addition, some of the basic principles in adult education originated in progressive thought: needs and interests, the scientific method, problem solving techniques, the centrality of experience, pragmatic and utilitarian goals, and the idea of social responsibility.

Many educators over a period of half a century contributed to the distinctive features of progressive education. The first part of this chapter will be an attempt to shed some light on the history of this complex movement. The historical section will be followed by a discussion of the basic principles of progressive education and their expression in adult education. A third section will examine some of the programs in adult education that have been inspired by progressive principles. Finally, an assessment of this movement in adult education will be presented.

An Historical Perspective on Progressive Education

The origins of progressive education lie in the rationalist, empirical, and scientific thought that developed first in Europe, and then became predominant in the United States. The traditional liberal education of the day was challenged by educators who proposed new ways of seeking knowledge. Reason, experience, and feeling began to replace tradition and authority as the chief ways of arriving at truth.

Progressivism's earliest threads can be traced back to the 16th century. Bishop John Comenius suggested allowing children to imitate nature for their education, rather than reading books. Rousseau carried this idea to an extreme in proposing that all learning until the age of twelve should come from experience. The natural freedom and spontaneity of the child that Rousseau advocated was stressed in the practical educational experiments of Pestalozzi and Froebel. They advocated contact with natural objects, the learning of manual skills, and the incorporation of play into educational experiences. In 18th century England, both Bacon and Locke put greater faith in empirical knowledge at the expense of knowledge based on the authority of the written word.

The development of the philosophy underlying the progressive education movement owes much to the seminal ideas of Darwin (1958). Darwin stressed inductive methods of science rather than deductive methods of philosophy and theology. He developed a scientific method of arriving at knowledge which entailed observation and the testing of hypotheses through experience. Nature provided the context and conditions within which human persons struggled for existence. These ideas of Darwin affected not only psychology, natural sciences, and philosophy, but also had an influence in shaping the new pedagogy being developed by progressive educators.

In applying Darwin's thought to a social context, Herbert Spencer (1860) also influenced progressive education. He developed a view of education which, through an emphasis on science, would lead to the betterment of the human condition. Societies and cultures evolve, he reasoned, just as the human species and lower forms of life have evolved. Spencer encouraged the progressives to see in an education based on science a powerful means of advancing cultural perfection and development. Others, however, interpreted Darwin's thought in a conservative manner implying that little could be done to bring about changes for the better.

Inspired by these various intellectual developments, a distinctive progressive movement evolved by the turn of the century. At that time, the United States was undergoing great social, economic, and political changes. Mass immigration was taking place in urban areas of the country, especially in the East. The industrialization that had begun after the Civil War accelerated at the turn of the century. In the face of these social, political, and economic problems, many American thinkers formed a great faith in the power of education for solving these problems (Perkinson, 1977). A school system from kindergarten through high school developed to socialize the new immigrants, ameliorate the social ills brought about by rapid urbanization, train workers and leaders needed for the growing industrial society, and contribute to the development of a democracy without corruption. A special teaching profession emerged with scientific training and high ideals. Vocational education was added to the traditional liberal arts education. Although the progressive dreams were not all realized (Perkinson, 1977), these reforms greatly influenced the direction of American education.

The theory of progressive education developed at this time was designed to liberate the talents and gifts of the child; thus it was child-centered in the tradition of Rousseau, Pestalozzi, and Froebel. It was indebted to Darwin for the concept of the child as a developing and evolving organism, and its practical, utilitarian bent was influenced by the thought of Spencer. The highest ideal of the progressive movement was education for democracy, defined by Dewey as people engaged in joint activity to solve their common problems. Thus, the goals of education as the early progressives saw them were both individual and social. In liberating the learner, a potential was released for the improvement of society and culture.

The philosophical basis of progressivism is pragmatism, a distinctively American philosophy that goes back to the 1870's and the writings of Charles Peirce, William James, and Chauncy Wright. As a philosophy, pragmatism has various dimensions. It accepts the methods of science for understanding the human person and solving human problems. Dewey described the inductive scientific method in his classic, *How We Think* (1910), and James (1902/ 1972) applied it to religious beliefs and values. Pragmatism accepts both the relativism and pluralism of world views. This attitude is most in keeping with the nature of human persons and the evolving world. The centrality of human experience is another dimension of pragmatic thought. Experience is placed in opposition to all authoritarian ways of arriving at knowledge. Pragmatism emphasizes the consequences of actions in the determination of truth or goodness. Thus, there are no absolutes in knowledge or in morality. A final characteristic of pragmatism is its emphasis on social reform as a legitimate concern of philosophers. In this aspect, some pragmatists were close to Marx in seeing the task of philosophy as not only understanding, but also changing the world in which we live.

Charles Peirce's contribution to pragmatism was his view of how persons arrive at their ideas (Rorty, 1966). In and of themselves, ideas are little more than hypotheses until tried on the anvil of experience. Pierce attempted to balance the concept of truth as changing, with the common sense awareness of stability, habit, and law in human life.

William James (1909) followed Peirce in his view of the process of arriving at knowledge. For him, an idea was true in terms of its workability. Truth is not absolute or immutable. It is made actual in real life events. James also made contributions to progressive thought in the area of psychology. He viewed the human mind as the product of environment, an accumulation of sensory data that comes from the outside world. The task of the educator was to attend to the formation of habits in students, for once these were formed, the students had the opportunity for freedom, creativity, and progressive thought.

The chief exponent of pragmatism and progressive thought, especially as it related to education, was John Dewey. This American philosopher was involved in all aspects of the progressive movement: politics, economics, social reform, and education. His writings are voluminous and have received constant evaluation and criticism. He is, without a doubt, the single most influential philosopher of education this country has produced, and his impact on all forms of education is immense. He has both defenders and detractors among educators. But for all practical purposes, his writings represent the definitive work in the progressive philosophy of education. Three distinct phases of the progressive movement in education can be seen in the following description of his ideas.

In its earliest stages, progressive education was most concerned with developing a child-centered approach to education. Dewey's early works, *School and Society* (1900/1956), and *The Schools of Tomorrow* (1915) are strong statements of this view. Rousseau, Pestalozzi, and Froebel were most influential in these works. The primary task of education was to develop the potential of the child. This necessitated removing the child from the passivity and uniformity of traditional education. Manual training was introduced into the curriculum, and an effort was made to begin the educational process with the needs and interests of the child. Using the child as a starting point, one could "facilitate and enrich the growth of the individual child" as well as continue to reap the benefits of traditional learning (Dewey, 1900/1956, p. 70).

The germ of the second stage in the development of progressive education is also found in *School and Society* (1900/1956). Education, Dewey felt, had a role to play in social reform and reconstruction. *Democracy and Education* (1916), Dewey's most enduring and influential work, places education at the very heart of social reform. The work explores the educational meanings of democracy, science, evolution, and industrialism. Dewey becomes critical of the ideas of Rousseau, Locke, Herbert, and Froebel. He also shows more awareness of contemporary developments in psychology and sociology. The social thrust of Dewey's thought at this time can be seen in his own summary of the leading ideas in his work. Three of the seven ideas involve social issues: the dependence of growth of the mind upon participation in shared activities; the influence of the physical environment on the development of culture; and the necessity of utilizing individual differences in desire and thinking to produce changes in society (1916, p. 377).

For Dewey, education would flourish if it took place in a democracy; democracy would develop only if there were true education. Democratic societies were intentionally progressive and aimed at a greater variety of mutually shared interests. Greater freedom was allowed its members and therefore there was a need to develop a social consciousness in individuals. Thus for Dewey a democratic society was committed to change. A democracy "is more than a form of government; it is primarily a mode of associated living, of conjoint communicated experience (1916, p. 90)." The goals of education in this work are seen primarily in social terms. A democratic education will produce a society that is constantly in a state of greater growth and development.

While Dewey saw the task of the schools as important in social change, he did not go as far as a radical social reconstructionist such as George Counts. As will be seen in the chapter on Radical Adult Education, Counts called upon the schools in the 1930's to clearly indoctrinate students in a socialist vision of society. Dewey maintained that the task of the schools was to educate individuals in democratic values. Students would then work for a better society. Thus the school was only indirectly involved in social change. Bowers (1969) has detailed the history of the split in progressivism between liberals like Dewey and radicals like Counts.

The third phase of progressive education, experimentalism, is found in Dewey's short but influential work, *Experience and Education* (1938). By 1938 the weaknesses of child-centered education had become apparent, and many of the goals of social reformists had been achieved through the politics and social programs of the New Deal. Dewey and other progressive educators took up the task of developing a statement of progressive education that avoided the extremes of the child-centered and social action themes of early progressivism. In *Experience and Education* Dewey was critical of both the subject-centered or traditional education, and the child-centered progressive education. He called for an education that entailed the critical and controlled type of learning exemplified in science. The methods of criticism, full public inspection, and testing became the moral principles to guide educational work. In this approach, there is need for the guidance and direction of learning that makes the teacher more important than in the traditional education. The concept of experience is restricted to those experiences that are truly educative. Individuals achieve freedom as they master the tools of learning that are available.

Experimentation, or this third facet of progressive education, represents the mature thought of Dewey. This view took into account many of the criticisms that had been leveled against progressive education: lack of discipline, child-centeredness, focusing on trivial problems, little attention to subject matter, anti-intellectualism, and a lack of a clear definition of the teacher's role.

After the Second World War, Dewey became, for some, the scapegoat for all that was perceived wrong in American education. In a letter to *Life* magazine (March 15, 1959), President Eisenhower joined the criticism:

> Educators, parents and students must be continuously stirred up by the defects in our educational system. They must be induced to abandon the educational path that, rather blindly they have been following as a result of John Dewey's teachings.

Dewey's ideas were returned to, however, in the 1960's and 1970's. Significantly, this was a period of social and political change in American society. Many saw in the progressive era and its philosophy of education a suitable theory for understanding and directing education's role in social change (Holt, 1970; Herndon, 1971; Silberman, 1970). Even in these decades though, progressivism was not without its critics. Radicals saw progressives as the originators of bureaucratization, social control, racism, and other ills (Katz, 1968; Karrier, et al., 1973). Conservatives, on the other hand, rejected progressive ideas and called for a return to traditional values and basic subjects (Conant, 1961; Kirk, 1965; Koerner, 1965). The identification of progressive thought with liberal political, social, and economic thought lies at the heart of the controversy over the impact of progressivism on American life in general, and on education in particular.

Progressive Education and the Adult Education Movement

A comparison between Cremin's classic on progressive education, *The Transformation of the Schools* (1957), and Knowles' *The History of the Adult Education Movement in the United States* (1977), makes clear the intimate connection between progressive and adult education. Progressive education's emphases upon vocational and utilitarian training, learning by experience, scientific inquiry, community involvement, and responsiveness to social problems found expression in the development of new forms of general and adult education. Both Cremin and Knowles present vocational education, university extension and cooperative extension, settlement houses for new immigrants, and Americanization education as forms of progressive education.

Knowles' history of the adult education movement recounts the story of a movement that attempted to separate itself from the narrow focus of many schools, colleges and universities in order to develop programs to meet the needs of large numbers of people and society in general. In the period between 1866 and 1920, the "'useful,' 'functional,' 'pragmatic' became the predominant standards for knowledge and science..." (Knowles, 1977, p. 36). Agricultural education and industrial training, part of the progressive movement in both politics and education, were important developments at this time. Extension work at universities was also inspired by progressive ideals.

> A new spirit was infused into the idea of extension representing a shift away from an emphasis on academic subjects toward an all embracing concept of the role of the university in serving all of the people of the state in relation to the full scope of life problems—agricultural, political, social, and moral. [Knowles, 1977, p. 49]

Other common interests between the progressives and the adult educators at this time included the introduction of vocational education into the adult evening schools, the development of voluntary associations and agencies, the providing of services to the poor through settlement houses and other social agencies, and an interest in parent education programs. Knowles' characterization of this period clearly reveals the relationship of the adult education movement to progressivism:

> The general character of adult educational content shifted from general knowledge to several pin-pointed areas of emphasis—vocational education, citizenship and Americanization, the education of women, civic and social reforms, public affairs, leisure time activity, and health. Adult education was clearly in tune with the needs of this era of

industrialization, immigration, emancipation, urbanization, and national maturation. [Knowles, 1977, p. 75]

When Knowles turns to the period between 1921 and 1961, the same link between progressive ideals and adult education can be seen. Business and industry, the broadening of the curriculum, the growth of extension, experiments with newer methodologies, involvement with government and social agencies, and labor education are common concerns of progressives and adult educators.

During this same period, two influential books by adult educators appeared which explicitly related the two movements. James H. Robinson in *The Humanizing of Knowledge* (1924) called for the utilization of the new knowledge from the social sciences. Robinson felt that this new knowledge would help free the minds of adults from traditional ideas about religion, politics, nationalism, economics, and race.

Though Robinson's work advocated the introduction of social science knowledge into adult education, it was not until Eduard Lindeman's book, *The Meaning of Adult Education*, appeared in 1926 that the ideas of the progressives were fully applied to the field of adult education. Lindeman was directly influenced by the ideas of John Dewey and other progressives. He saw education as having as its primary aim the development of social intelligence, that is, the practical understanding of the world in which we live. Lindeman primarily identified with that aspect of progressive education that envisioned the reform of society as the principal aim of education. Like Dewey, he saw citizens involved in education as it related to their life situation:

> Every adult person finds himself in specific situations with respect to his work, his recreation, his family-life, his community-life, et cetera—situations which call for adjustments. Adult education begins at this point. Subject matter is brought into education, is put to work, when needed. Texts and teachers play a new and secondary role in this type of education; they must give way to the primary importance of the learner. [Lindeman, 1926, pp. 8-9]

Lindeman's influence and thus Dewey's is seen in the development of the American Association for Adult Education in 1926. Knowles reports that an early policy decision of this institution was to resist all pressures for a rigid definition of adult education and to allow a concept that included many areas of adult activity. Rejecting the narrow base of liberal adult education, early organizers recognized cultural, vocational, and recreational interests as legitimate facets of adult education (Knowles, 1977, pp. 196-197). In the chapter on analytic philosophy, it will be seen that British philosophers of adult education prefer to restrict the term adult education to mean liberal adult education.

The founding of the Adult Education Association in 1951 was marked with similar debates over the nature of adult education. The impetus for the founding of the Association came from the Fund for Adult Education which, as was noted, favored the liberal arts approach to adult education. In order to receive the support of the Fund, the founding adult educators developed goals for the organization that reflected adult liberal education while at the same time responded to the more practical needs of the field (Knowles, 1977, pp. 221-223). Over the years, the Association has broadened its base to include a wide variety of educational activities in line with the broad goals of progressive adult education.

In its development, adult education has been more faithful in many ways to the pragmatic principles that inspired its beginnings than have the public schools. Adult education, as it has been theorized about and actually practiced in this country, has been thoroughly pragmatic, utilitarian, and, thus, progressive. This factor accounts for many of its strengths and some of its weaknesses. To better understand adult education's pragmatic orientation, the fundamental principles of progressive education and their manifestations in adult education theory and practice will be examined in the following section.

Basic Principles of Adult Progressive Education

Most of the basic principles of the progressive education movement were at least touched upon in the previous section covering the theory's historical development. Following is a more systematic treatment of this theory, drawing from Dewey and adult educators whose views are consistent with this school of thought. Some criticisms of these principles will also be offered.

1. *A Broadened View of Education.* One of the major contributions of progressive education was to broaden the concept of education. The traditional or liberal philosophy of education confined the aims of education to intellectual development through a study of certain academic disciplines. Education was first of all broadened by the progressives to include what sociologists call socialization and anthropologists call inculturation. Education is thus not restricted to schooling, but includes all those incidental and intentional activities that society uses to pass on values, attitudes, knowledge, and skills. Education in this view becomes extensive. It includes the work of many institutions of society: family, workplace, school, churches, the entire community, in fact. In this scheme of things, the school is just one agency responsible for transmitting culture.

Secondly, in viewing education as socialization, the progressives took the logical step of placing some importance upon adult learning. Dewey argued for an education that was truly lifelong:

> Education must be reconceived, not as merely a preparation for maturity (whence our absurd idea that it should stop after adolescence) but as a continuous growth of the mind and a continuous illumination of life. In a sense, the school can give us only the instrumentalities of mental growth; the rest depends upon an absorption and interpretation of experience. Real education comes after we leave school and there is no reason why it should stop before death. [Dewey, 1916, p. 25]

The unfortunate thing about Dewey was that after laying the basis for lifelong learning, he devoted most of his efforts to one education institution, the school. Thus, in the truest sense, Dewey's theory of education is a theory of schooling, though his views are certainly applicable to other forms of education and learning.

A third way in which the progressives broadened the concept of education was through advocating the introduction of the practical, pragmatic, and utilitarian into the curriculum. Their struggles in this area were long and uphill against entrenched interests in colleges, schools, and universities. Dewey argued that education appropriate to American society must include both the liberal and the practical, both education for work and education for leisure, and both the humanities and the sciences (1916, ch. 19, 20). He contended that Aristotle's distinction between the liberal arts and the servile arts of work was based not on philosophical grounds, but was a result of the cultural situation in Greece where work was done by slaves. Dewey called for an education that was both liberal and practical. A broadened view of education in Dewey's view

> reconciles liberal nurture with training in social service-ableness, with ability to share effectively and happily in occupations which are productive. . . . The problem of education in a democratic society is to do away with the dualism and to construct a course of studies which makes thought a guide for free practice for all and which makes leisure a reward of accepting responsibility for service, rather than an exemption from it. [Dewey, 1916, pp. 260-261]

It will be seen that the British philosophers prefer a concept of adult education that is limited to liberal studies. In this country, however, the influence of the progressives in the theory and practice of adult education has served to broaden the range of endeavors considered to be educational.

A fourth way in which the progressives broadened the concept of education was in their emphasis on the centrality of experience. Dewey defined education as the reconstruction and reorganization of experience which increases our ability to direct the course of subsequent experience. Experience for the progressives has both an active and a passive component. It is not just what has happened to a person but also what a person does. It is, more precisely, the interaction of the individual with the environment (Dewey, 1938, p. 42).

The emphasis of the progressives upon experience has to be seen in relation to traditional education which centered upon books that reported the experiences of other people. The progressives felt that the learners' experiences were an equally valid center for education. Dewey was careful in his treatment of experience to point out that education and experience were not identical, for there were also experiences that were miseducative. Educative experiences had a special quality of agreeableness and exerted positive influences on later experiences. The role of the teacher was important, for educational experiences were likely to happen in situations where there were teacher-guided interactions between persons and the environment (Dewey, 1938, p. 42).

In summary, the broadened view that the progressives took to education has been adopted by adult educators. Adult educators view education as a lifelong process and have long fought a definition of education restricted to notions of schooling. In addition, research has shown that adults of all ages are capable of learning and do learn in a multitude of settings and programs. With regard to curriculum, adult education has always included the pragmatic, utilitarian, and vocationally oriented dimensions. Finally, adult education values the experience-centeredness emphasized by progressives. Knowles (1970) has contended that the quality and volume of personal experiences of adults provide a rich learning resource that can contribute to a more mature approach to education.

2. *A New Focal Point in Education.* In broadening the view of education to include the personal experiences and interactions of students, the progressives gave education a new focus—the learners with their personal needs, interests, experiences, and desires. As we have seen above in the historical survey, this was the first stage of development in progressive education. Although it was somewhat modified under the attack of later criticisms, progressives have never abandoned their original insight which they took from Rousseau, Pestalozzi, and Froebel. This view was sloganized into the expression "We teach children, not subjects." Dewey corrected this to include both children and subjects, but there was no doubt where the emphasis lay.

Besides placing the learner at the center of educational concern, the progressives also developed a new concept of the human person. Contrary to some pessimistic religious views of human nature, progressives contended that persons were born neither good nor bad. Rather, they were born with unlimited potential for development and growth. Growth is a series of approximations toward a final goal which is never to be reached. Humans have biological continuity with animals, but they can, within limits, adapt the environment to their own needs by the use of intelligence. Dewey and other progressives tended to be optimistic about the potential for human growth given the right environmental situations. Thus the human person could, through scientific method and experimental thinking, achieve a more satisfying life.

Dewey and other progressives criticized traditional education for being too concerned with the learning of certain academic disciplines and not attending sufficiently to the impulses, interests, and purposes of learners. The progressives were deeply committed to the insights of the newly developing psychology which explored stages in psychological development and differences among individual learners. With this information as a starting point, progressives in education attempted to make use of the interests, needs, and desires of learners in forging educational experiences. They were aware that these interests provided the energy for learning and instruction. The teacher's task was not just to capitalize on the interests that already existed in the learner, but to arouse interests in those things that were educationally desirable.

Adult educators adopted this new focal point of education. As early as 1926, Lindeman spoke of the individual needs and goals that defined the adult educator's task:

> In what areas do most people appear to find life's meaning? We have only one pragmatic guide: meaning must reside in the things for which people strive, the goals which they set for themselves, their wants, needs, desires, and wishes. [Lindeman, 1926, pp. 13-14]

Emphasis in adult education upon conducting needs assessments for program development and instructional purposes gives expression to this basic progressive orientation. In addition, current research efforts to determine the extent of independent learning among adults are based upon the progressive and humanist assumption that a person is "a self-directing organism with initiative, intentions, choices, freedom, energy and responsibility" (Tough, 1971, p. 5).

The progressives' centering upon individuals and their needs has been subject to criticism from various philosophical viewpoints.

Liberal educators tend to see the primary focus still in disciplines to be taught. Behaviorists feel that needs and interests are learned from the environment and so can be changed by manipulation of the environment. And analytical adult education philosophers like Lawson (1975), Paterson (1979), and Monette (1977, 1979), seriously question the assumption that learners can articulate and plan for their own educational needs.

3. *A New Educational Methodology.* In the popular mind, progressive education has been equated with the introduction of new instructional methodologies. The progressives attacked the rigid methods of assign, study, and recite of traditional or liberal education. They contend that only static or inert knowledge resulted from this approach. Dewey characterized traditional methods as short-sighted and faulted them for bringing about "a deliberate closing-in of surroundings upon growth" (1916, p. 49).

Progressives approached the question of method at both the theoretical and the practical level. At the theoretical level, they pointed to the inherent unity between method and subject matter. How we teach is intimately related to why we teach and what we teach. Progressives saw value in learning the methods that have been used by others, but they laid more stress on the individual teacher developing his or her own method of teaching suitable for the group being taught.

A method of teaching given prominence by progressive educators was the scientific method of arriving at knowledge. This can also be termed the problem-solving method, the project method, or the activity method. This method, as described by Dewey and others, entailed the clarification of a problem to be solved, the development of ideas or hypotheses about this problem, and the testing of these hypotheses by an examination of empirical evidence. Progressives felt that this method could be used in most subject areas and that it was based on the natural inclination of learners to grapple with problems. This experimental method was an attempt to discover the truths about the world in which one lives.

Adult educators have, for the most part, accepted the methodology proposed by the progressives. Bergevin (1967), for example, called for adult education to be problem-centered or situation-centered. "Programs of learning for adults must," he emphasized, "be adjusted to the learners, to the problems they need solved, to the situations confronting them. Adult education must start there." The alternative—the subject-centered approach—was, in Bergevin's words, "a wasteful procedure" (1967, p. 149). Broudy (1960) made a similar observation noting that since adult education was *not* a preparation for the future, a more creative problem-solving curriculum was needed.

Clearly, Lindeman incorporated progressive ideas about method into his concept of adult education:

> I am conceiving adult education in terms of a new technique for learning, a technique as essential to the college graduate as to the unlettered manual worker. It represents a process by which the adult learns to become aware of and to evaluate his experience. To do this he cannot begin by studying subjects in the hope that some day this information will be useful. On the contrary, he begins by giving attention to situations in which he finds himself, to problems which include obstacles to his self-fulfillment. Facts and information from the differentiated spheres of knowledge are used, not for the purpose of accumulation, but because of need in solving problems. [Lindeman, 1956, p. 160]

While Lindeman seems to equate the two terms, methods and techniques, Coolie Verner has made an important distinction between the two. Method for him is "the relationship that exists between the learner, the knowledge, and the institution which has knowledge to diffuse" (Verner, 1959). Verner considers techniques to be the various devices that are used in learning: role playing, symposiums, forums, buzz groups, panels, etc. Other adult educators (Knowles, 1970, Kidd, 1973; Houle, 1972; Bergevin and McKinley, 1968) have given great attention to describing and promoting methods that are largely in keeping with the progressive approach to education. In an introductory essay tracing various systems of thought, Houle (1972) also notes Dewey's permanent influence on methodology and program planning in adult education. Some later systems, Houle points out, have not had the openness and fluidity of Dewey's thought (1972, p. 13).

Other adult philosophers of education who have taken a progressive or experimental view of methodology include Paul Sheats and Kenneth Benne. Sheats (1938) has attempted to forge a middle path between those who want to impose a definite curriculum and those who want education to bring about radical social change. He advocates an experimental attitude toward the work of adult education. Benne, in arguing the merits of various philosophical approaches to adult education, concludes that

> A broadened method still must be an experimental method, rather than a method of authority, of intuition, of deduction, or of induction. Rationality, for our time at least, must be defined in experimental terms. [Benne, 1957, p. 79]

In this experimental view, learning is a "series of experiments with respect to problems encountered and constructed" (p. 77). The preferred methodology in adult education, according to Benne, is problem-solving, for "programs of learning for adults must be adjusted to the learners, to the problems they need solved, to the situations confronting them" (1957, p. 149).

Though progressive education has made its mark on education through the introduction of a new methodology, in the last analysis it is not in this area that its greatest impact on adult education lies. Its greatest influence is found in the new relationship between teachers and learners.

4. *A Changed Relationship Between Teachers and Learners.* The broadened view of education, the new focal point, and the new methodology that the progressives proposed led logically to a new role for the teacher in the educational process. Progressives opposed viewing the teacher as the sole source of knowledge whose task was to put, or as Freire would have it, "bank" knowledge into the minds of students. In an educational theory that values the learning of subject matter or academic disciplines as the heart of the educational effort, this concept is functional. But if education is seen as the progressives viewed it—as the reconstruction of experiences through interactive processes with one's environment—then the traditional view of the teacher-learner relationship is inadequate.

Learning, according to Dewey, is something that students do for themselves. The teacher's responsibility is to organize, stimulate, instigate, and evaluate the highly complex process of education. The teacher provides the setting that is conducive to learning. In so doing, the teacher also becomes a learner, for the relationships between teachers and learners are reciprocal. Both should plan and learn from each other.

Dewey's earliest writings tended to downplay the role of the teacher. At that time he was perhaps overreacting against the traditional authoritarian stance of the teacher. In *Democracy and Education,* he stated that

> When the parent or teacher has provided the conditions which stimulate thinking, and has taken a sympathetic attitude toward the activities of the learner by entering into a common or conjoint experience, all has been done which a second party can do to instigate learning. The rest lies with the one directly concerned. [Dewey, 1916, p. 160]

Dewey rejected the view that the teacher merely stands off and looks on. He wanted teachers to participate and share in all the learning activities:

> In such shared activity, the teacher is a learner, and the learner is, without knowing it, a teacher, and upon the whole the less consciousness there is, on either side of either giving or receiving instruction, the better. [Dewey, 1916, p. 160]

By the time that Dewey wrote his most mature statement on educational theory in *Experience and Education* (1938), this view was modified and broadened. By then progressive education had come under severe criticism both for the learner-centeredness of its approach and its apparent denial of any real teacher role and authority. In his 1938 work, Dewey gave a more sophisticated appraisal of the teacher's role and tried to avoid the extremes of permissiveness and manipulation. Dewey still saw learning as based in the personal experiences of the student. The important tasks of the educator were to guide, direct, and evaluate the experiences in terms of their educational component. Teachers were also to share with learners insights that had come from their own experiences. Dewey admitted that to do this without imposing one's own views upon learners made the teacher's role more difficult than in traditional education.

Another task that Dewey allotted the teacher in *Experience and Education* (1916) was that of exercising social control without violating the freedom of the learners. When control is exercised by teachers, it is not a matter of personal power, but of acting in behalf of the group (p. 54). Dewey observed that the primary source of social control could be found in the work itself. This work must be thought out and planned:

> The educator is responsible for a knowledge of individuals and for a knowledge of subject-matter that will enable activities to be selected which lend themselves to social organization, an organization in which all individuals have an opportunity to contribute something, and in which the activities in which all participate are the chief carriers of control. [Dewey, 1938, p. 56]

For Dewey, the term social control meant both classroom discipline and discipline of learning. Since progressive education was considered weak in discipline, Dewey felt it necessary to defend the purposes and methods of discipline in progressive schools.

Though Dewey stresses at length the role of the teacher in exercising social control, perhaps his most adequate description of a teacher was that of leader of group activities:

> The educator must survey the capacities and needs of the particular set of individuals with whom he is dealing and must at the same time arrange the conditions which provide the subject matter or content for experiences that satisfy these needs and develop these capacities. The planning must be flexible enough to permit free play for individuality of experience and yet firm enough to give direction towards continuous development of power. [Dewey, 1938, p. 580]

Progressives recognized the difficulty of this proposed balancing act, but such a view was necessary to both safeguard freedom and to ensure that genuine educational experiences resulted.

Dewey wanted learners to have freedom. But he also criticized the attitudes of some progressive teachers who would put materials before learners and then not even suggest what should be done with them (1938, p. 71). Dewey argued that suggestions from teachers with broad experiences and wider horizons were more valuable than suggestions from accidental sources. But still, Dewey wanted only suggestions for students in planning and carrying out their learning experiences.

Dewey recognized the weakness of the progressive theory when it came to the learning of subject matter. He contended that improvisation in education could not take the place of the selection and organization of subject matter. He called for the organization of curriculum around problems that would relate to experiences of the learners. In discussing this issue, Dewey used the learning of science as an example. It would have been more telling if Dewey had chosen other fields like history, languages, humanities, mathematics, and skills learning. The progressives tended to see scientific learning as the ideal form of learning. Because of this approach, critics tend to see the progressive theory as best adapted to science learning and less suitable for other forms of learning.

It should be clear to anyone familiar with the work of adult educators in the past half century that the progressive view of the teacher has greatly influenced the descriptions of the role of the adult educator. Lindeman incorporated the progressive view of the teacher into his theory of education. He stated that in adult education

> The teacher finds a new function. He is no longer the oracle who speaks from the platform of authority, but rather the guide, the pointer-out, who also participates in learning in proportion to the vitality and relevancy of his facts and experiences. [Lindeman, 1956, p. 160]

Lindeman goes on to give a definition of adult education that is truly Deweyan and progressive, and that underlies the theoretical and practical thinking of many adult educators today. Following is his conception of adult education:

> A cooperative venture is nonauthoritarian, informal learning, the chief purpose of which is to discover the meaning of experience; a quest of the mind which digs down to the roots of the preoccupations which formulate our conduct; a technique of learning for adults which makes education coterminous with life and hence elevates living itself to the level of adventurous experiment. [Lindeman, 1956, p. 160]

Knowles is also indebted to this progressive concept of the role of the teacher. He characterizes the adult educator as that of a "helper, guide, encourager, consultant, and resource, not that of transmitter, disciplinarian, judge and authority" (1970, p. 34). Knowles' description of the adult educator as andragogue rather than pedagogue is in reality a contrast between the view of the teacher of traditional education and that proposed by the progressives (Elias, 1979).

Benne (1957) has presented a view of the teacher-learner relationship that is clearly in the progressive spirit. He prefers to view the teacher as a helper in the learning process. The teacher as helper must not only possess knowledge, but must also evaluate the knowledge that the learner acquires. The teacher-helper is a resource person who knows more about what is being studied. It is also the task of this helper to aid the learner in removing some of the emotional blocks to learning. Finally, the role of the teacher-learner is to establish the appropriate methodology for learning, which for Benne is the experimental method (1957, pp. 79-81). Benne is truly a progressive educator when he discusses the source of the teacher's authority. Rejecting views that place educational authority in a mandate from God, the content of the Great Tradition or Great Books, the dominant ideology of a society, or the realities of the situation, Benne locates the educator's authority in "the widening of a community of shared and evaluated experiences" (Benne, 1957, p. 82).

Another educator who has also been greatly influenced by the progressive description of the relationship between teachers and learners is Paul Bergevin. Although Bergevin in his influential *A Philosophy for Adult Education* (1967) gives no reference to John Dewey and the progressives, his indebtedness to this tradition is clear in many areas, but especially in the role that the teacher plays in the educational process. Bergevin argues for full participation of the learner in the teaching-learning process. He does not elaborate on the role of the teacher or the learning process except to say that both must carry out the program. Later in the chapter we will discuss the participation model of the Indiana School which more fully exemplifies these principles.

5. *Education as an Instrument of Social Change.* From the historical perspective presented in this chapter, it might be recalled

that progressive education placed a strong emphasis upon education's role in promoting social change. Progressives believed that the function of education was not merely to prepare learners for fitting into the existing society, but also to provide a means for changing society. For the progressives, education was to foster creativity and stability, as well as individuality and social consciousness.

As in other areas, the ideas of the progressives were brought into adult education through the powerful influence of Lindeman. The relationship between education and social change and action was a special concern of Lindeman, a professor of social philosophy at the New York School of Social Work. Lindeman believed that in a democratic society education and participation were necessary for bringing about change:

> Adult Education turns out to be the most reliable instrument for social actionists. If they learn how to educate the adherents of their movement, they can continue to utilize the compelling power of a group and still remain within the scope of democratic behavior. When they substitute something other than intelligence and reason, social action emanates as sheer power and soon degenerates into habits which tend toward an anti-democratic direction. Every social-action group should at the same time be an adult-education group, and I go even so far as to believe that all successful adult education groups sooner or later become social-action groups. [Lindeman quoted in Kidd, 1973, p. 154]

Although Lindeman was adult education's most eloquent spokesman for the progressive point of view, two other adult educators writing from a progressive orientation addressed the issue of social order and social change. Bergevin (1967) saw adult education as essential in contributing to what he called "the civilizing process." The civilizing process had an individual and societal dimension, each having responsibility for the other. At the individual level, the civilizing process referred to a person's "maturing" from a "mere survival" level to a "responsible member of social order" (p. 7). From the societal perspective, the civilizing process was a "corporate, social movement involving the whole of society, as it moves from barbarism toward refinement in behavior, tastes, and thought" (p. 8). Adult education, then, consisted of

> a consciously elaborated program aiding and reinforcing the civilizing process. The over-all aim of the professional or lay adult educator, then, will be to bring each of us into some kind of constructive relationship with the civilizing process, always remembering that this process should represent those positive elements in environment and society that help us develop mature rationality in our lives and institutions. [1967, pp. 9-10]

For Bergevin, the continuing education of adults was essential in preserving and enhancing a democratic way of life. It was a necessity, a "built-in requirement of a society emerging from control by the few to control by the many" (p. 35). Speaking from the progressive's view of human nature as being neither inherently good nor inherently evil, Bergevin presented adult education as a most serious and urgent matter—"a determining factor in the race between building and destroying, between the civilizing process and barbarism. We adults are capable of either and both" (p. 14).

Robert Blakely (1958, 1967) also explored the role of education in social change. Learning, especially adult learning, was, in his words, "fundamental to the solution of all social problems" (1967, p. 54). Like Bergevin, Blakely delineated both an individual and a social dimension to adult education. Education would lead to a better, more fulfilling personal life, while at the same time making a better citizenry and a better world (1958). While Bergevin spoke of the "civilizing process," Blakely wanted to see education working toward a "homeodynamic" society—that is, a society in which a balance could be achieved between cultural components that imitated the past, and components that were inventive of the future. Survival of individuals and society depended upon achieving this balance (1967). Other than to mention the value of group process, Blakely offers little in the way of specific suggestions for achieving a homeodynamic society.

Though not commonly propounded by leading adult educators at the present time, the social action thrust in adult progressive education inspired the founding of Myles Horton's Highlander Folk School in Tennessee. Although considered by some to be an example of radical adult education, as Adams (1972) describes the Highlander idea, Horton drew his inspiration from both Dewey and Lindeman in developing the adult residential center for the development of community leaders among school, church, civic, labor, and farm groups (p. 520). Participants in the Highlander School have been involved in worker education, civil rights struggles, and other liberal social causes. Adams judges the Highlander School as committed to democracy, brotherhood, mutuality, and united social action. The school's governing concepts are deliberately vague, "letting the people it serves and the times they live in define precisely what they mean" (p. 520). This is a good description of the progressive ideal in social action: education for social change, but always respecting the freedom of individuals to be true to their own convictions and commitments.

In summary, only a few adult educators have taken up the social thrust of the progressive education movement. The learner-centeredness and methodology of the progressives have had a much greater impact upon the field of adult education. It was left to the radicals, treated in the chapter on Adult Radical Education, to highlight the social change dimension of adult education. The work of Paulo Freire in particular has raised the consciousness of many North American adult educators about the potential of adult education for social and political change.

Contemporary Programs Inspired by Progressive Adult Education

In previous sections of this chapter the influence of progressive ideas on contemporary adult educators has been indicated. There is scarcely an adult educator whose ideas cannot be traced at least in some indirect form to the seminal ideas of Dewey and Lindeman. It could be argued that humanistic, radical, and behavioristic adult education are all in some ways dependent upon the progressive education for some of their chief ideas. Humanism took hold of the learner-centeredness of this approach, radicalism carried to further lengths the social change impulse of progressivism, and behaviorism placed an emphasis on the experimental and scientific dimensions of progressive thought.

Besides inspiring contemporary forms of adult education theory and practice, progressivism's influence can be seen in a number of programs currently in operation in adult education. Three of these programs—Americanization education, the Indiana Plan, and the Community Education Movement—will be discussed in the following section.

Americanization Education. Americanization education or Schools for the Foreign Born arose at a time when progressive ideas permeated educational circles. The great influx of immigrants in the early decades of the 20th century led to social concern for their welfare as well as fear that their numbers would produce an unstable political condition. Adult education's role in the "civilizing process" was enthusiastically put into practice by the adult evening schools primarily, but also by churches, factories, settlement houses, the YMCA, and other organizations. Seller (1978) reviews the curriculum of these programs:

> their major emphasis between 1914 and 1924 (even more than in the earlier years) was English lessons for all. For men, they stressed citizenship training (with emphasis upon the virtues of democracy and capitalism) and instruction in the factories in work habits and safety. For women, they stressed lessons in hygiene, childcare, and American-style cooking and homemaking. [Seller, 1978, p. 85]

Such campaigns were failures in the sense that only a small percent of the target population was involved. Immigrants desired literacy in their own native language as well as opportunities to develop cultural and intellectual interests. As a result, organizations within ethnic communities more effectively met the educational needs of immigrants (Seller, 1978).

Another critic (Carlson, 1975) argues that even today Americanization education can be faulted for imposing values on immigrants to such an extent that they have been encouraged to give up their unique qualities of religion and culture. While the complexity of this issue cannot be treated here, Carlson's study gives educators involved in such programs pause for thought.

Today, Americanization education or classes for the foreign born exist in communities throughout the United States. The emphasis in these programs is upon preparation for citizenship. English as a Second Language (ESL) or English for the Foreign Born (EFB) classes are usually held apart from citizenship preparation classes. While any number of community organizations might sponsor Americanization education, the adult school remains the primary deliverer of such programs.

Community Education Movement. The origin of the Community Education movement can be found in the ideals of early progressive educators. Dewey, in his attempt to shift education's focus from subject matter to learner needs and experiences wrote:

> From the standpoint of the child, the great waste in school comes from his inability to utilize the experiences he gets outside the school within the school itself; he is unable to apply in daily life what he is learning at school. That is the isolation of the school—its isolation from life. [Dewey, 1900/1956, p. 75]

Community Education as it has developed over the last fifty years can be characterized by its two major thrusts more easily than by a single definition. The two thrusts are (1) the enhancement of school programs by involving the community in the schools; and (2) the enhancement of the community through providing educational experiences for all people of all ages in the community.

Numerous programs in diverse settings developed in the first years of the movement. Welser (1978) points out that the movement had rural beginnings in Kentucky and Tennessee, and urban forms which sought to deal with community problems of crime, unemployment, delinquency, etc. It also thrived in times of social calm and times of great social upheaval, such as during the Great Depression (Welser, 1978). Welser's conceptualization of community education could have been written by Dewey:

> Education is a natural community process, of which the traditional school system is but a single component. In every community, all of the people are being educated all the time by everything that is happening in that community. It is both the amount and the overall quality of education that

distinguishes one community from another. [Welser, 1978, p. 544]

The breadth of the community education idea can be better grasped by a closer look at its components. Parson's adaptation of the basic components of community education, originally proposed by Minzey (1974), are as follows:

1. Educational Programs for Children and Youth—a key component of community education in which the use of community resources to enhance classroom teaching is emphasized.
2. The Expanded Use of Community Facilities—school buildings are looked to for community activities and services.
3. Enrichment Programs for School-Aged Children and Youth—programs over and above those offered during regular school hours. These are typically enrichment programs designed to present opportunities to develop interests and skills for which there is little time during the day.
4. Adult Education Programs—designed to meet the needs and interests of adult members of the community.
5. Recreation Programs for Adults, Youth, and Families.
6. Coordination and Delivery of Community Services—the school, through its building and personnel helps communities identify problems and resources and provides coordination necessary to bring these two together.
7. Community Development and Citizen Participation—the community school coordinator can play an important role in stimulating participation and facilitating community development. [Parson, 1978, pp. 614-616]

A discussion of community education, no matter how brief, cannot overlook the importance of the Mott Foundation's contribution to the Community Education Movement. In 1936, Charles Mott supported the opening of five school buildings as community centers in Flint, Michigan. Thriving today, the Flint Community Education Program has served as a model for countless other programs. In addition, the Mott Foundation trains community school leaders and supports Centers for Community Education Development throughout the United States.

As of this writing, there are over 1400 Community Education school districts involving more than 5000 Community Education programs in separate buildings. Eleven states have passed supporting legislation, and forty-two states have Community Education directors (Welser, 1978). While community education has developed as a movement somewhat separate from adult education, the connections between the two are clear. Both are interested in lifelong learning and in the continuing education of adults.

Participation Training—The Indiana Plan. Another approach to adult education clearly based on progressive principles has been developed by professors of adult education at Indiana University. Paul Bergevin has given the philosophical or theoretical foundation for the approach in his *A Philosophy for Adult Education* (1967). Bergevin and John McKinley have described the mechanics of the program in *Participation Training for Adult Education* (1965) and in *Design for Adult Education in the Church* (1958).

The underlying assumption of participation training, or the Indiana Plan, is that persons can be trained to participate actively in the learning experience and to assume responsibility for the success of the program. In this training, persons, not subjects, are taught. The particpants group themselves according to patterns that they choose. Learing is not enough in the program for, sooner or later, persons must act as a consequence of their learning. In this training, the nature of each learner is explored, relationships are forged with fellow learners, and the subject matter is treated (Bergevin, 1967, pp. 56-58).

The progressive influence can be clearly seen in an analysis of the systematic learning in participation training. The focus is upon adult learning for credit or non-credit. This form of adult learning can take place in many different types of community organizations. It encourages the full cooperation and participation of all members of the learning team and it depends upon continuing educational relationships between adults who teach and adults who learn (Bergevin, 1967, pp. 58-59).

Basic principles for participation training presented by Bergevin and McKinley (1968) are either derived from or consonant with progressive adult education. First, adult education begins with a consideration of the problems and principles of adult learning. Second, the training program demands a freedom in which individuals feel that they are secure in making contributions to the group. Third, they are encouraged to participate actively in the program. Fourth, both learners and teachers share in the program development by expressing their needs and relating the information to their experiences. Fifth, shared goals are developed which give direction to the program. Sixth, there is a balance between content and process in the programming. Seventh, a wide variety of methods are utilized, beyond the traditional methods of lecture and assignments. Finally, evaluation is a cooperative effort between teachers and learners (Bergevin and McKinley, 1958).

The strong emphasis on education as a means of social change and progress is one progressive ideal not clearly developed in this program. This goal is not excluded, but the method does not dwell on the potential of the training to involve people in change efforts in local communities. In general terms, social change as a goal of education is found in the philosophy of the Indiana Plan, but this function seems to be added on to objectives that are more concerned with personal development and fulfillment. The Plan speaks vaguely about promoting democracy, but contains no socio-cultural analyses of contexts in which these goals are to be pursued.

Assessment of Progressive Adult Education

In one sense it is possible to speak of progressive education as a theory of the past. The Progressive Education Association died in the 1950's. No contemporary philosopher of education would align himself or herself totally with this movement. No major adult educator is clearly a progressive in the sense that Dewey and Lindeman were progressives. The strength of the movement may have been in its particular response to social conditions that were present in this country between 1890 and 1950.

But to consider progressive education a theory of the past is to miss the powerful influence that this theory has exercised to this day both in general and adult education. Silberman (1970) showed that reforms in American education in the sixties were partly inspired by the philosophy of John Dewey. Many educational reforms of this period—open classrooms, renewed interest in moral education, student-centered learning, intelligent use of the environment in education, schools without walls, the introduction of creative methods into education, the emphasis on the role of education in social change, the reintroduction of the problem or situation curriculum—these are all elements of progressive education that were rediscovered by such educational reformers as John Holt, George Dennison, Jonathan Kozol, Joseph Featherstone, and Paulo Freire. In fact, a strong case can be made that the reform movements of this time were led by neo-progressives, some of whom read their Dewey, and others of whom arrived independently at similar conclusions and suggestions for educational reform.

As has been pointed out in this chapter, the distinctive features of progressive education have been incorporated in one fashion or another into the theory and practice of adult education. Learner centeredness, the experimental method, and social activism are part of the legacy that the progressives have left to American education. In varying degrees, these elements are found in the philosophies of adult educators. All adult educators accept the basic progressive premise that education is a process of reflective inquiry.

In the passage of time, however, some of the weaknesses of progressive education have come to light, especially those pointed out by liberal educators. This philosophy at times emphasizes science at the expense of the humanities, history, literature, and the arts. Progressives have often replaced the fixity of ideas with the fixity of the problem. Too great influence has been ascribed by this theory to the power of education to bring about social change. The view of education and human life appears too optimistic in its failure to take account of the tragic in life. In placing the learner at the center of the process of education, at times insufficient attention is given to the role of the teacher and to the importance of subject matter.

It is not only the liberal educators that have criticized progressive education. In the next four chapters we shall see four contemporary philosophies of education that have been inspired in some form by progressive principles, but are also critical of this philosophy at certain points. This pluralism of philosophic viewpoints is to be expected in such an endeavor as education which is closely related to both individual and social goals.

REFERENCES

Adams, Frank. "Highlander Folk School: Getting Information, Going Back and Teaching It," *Harvard Educational Review*, 1972, 2, 497-520.

Benne, Kenneth. "Some Philosophical Issues in Adult Education," *Adult Education*, 1957, 7, 67-82.

Bergevin, Paul and John McKinley. *Design for Adult Education in the Church: The Indiana Plan.* New York: Seabury, 1958.

Bergevin, Paul, Dwight Morris, and Robert Smith. *Adult Education Procedures: A Handbook of Tested Patterns for Effective Participation.* New York: Seabury, 1963.

Bergevin, Paul and John McKinley. *Participation Training for Adult Education.* New York: Seabury, 1965.

Bergevin, Paul. *A Philosophy for Adult Education.* New York: Seabury, 1967.

Blakely, Robert J. *Adult Education in a Free Society.* Toronto: Guardian Bird Publications, 1958.

Blakely, Robert J. *Toward a Homeodynamic Society.* Boston: Center for the Study of Liberal Education for Adults, 1965.

Bowers, C. A. *The Progressive Educator and the Depression: The Radical Years.* New York: Random House, 1969.

Broudy, Harry. *Aims in Adult Education: A Realist's View.* New York: Seabury, 1967.

Carlson, Robert A. *The Quest for Conformity: Americanization Through Education.* New York: John Wiley Sons, 1975.

Conant, James. *Slums and Suburbs.* New York: McGraw Hill, 196 .

Cremin, Lawrence A. *The Transformation of the School: Progressivism in American Education, 1876—1957.* New York: Random House, 1961.

Darwin, Charles. *The Origin of Species by Means of Natural Selection.* London: Oxford University Press, 1958. (Originally published in 1857.)

Dewey, John. *How We Think.* Chicago: University of Chicago, 1910.

Dewey, John and Evelyn Dewey. *Schools of Tomorrow.* New York: Dutton, 1915.

Dewey, John. *Democracy and Education.* New York: Macmillan, 1916.

Dewey, John. *Experience and Education.* New York: Macmillan, 1938.

Dewey, John. *The Child and Curriculum and The School and Society.* Chicago: University of Chicago Press, 1956. (Originally published as *The School and Society*, 1900; and *The Child and the Curriculum*, 1902.)

Elias, John. "Neither Andragogy nor Pedagogy, but Education," *Adult Education.* 1979, 29, 525-256.

Herndon, James. *How to Survive in Your Native Land.* New York: Simon and Schuster, 1971.

Holt, John. *How Children Learn.* New York: Pitman, 1967.

Houle, Cyril. *The Design of Education.* San Francisco: Jossey-Bass, 1972.

James, William. *The Varieties of Religious Experience.* London: Longmann, 1972. (Originally published, 1902.)

James, William. *The Meaning of Truth: A Sequel to Pragmatism.* New York: Appleton, 1909.

Karrier, Clarence, Paul Violas, and Joel Spring. *Roots of Crisis: American Education in the Twentieth Century.* Chicago: Rand McNally, 1973.

Katz, Michael B. *The Irony of Early School Reform.* Boston: Beacon, 1968.

Kidd, J. R. *How Adults Learn* (Rev. ed.). New York: Association Press, 1973.

Kirk, Russell. "A Conservative View of Education," In P. Phenix (ed.), *Philosophies of Education.* New York: Wiley, 1965.

Knowles, Malcolm. *The Modern Practice of Adult Education.* New York: Association Press, 1970.

Knowles, Malcolm. *The History of the Adult Education Movement in the United States* (Rev. ed.). New York: Krieger, 1977.

Koerner, James. *The Miseducation of American Teachers.* Baltimore: Penguin, 1965.

Lawson, K. H. *Philosophical Concepts and Values in Adult Education.* Nottingham, England: Barnes and Humby, 1975.

Lindeman, Eduard C. *The Meaning of Adult Education.* Montreal: Harvest House, 1961. (Originally published 1926.)

Lindeman, Eduard C. *The Democratic Man: Selected Writings of Eduard Lindeman.* Edited by Robert Glessner. Boston: Beacon, 1956.

Minzey, Jack. "Community Education—Another Perception," *Community Education Journal,* 1977, *4*, 3, 58-61.

Monette, Maurice L. "The Concept of Need: An Analysis of Selected Literature," *Adult Education,* 1977, *27*, 116-127.

Monette, Maurice L. "Need Assessment: A Critique of Philosophical Assumptions," *Adult Education,* 1979, *29*, 83-95.

Parson, Steve. "Cooperative Extension Guide to Community Education Development," In *Yearbook of Adult and Continuing Education, 1978—1979,* Chicago: Marquis Academic Media, 1978.

Paterson, R. W. K. *Values, Education and the Adult.* Boston: Routledge and Kegan Paul, 1979.

Perkinson, Henry. *The Imperfect Panacea: American Faith in Education, 1865—1976* (2nd ed.). New York: Random House, 1977.

Robinson, James. *The Humanizing of Knowledge.* New York: George H. Doran, 1924.

Rorty, Amelia (ed.). *Pragmatic Philosophy: An Anthology.* New York: Doubleday, 1966.

Seller, Maxine S. "Success and Failure in Adult Education: The Immigrant Experience, 1914—1924," *Adult Education,* 1978, *28*, 83-99.

Sheats, Paul. *Education and the Quest for a Middle Way.* New York: Macmillan, 1938.

Silberman, Charles. *Crisis in the Classroom. The Remaking of American Education.* New York: Random House, 1970.

Spencer, Herbert. *Education: Intellectual, Moral and Physical.* New York: Appleton, 1860.

Tough, Allen. *The Adult's Learning Projects: A Fresh Approach to Theory and Practice in Adult Learning.* Ontario: Ontario Institute for Studies in Education, 1971.

Verner, Coolie. *Methods and Techniques: An Overview of Adult Learning Research.* Chicago: American Education Association, 1959.

Welser, Carl F. "The Flow of Community Education in Historical Perspective," In *Yearbook of Adult and Community Education, 1978—1979.* Chicago: Marquis Academic Media, 1978.

CHAPTER IV

BEHAVIORIST
ADULT EDUCATION

Probably no other system of psychology has had as much impact on general and adult education, or had its principles be the cause of as much debate as behaviorism. Founded by John B. Watson in the 1920's, behaviorism focuses upon the overt, observable behavior of an organism. Animal and human behavior is studied in laboratory settings employing scientific principles and methodology used so successfully in the "hard" sciences such as chemistry and physics. The intellect, feelings, emotions, a person's "inner" life are not observable or measurable and therefore not investigated in and of themselves. Behaviorists from Watson through Skinner believe all human behavior is the result of a person's prior conditioning and is determined by external forces in the environment over which a person has little or no control.

Although behaviorism is ordinarily considered a psychological system, the fundamental questions raised by this approach are clearly philosophical in nature. Are people more than complex machines? What differentiates humans from animals? To what extent are men and women free agents? What is the relationship between education and the shaping of culture? Is education no more than training, than arranging certain stimuli to elicit predetermined responses? As will be seen in the next chapter, humanism and humanistic psychology grapple with these questions and provide an alternative to a behaviorist view of the world.

This chapter will begin with a brief discussion of the historical antecedents of behaviorism, and the major contributors to its development in the twentieth century. A second section will examine the application of behaviorism to education—the roles of the teacher and learner, accountability, behavioral objectives, programmed instruction, etc. Behaviorism's impact on adult and continuing education will also be examined through analyzing its manifestation in continuing professional education, business and industry, and adult literacy programs.

Antecedents of 20th Century Behaviorism

Though modern psychological behaviorism has arrived at its conclusions through scientific research, it is clear that behaviorism as a system of thought has its roots in a number of philosophical traditions. The first of these traditions is *materialism*, the theory that reality can be explained by the laws of matter and motion, without any appeal to mind or spiritual reality. In the materialist viewpoint, humans are part of nature, though complex parts. This materialist point of view is found in the writings of Hobbes who was both a materialist and a determinist. This British philosopher contended that the psychological make-up of persons could be explained in mechanistic terms.

A second philosophic tradition to which modern behaviorism is allied is *scientific realism and empiricism.* Francis Bacon introduced into Western thought the inductive method by which one arrived at truth through an examination of information gained through the senses alone. Bacon was followed in this viewpoint by John Locke who denied the innateness of ideas and explained human knowing through empirical processes. Bertrand Russell contributed to this tradition by his preference for the "hard" data of science over the "soft" data of the humanities.

Positivism is the third philosophic tradition to which modern behaviorism is allied. Philosophical positivism was proposed by Comte who contended that one arrived at knowledge not through theology or traditional philosophy, but through scientific observation and the measurement of facts. Logical positivism, prevalent in Germany and England, placed greater emphasis on developing a language that corresponded to reality and that did not go beyond reality that could be experienced. Finally, British philosopher Gilbert Ryle (1943) developed a philosophical behaviorism through an analysis of language. In his thought, the causes of behavior can be explained by the behavior itself and not by any self, mind, consciousness, or "ghost in the machine."

A distinctive psychological orientation toward the study of human behavior is rooted in the thought of the 17th century French philosopher Rene Descartes. He viewed behavior systematically when he suggested that all instances of behavior could be classified as voluntary or involuntary. The involuntary or automatic behavior identified by Descartes led to the development of the "reflex" concept in the 18th and 19th centuries. Reflexology culminated in the work of Sir Charles Sherrington and Ivan Pavlov. Sherrington demonstrated the usefulness of the experimental scientific method in revealing lawful properties of behavior—specifically reflex action in animals. Pavlov, through his famous experiments with salivating dogs, explored mechanisms for the acquisition and extinction of conditioned reflexes. The concept of classical conditioning emerged from his work. Classical conditioning emphasizes the importance of controlling the behavior by controlling the stimulus. It differs from Skinner's operant conditioning which involves control of both the stimulus before the behavior, and the environmental contingencies after the behavior is exhibited.

Charles Darwin's work provided another impetus for the emergence of behaviorism. The instinctual behavior in animals delineated by Darwin was viewed as involuntary, reflexive, and dependent upon internal stimuli. His *Origin of Species* (1859) also proposed the notion of biological continuity which implied that humans were more intelligent, perhaps, but not separate from other species. Humans were thus at the mercy of their environment and if humans thought they could plan their behavior and affect their environment, then so could animals. Such ideas gave rise to research into animal intelligence in the late 19th and early 20th centuries.

E. L. Thorndike, a psychologist and contemporary of Watson, investigated both animal and human intelligence. Using animals in controlled laboratory experiments, Thorndike explained learning as a process of association. An organism, when presented with a stimulus, formed a connection or bond with a response. Hence, his work became known as "connectionism" or the "S-R" theory of learning. Thorndike's laws of learning were major contributions to the psychology of learning and have long been viewed as applicable to learners of any age. According to Thorndike, organisms will acquire and remember those responses that lead to satisfying after effects (law of effect); repetition in itself does not establish a connection, but repetition of a meaningful bond will strengthen the learning (law of exercise); and a pleasurable bond, hence maximized learning, occurs if the organism is ready (law of readiness) (Thorndike, 1932).

John B. Watson, Founder of Behaviorism

With the publication of two important texts, *Behavior—An Introduction to Comparative Psychology* (1914) and *Psychology from the Standpoint of a Behaviorist* (1919), John B. Watson became the acknowledged leader of behaviorism. Watson adamantly endorsed the idea that psychology was a science of behavior, not a study of the mind or mental activity. The way to understand humans, he insisted, was through observing their behavior, not exploring the inner, unobservable recesses of mind and emotion. Emotion he defined as "a hereditary pattern of response in which implicit visceral and glandular responses were predominant." The concept of instinct he rejected entirely. For Watson, "the genesis of behavior, from the squirming and squallings of the new-born child to the complex skills and language responses of the adult, he ascribed to Pavlov's principle of conditioning" (Keller, 1977).

Using Pavlov's techniques, Watson, in a famous experiment with an eleven-month-old child, successfully conditioned the boy to fear a white rat. Watson argued that emotional responses together with motor reflexes can be conditioned to evoke reflexes. All behavior, from the fear response of the rat to the most complex activity of the adult, could be explained in terms of conditioning. As an extreme environmentalist, Watson maintained that he could take any healthy infant and through environmental conditioning produce anything from a doctor to a beggar.

Through books, articles, and lectures, Watson brought the science of behaviorism to the attention of the American public and to other psychologists. Child-rearing practices of rigid feeding schedules and strict discipline reflected his influence. Classical conditioning, although considered today to be inadequate to explain all behavior, is still a useful strategy for reversing inappropriate fear responses such as fear of crowds, snakes, or darkness (Herman, 1977).

Between the 1920's and 1950's other behaviorists expanded upon the work of Watson and Pavlov and attempted to explain, control, and predict more complex behaviors. E. R. Guthrie proposed that contiguity was important; that is, the only significant aspects of a response were in what they made the organism do next. Tolman investigated latent learning and the intervening variables between a stimulus and a response. Hull, and his colleague Spence, considered drive, habit, strength, and motivation as salient aspects of response behavior. Important as the work of these researchers was, behaviorism received its greatest boost from the contemporary successor to Watson, B. F. Skinner.

B. F. Skinner and Modern Behaviorism

Burrhus Frederick Skinner became known in psychological circles in the 1930's with his book, *The Behavior of Organisms.* As a radical determinist and behaviorist, Skinner firmly believes that humans are controlled by their environment, the conditions of which can be studied, specified, and manipulated. An individual's behavior is determined by the events experienced in an objective environment. "The effects of exposure to various events during one's life-span are critically important . . . and it is assumed that only knowledge of the relationships between such events and the resultant behaviors will allow an adequate account of a person's functioning . . . it is psychology's business to investigate these relationships" (Nye, 1975, p. 39). Through refined research techniques and an amassing of experimental data, Skinner and his followers have made significant theoretical contributions to understanding human behavior. Following is a brief discussion of several principles of modern behaviorism.

Skinner's major contribution has been to distinguish between classical and operant conditioning. In classical conditioning, responses are conditioned or unconditioned reflexes. The stimuli that evoke the responses are all that matter; reward, reinforcement, and feedback are not necessary. In operant conditioning the response is as important as the stimulus and, if reinforced, will solidify the bond to the stimulus. According to Skinner, the behavior is *"strengthened* by its consequences, and for that reason the consequences themselves are called 'reinforcers'." He goes on to point out that "the standard distinction between operant and reflex behavior is that one is voluntary and the other involuntary" (Skinner, 1974, pp. 39-40).

The principle of reinforcement is essential to understanding operant conditioning. If a behavior is reinforced, the response is more likely to occur again under similar circumstances. Behavior that is not reinforced or rewarded is likely to become less frequent and may even disappear. Even something as complex as personality can be understood in terms of operant conditioning. Personality, according to Skinner, is a "repertoire of behavior imported by an organized set of contingencies"—in effect, a personal history of reinforcements (Skinner, 1974, p. 149). Reinforcements can be both positive and negative:

> Positive reinforcement involves the *addition* of something (a positive reinforcer) to a situation when a response is made. For example, a response may be positively reinforced if the obtaining of food, water, sexual contact, money, or praise is a consequence. Negative reinforcement involves the *removal* of something (called either a negative reinforcer or an aversive stimulus) from a situation when a response is made. For example, a response may be negatively reinforced if the removal of extreme cold or heat, a loud noise, a threat, a tedious task, or a headache is a consequence. In short, much of our behavior is conditioned because it gains us something (in the case of positive reinforcement) or because it allows us to escape or avoid something (in the case of negative reinforcement). [Nye, 1975, p. 48]

Reinforcement, in the behaviorist view, can both explain our own behavior and be used to modify another's behavior. Particular reinforcers might be difficult to identify, but that doesn't mean they aren't there. They might, in fact, be intrinsic rather than extrinsic. That is, the behavior itself is rewarding. The key to controlling behavior is being able to identify the most effective reinforcers, the amount they should be employed, and the timing of their use.

The timing of reinforcements has been another area of experimentation by Skinner and modern behaviorists. Skinner distinguishes between continuous and intermittent reinforcement schedules. In continuous schedules, a response is reinforced each time it is made. Behavior that is maintained by continuous reinforcement has been found to extinguish rapidly when reinforcement is not forthcoming. On the other hand, behavior that is only intermittently reinforced is likely to be maintained longer. Intermittent reinforcement schedules can be fixed, that is, occurring not continually but regularly in relation to time or number of responses, or variable, having no set pattern. Knowing the most effective scheduling of reinforcements for eliciting desired behavior has been a continuing area of interest of behavioral psychologists. Educational settings, where certain learning behaviors are desired, are but one area of application of such knowledge.

Skinner differentiates between negative reinforcement and punishment, two forms of aversive control. A negative reinforcer is something a person tries to avoid or escape; it generates behavior in the same way as a positive reinforcer does. For example, people pay taxes because they want to avoid a fine or going to jail; a student memorizes spelling words to avoid a failing grade. Punishment, on the other hand, is used to *eliminate* a specific behavior. Skinner opposes the use of both negative reinforcement and punishment.

Operant conditioning, positive and negative reinforcement, extinction and avoidance behavior, and reinforcement schedules are Skinner's experimentally derived contributions to better understanding human behavior. It is the philosophical assumptions underlying his approach, however, that have brought much criticism and debate from non-behaviorists. While these assumptions are implicit in most of his writings, *Beyond Freedom and Dignity* (1972) squarely confronts the role of man, human will, freedom, dignity, and the concept of self-determinism in a behavioristic society.

The purposes of psychology according to Skinner are to understand, predict, and control human behavior. Since most of the problems of any society involve the behavior of humans who live in that society, controlling human behavior can result in a better society. If we want to improve our society, Skinner reasons, we must first give up the notion of personal freedom and its accompanying sense of dignity and personal worth. Personal freedom is, in fact, an illusion. "Man's struggle for freedom is not due to a will to be free, but to certain behavioral processes characteristic of the human organism, the chief effect of which is the avoidance of or escape from the so-called 'aversive' features of the environment" (Skinner, 1971, p. 42). The task for society, according to Skinner, is "not to free man from control but to analyze and change the kinds of control to which they are exposed" (Skinner, 1971, p. 43).

Autonomous man becomes a scapegoat for behavior that we do not yet understand. The role of environment in shaping and maintaining behavior is in its nascent stages. Skinner is convinced, however, that a "technology of behavior" is the only means of solving social problems and ensuring survival of the human species. "The task of parents and professional educators and society at large, according to Skinner, is to define the kinds of behavior wanted in their societies and then to produce people who will behave in those ways" (Kolesnik, 1975, p. 106). *Walden Two* (1948) is Skinner's fictional account of a utopian society based upon behavioral engineering. At least one community, founded in 1967 and still in existence, has attempted to put Skinner's ideas into practice (Kinkade, *A Walden Two Experiment: The First Five Years of Twin Oaks Community*, 1972).

It is difficult to argue with a behaviorist world view. Instances of puzzling human behavior, consciousness, feelings, mind, notions of free will, dignity, and freedom are at least potentially explainable if, according to behaviorists, one looks long and hard enough for determinants of reinforcement in the environment. The more unanswerable questions have to do with the mechanisms of control in a society. The potential for misuse of a technology of behavior exists. Skinner himself notes the question of "values" involved in designing a society. "Who," he asks, "will use a technology and to what ends?" (Skinner, 1971, p. 25).

Regardless of the extent to which one concurs with Skinner's underlying philosophical assumptions or plans for restructuring society, one can make use of the techniques and principles of behavior proposed by this school of psychology. Behaviorism has, in fact, had a significant impact upon various facets of our society. The following section deals with behaviorism's influence upon education.

Behaviorism Applied to Education

The educational patterns of any society reflect the underlying values of that society. According to Skinner (1974), survival is the fundamental value for individuals and societies:

What is good for the species is what makes for its survival. What is good for the individual is what promotes his well being. What is good for a culture is what permits it to solve its problems. There are . . . other kinds of values, but they eventually take second place to survival. [Skinner, 1974, p. 205]

An educational system can ensure the survival of individuals and of society by carefully arranging the contingencies of reinforcement to meet these ends. On the individual level, behavioristic education emphasizes the acquisition of job skills so that a person can "survive" in our society. Learning how to learn is also an important skill needed if one is to adapt successfully to a changing environment. Behaviorists would also de-emphasize competition and individual success. Education, they feel, should reinforce cooperation and interdependence on a global level in order that the world's problems can be addressed. Education should produce people who can work with each other to design and build a society that minimizes suffering and maximizes the chances of survival.

In *The Technology of Teaching* (1968), Skinner addresses the issues of who and what should be taught as well as the administrative concerns of student control and individual differences. In his view, "that culture is strongest which educates as many of its members as possible" (p. 233). Thus, both school entry age could be lowered and opportunities for adults extended. With regard to what should be taught, Skinner advocates allowing for novelty and diversity for "both cultures and species increase their strength with respect to a far wider range of contingencies when subject to variations and selection" (1968, p. 235). The diversity should be carefully planned, however, and not left to accident or chance. Finally, teaching should take place under favorable conditions, student behavior can and should be controlled through positive rather than negative reinforcement, and individual differences need to be more efficiently dealt with.

The roles of teacher and learner are quite defined in the behaviorist framework. The ultimate goal of education is to bring about behavior that will ensure survival of the human species, societies and individuals. The role of the teacher is to design an environment that elicits desired behavior toward meeting these goals and to extinguish behavior that is not desirable. The teacher, then, is a contingency manager, an environmental controller, or behavioral engineer who plans in detail the conditions necessary to bring about desired behavior. One source (Karen, 1974) has identified several "principles of effective contingency management" for evoking desired learning behavior:

1. Consequence Identification—the consequences for an educational program (reinforcers and punishers), must be identified by their effects on the pupil's behavior—not on the teacher's.
2. Automaticity—consequences affect student behavior automatically, whether or not the relationship between behavior and consequences can be verbalized.
3. Relevant Criteria—consequences of an educational accomplishment should be closely related to the criteria of accomplishment.
4. Consistency—the consequences of student's behavior should be attended to in a consistent manner.
5. Immediacy—consequences should be presented immediately following the behavior responsible for them.
6. Frequency—reinforcements should occur often enough to strengthen desired behavior.
7. Small Steps—educational material should consist of units and subunits small enough to allow for a reasonable reinforcement schedule.
8. Unplanned Punishment Effects—the threat or actual withdrawal of possible reinforcements or punishment weakens the effect of using positive reinforcement alone.
9. Effective Contingency Contracting—a learning contract between student and teacher should be clear, fair, and honest. [Karen, 1974, pp. 409-411]

The student role in behavioral education is active rather than passive. The environment is arranged in such a way that certain student behaviors are emitted. It is essential that students act so that their behavior can be reinforced. A student has learned something if there is a change in behavior, and if his or her response occurs again under similar circumstances.

Behavioral psychology applied to the educational context has also resulted in several policy emphases and specific instructional practices. Following is a brief discussion of behavioral objectives, accountability, competency-based education, and instructional strategies.

Behavioral Objectives

The use of behavioral objectives in educational settings is a direct outgrowth of behavioral psychology. Behaviorism focuses upon the measureable, overt activity of an organism. Learning, in behavioral terms, is a change in behavior. Behavioral objectives, then, specify the behavior to be exhibited by learners after completing a unit of instruction. Also called "instructional objectives," behavioral objectives contain three components: (1) the relevant *conditions* or stimuli under which a student is expected to perform; (2) the *behavior* a student is to perform including a general reference to the product of the student's behavior; and (3) a description of the *criteria* by which the behavior will be judged acceptable or unacceptable, successful or unsuccessful.

Advocates of behavioral objectives maintain that learning outcomes can be measured objectively and precisely, thus revealing how much progress has been made on the part of the learner. Evaluation based on behavioral objectives eliminates subjective, capricious estimates of student performance. Behavioral objectives also provide the teachers with a means of clarifying just what is going to be taught, and hence, what a student is supposed to learn. Advocates further claim that using behavioral objectives leads to more effective teaching and learning. While this claim is not clearly substantiated by research (Herman, 1977), it does make sense that the use of behavioral objectives can lead to improved communication among different segments of the educational process. Gagne (1973, pp. 86-88) makes a case for *communicating* as the primary purpose of statements describing instructional objectives. Such communicating is facilitated on four levels: instructional designer to course planner, designer or planner to the teacher, teacher to the student, and teacher or administrator to the parent.

The criticisms of behavioral objectives appear to cluster around the concept of learning. Opponents argue that learning is a complex phenomenon, that many kinds of behaviors might reveal that learning has occurred, that outcomes can be creative and unpredictable, and that learning can be unstructured or latent and approached from the whole rather than bits and parts. Also, say opponents, behavioral objectives are more appropriate for certain subjects and types of learning than others, and they do not ensure that what is learned in one situation will transfer to a new situation.

Whether or not one supports the concept of behavioral objectives, they are widely used by teachers, curriculum designers, administrators, and adult educators in a variety of settings. Adult basic education, continuing professional education, and training in business and industry are three program areas in adult education that make extensive use of behavioral objectives.

The increased use of behavioral objectives reflects the demand at all levels of education for accountability—the idea that all those involved with the educational process must be held accountable for bringing about what education is designed to accomplish. The link between behavioral objectives and accountability is expressed by Popham (1971): "Those who discourage educators from precisely explicating their instructional objectives are often permitting, if not promoting, the same kind of unclear thinking that has led in part to the generally abysmal quality of instruction in this country" (p. 78).

Accountability

Behaviorist education, with its emphasis upon arranging the contingencies of learning and then measuring the change in behavior, provides a basis for the notion of accountability. According to Popham (1973):

> The concept of educational accountability involves the teacher's producing *evidence* regarding the quality of his or her teaching, usually in terms of what happens to pupils, then standing ready to be judged on the basis of the evidence. Any accountable teacher, therefore, takes *responsibility* for the results his or her instruction produces in learners. [p. 41]

Other educators hold a somewhat broader view of accountability in that all the professionals involved in an educational activity should be held responsible for its outcomes. The result of making professionals responsible for their product, speculates Barro (1973, p. 13), will be "higher quality education." The taxpayer's concern with making schools cost effective, the inevitable evaluations that accompany such a demand, the need to effectively reach disadvantaged groups, and a drive to be responsible to individual needs are forces that have led to attempts to make education more accountable.

Behavioral objectives provide one mechanism for looking at the effectiveness of a school system, curriculum, administrator or teacher. Barro (1973) lists other tools that could be employed to achieve high quality education through accountability. Several make use of behavioral concepts of reward, reinforcement, and measured results:

- Use of improved output-oriented management methods
- Institutionalization of external evaluations or educational audits
- Performance incentives for school personnel
- Performance or incentive contracting
- Decentralization and community control
- Alternative educational systems. [pp. 15-17]

Performance contracting and educational vouchers are two of the more intriguing ways in which school systems have sought to deal with accountability. In performance contracting, businesses or industries using modern technology and principles of behavioral design contract to bring about better student performance more efficiently than the public school system. The results of such attempts to date have been inconclusive (Kolesnik, 1975). Educational vouchers essentially present an economic incentive for bringing about quality education. Although various plans exist, each provides a process for allocating funds through a governmental agency to parents of school children. Parents then "purchase" education for their children at a school of their own choosing. This would then force schools to provide quality education in order to remain solvent. In adult education, educational vouchers and entitlement programs have been proposed for consideration as one means of implementing lifelong learning (Lifelong Learning Act, 1976). The G.I. Bill is another example of a voucher-like method of financing adult education. The educational section of the Bill allows service personnel to receive a fixed sum of money if they are enrolled in an accredited or degree-granting program more than half time. A veteran enrolled in a course of study less than half time can be reimbursed for the cost of the course. Each state has a State Approving Agency which "approves" programs for which veterans can be funded.

Employer tuition-aid programs in business and industry also allow adults to purchase education thus causing deliverers to be more accountable. It has been estimated that as many as 80 per cent of U.S. employers provide some kind of educational aid for courses at outside institutions ("Tuitition-Aid Concepts . . . ," 1977). Most programs, however, require that the courses be job-related, reimburse according to completion and/or grade obtained, and have a low rate of participation (4 to 5 per cent). Companies experimenting with more liberal policies have had better results. Kimberly-Clark, for example, allows its employees to take courses that are "culturally self-improving" as well as job related; pays for tuition, travel, books, etc., *prior* to the course; grants paid educational leave; and contributes to a fund for educational expenses for immediate family members. Eighty-nine per cent of the people who have taken courses have taken job-related classes. And of the 7,000 employees, 38 per cent have taken advantage of their educational plan ("Tuition-Aid Concepts . . . ," 1977).

A systems approach to administration and planning for schools and adult education activities is yet another manifestation of the accountability movement. Systems is a way of looking at the educational organization, its various components, and how they fit together to bring about a specified end product. The three basic components of any systems model are the input, that which enters the system to be processed to bring about the desired results; throughput, or the heart of the system where the inputs are processed in an orderly fashion; and output, or the end result of the inputs being processed. The systems approach includes a flow chart that visually represents the structure of the subsystems, including elements of directionality, time allotment, and decision points.

Any number of systems including the more popular planning-programming budgeting systems (PPBS) and program evaluation review technique (PERT) are being used by the field of education as a tool for guiding administrative policies, designing curriculum, and improving units of instruction. In adult education the systems approach has been utilized for state-wide planning of adult basic education, in university extension, cooperative extension, business and industry, and continuing education. According to Londoner (1972), the typical application of systems analysis to administrative and/or program planning activities of adult educators and trainers involves the following basic steps:

Need—the definition of the real underlying need and problem the program is trying to satisfy.

Objectives—the statement and definition of the educational objectives in terms of measurable learning goals.

Constraints—the definition of the real-world limitations or restraints which must be satisfied by the system before reaching the desired outcome.

Alternatives—the generation or adoption of possible approaches to attaining the desirable outcomes.

Selection—the analysis and evaluation of all alternatives in light of the desired outcomes and the possible constraints with which the system must cope.

Implementation—the first adoption of the selected alternative to meet the desired outcome.

Evaluation—the assessment of the conformance or discrepancy between the initially specified objectives and the actual system performance.

Feedback and Modification—the process of modifying the designed system based on deficiencies in meeting the stated objectives. [Londoner, 1972, pp. 25-26]

While new tools have been developed for its implementation, the concept of accountability is not a recent phenomenon in adult education. The voluntary nature of most of adult education has mandated that teachers and programs of study effectively meet the needs of students. Programs have also had to be cost effective to justify continued support from parent institutions or public funds. The issue of accountability has, in fact, been philosophical as well as economic. In a society that emphasizes preparatory education of youth and values education for becoming a more productive member of society, most of adult education has had to be remedial or job-oriented. Activities focusing on personal growth and development, leisure and recreation, have also had to be "accounted" for largely because of adult education's structurally and financially subordinate position in the educational hierarchy.

Competency-Based Education

The demand that educational institutions and agencies be held accountable for their products, and the desire to make the educational process more effective has led to the concept of competency-based education. Competency-based education is being used to describe a range of educational activities from total curriculums to individual instructional units to self-instructional packets to teacher training. Briefly, competency-based education (CBE) or competency-based instruction (CBI) is an educational program in which required performances are specified and agreed to in advance of instruction. CBE programs specify, in behavioral terms, the goals and objectives to be met, the learning experiences to be engaged in, and the method of evaluation used to demonstrate achievement of the predetermined goals. Implicit in such an approach is the behavioristic definition of learning as a change in behavior that can be observed and measured.

The emphases in competency-based education are on the outcomes rather than the process of learning, on exit rather than entrance requirements, and on criterion-referenced evaluation rather than norm-referenced evaluation.

Criterion-referenced evaluation is an important concept in CBE and in behavioral psychology. In criterion-referenced evaluation, the learner's progress or accomplishments are compared to a fixed standard or criterion of mastery rather than to the performance of other students. It is based on the assumption that learning objectives can be predetermined, and that given sufficient time and proper reinforcements nearly all students can accomplish the objectives. Criterion-referenced testing also de-emphasizes competition among learners, an element in our educational system that behaviorists would like to replace with cooperation.

An attempt has been made to apply CBE to teachers as well as learners. Advocates of competency-based teacher education (CBTE) would like to see teacher certification based on demonstrated competencies and skills rather than a specified number of college courses. The problem with this approach to teacher certification is that there is little consensus as to the competencies a person must have to be considered a certified teacher (Kolesnik, 1975). The CBE movement, in fact, assumes that measurable competencies can be spelled out for all areas of knowledge. Competency-based education thus suffers from some of the same criticisms that have been aimed at behavioral objectives. Both CBE and behavioral objectives predetermine the end product of a learning experience. Other learning that may occur during the process *or* shifting to different outcomes as a result of formative evaluations are changes not easily accommodated in the behavioristic framework.

Competency-Based Adult Education

Competency-based education or instruction is well suited to adult education for several reasons: it allows for individual differences in terms of the starting point for instruction; the time it takes a student to master competencies is flexible and dependent upon individual ability; learning specified competencies may be done in a variety of ways from formal class activities to life or work experiences; criterion-referenced evaluation is non-threatening; it is an ideal vehicle for a self-directed individual learning experience. Concepts of competency-based education have been widely incorporated into programs in adult vocational education, continuing education, and adult basic education.

Vocational education has, to some extent, been "competency-based." Preparation for a vocation of necessity means identifying the skills needed to perform in an occupation, teaching those skills, and requiring a certain standard of performance in those skills. "What is new is the insistence on the use of validated competencies, thoroughly systematic procedures for delivering instruction, and more objective student assessment devices. Taken together, the principles of the competency-based approach constitute a revolution in the presentation of vocational training and in the significantly increased degree of certainty in certifying student proficiency" *(Competency-Based Vocational Education,* 1977, p. 9).

Developing a curriculum or course for competency-based vocational technical instruction begins with a detailed job description. These descriptions include location and general working conditions, job functions, general duties, contingent responsibilities, and so on. The job description provides the basis for a detailed task analysis, a process that breaks the basic job down into successively more detailed components. For many occupations, task analyses are already in existence and can be obtained through various vocational-technical publications, the U.S. military, and business and industry. A detailed task analysis of a specific job is then used as a basis for developing instructional objectives and materials. Finally, criterion-referenced measures are developed and are used to evaluate student performance on each task.

Competency-based vocational education (CBVE) exhibits characteristics which are common to all programs, regardless of the specific job or occupation. To begin with, the *competencies* (knowledge, skills, behaviors) to be demonstrated by the learner are derived from analysis of worker roles, stated in behavioral terms and made public in advance. Second, the *criteria* to be used in assessing student competency are direct outgrowths of the competencies themselves, stated explicitly and in advance, including specified conditions for mastery. The *assessment* of a student's competency uses performance as the primary source of evidence, while at the same time taking into account evidences of a student's knowledge. Student progress is determined by demonstrated competency rather than time or course completion. Finally, the individual's learning experience is guided by *feedback*, and the program as a whole is systematic *(Competency-Based Vocational Education*, 1977).

The advantages of CBVE, especially for adult learners, would appear to outweigh the problems. There are, however, constraints or at least potential pitfalls when competency-based concepts are applied to vocational training. Such an approach depends upon an accurate identification of tasks performed in thousands of occupations and the availability of such task inventories to curriculum developers. Also, some competencies desirable for certain occupations might be difficult to specify from task inventories and, if identified, difficult to perform. For some tasks, identifying what constitutes minimum performance standards or criteria for mastery might be difficult. These drawbacks are in addition to basic philosophical differences between a behaviorist and humanistic orientation. Competency-based education has been criticized because it has been seen as dehumanizing or nonhumanistic, lacking in concern for the student, and inhibiting creativity. It has also been attacked for forcing all students into the same mold, and fragmenting curriculum into bits and pieces while overlooking the whole (Verduin, Miller & Greer, 1977).

Continuing education is another area where competency based education programs are becoming increasingly popular. It provides one mechanism whereby employed persons can enhance their knowledge and skills in their field and do so under conditions that allow for individual differences in pacing, background and motivation. Competency-based modules in the areas of health, education, and business, for example, follow the same steps of task analysis, development of behavioral objectives and instructional materials, and criterion referenced measures of performance as in competency-based vocational education. The difference lies in content and focus. For the most part, CBVE prepares people to enter a job, occupation, or profession. Continuing education takes place after one is employed and reflects the need to remain current with developments in the field, retraining, and the increasing concern with credentialization, certification, and licensing.

Training in business and industry is one aspect of continuing education. The greatest majority of employee education and training is seen by company executives as necessary to carrying out company goals. Lusterman (1978a, p. 9) has delineated three characteristics of the corporate education system which set it apart from more traditional systems: (1) high motivation on the part of adult participants "who are learning under circumstances in which the rewards for success and the penalties for failure are perceived by them to be high"; (2) the work place is the setting for both the learning and the doing; and (3) corporate education is pragmatic—it is a means of achieving other goals such as profit. As in other areas of education, accountability is an important facet of corporate education. Concerned with the most economic and efficient way to accomplish a task, corporate training makes use of competency-based concepts and modern instructional technologies. The greatest emphasis in corporate training, Lusterman (1978b, p. 478) points out, is placed "on the importance of thinking through and specifying the desired outcomes of particular learning programs with respect to changes in the knowledge, behaviors, attitudes, or sensibilities of the learner— and on making reasonable effort to appraise results and make appropriate modifications."

Adult Basic Education (ABE) is another area of adult education deeply involved in competency-based education. Many states are experimenting with competency-based high school completion programs which emphasize the mastery of basic requirements rather than the number of hours of instruction or the number of courses completed. The Adult Performance Level (APL) Study conducted by the University of Texas and funded by the U.S. Office of Education has been a major impetus towards the development of a competency-based high school and curriculum in adult basic education. The purposes of this study were to (1) define adult literacy in terms of the competencies needed to function successfully in today's society, and (2) to assess those competencies in the adult population of the United States.

The study identified five general knowledge areas (Consumer Economics, Occupational Knowledge, Community Resources, Health, Government and Law) as necessary for adequate functioning in society. In addition, the four skills of Communication, Computation, Problem Solving, and Interpersonal Relations were also identified. Functionally competent adults were defined as ones who could employ the four skills across the five content areas. In surveys measuring functional adult literacy based upon APL competencies, 20 per cent of adults were found to be functionally incompetent, 34 per cent functional, but not proficient in performing everyday life tasks, and 46 per cent were proficient (APL, March 1975).

The competencies identified by the APL Study have formed the basis for assessment procedures and curriculum development in adult basic education. The competencies are delineated at three levels. The first level is the *goal* statement, or broad description of the capability that an adult should possess, such as "to manage a family economy and to demonstrate an awareness of sound purchasing principles" (APL, March 1975). The second level consists of *objectives* derived from the goal which must be mastered for an adult to be "functionally competent"—"to be aware of factors that affect costs of goods and services and to determine the most economical places to shop" (APL, March 1975), for example. Finally, there are situation-specific *tasks* which need to be performed as evidence that an objective has been mastered. A student might be asked to compute the unit price of a grocery item.

While aspects of the APL's research procedures and the competencies themselves have been questioned (Griffith and Cervero, 1977), "studies in New Jersey, Region X, Pennsylvania, and the Southeast, as well as the experiences in New England, Louisiana, Illinois, and other programs, support the applicability of many of the objectives to students currently enrolled in ABE programs" (Fischer, 1978). In a review of the research and activities in Competency-Based Adult Education, Fischer (1978) points out that CBAE has come to be associated with the acquisition of skills needed to cope socially and economically in our society. She concludes that "there is a great potential" in the functional competency movement, yet

> there is much to be done before this potential is fully realized. We are developing the means of providing instruction while still determining the competencies and the best ways of measuring competency. The identification of competencies is in itself an enormous task; the list may be endless and continually in flux. Society changes, people in that society change. It is, therefore, doubtful that all competencies will be applicable to all people at any point in their lives. . . . The concurrent development of different components of functional competency adult education is not, however, a bad situation. Development in each area can benefit development of the others if we continue to and strive for exchange of information. [Fischer, 1978, p. 30]

Competency-based adult education is a concept growing in popularity. Its application cuts across delivery systems and clienteles of adult education. As part of the accountability movement in education in general, CBAE is an effort to demonstrate the effectiveness of a complex and often times costly investment. As a manifestation of the behaviorist orientation to education, competency-based education emphasizes setting behavioral goals, objectives or outcomes, demonstrating behavioral change, and measuring the amount of change against pre-determined criteria.

Program Planning in Adult Education

Behaviorism has perhaps had its greatest impact in adult education in curriculum design and program development. While no single individual can be singled out as the major proponent of this philosophical orientation, Ralph Tyler can be credited with having a major influence on the program development models proposed by Houle (1972), Knowles (1970) and others.

In *Basic Principles of Curriculum and Instruction* (1949), Tyler presents a generic model for designing an educational activity whether it be a single instructional unit or a comprehensive program. Tyler bases his model upon the assumption that "education is a process of changing the behavior patterns of people" (p. 5). Each educational program should have clearly defined purposes. Defining these purposes is the first step in program design. Purposes can be derived from many sources including the learners themselves, contemporary life outside of school, and subject specialists. Information derived from these sources is then filtered through the philosophical orientation of the designer and institution, and through psychological findings related to learning. This process should lead one to formulate specific objectives that would guide in the selection of learning activities.

Writing specific objectives that can be used to guide learning experiences is the second step in planning. The nature of these objectives is identical to behavioral objectives discussed earlier in this chapter. Tyler (1949) reminds his readers that "since the real purpose of education is not to have the instructor perform certain activities but to bring about significant changes in the students' patterns of behavior," an objective should be "a statement of changes to take place in students." Each objective should specify "both the kind of behavior to be developed in the student and the content or area of life in which this behavior is to operate" (p. 44).

Learning experiences are then selected that will facilitate obtaining the objectives. Tyler defines a learning experience in behavioral terms as "the interaction between the learner and the external conditions in the environment to which he can react" (p. 63). The role of the teacher is that of a contingency manager who sets up the environment or structures the situation to elicit predetermined responses. Tyler states that "the teacher's method of controlling the learning experience is through the manipulation of the environment in such a way as to set up stimulating situations—situations that will evoke the kind of behavior desired" (p. 64). It is not enough to select appropriate learning experiences. They must also be organized so as to reinforce each other. Tyler posits three major criteria for organizing a group of learning experiences. The experiences should be (1) continuous— provide recurring opportunities for experiencing particular elements, (2) sequential—each successive experience builds up the preceding so as to increase the learner's depth and breadth of understanding, and (3) integrated—arranged so that the segments of learning experiences can be united into the learner's behavior (pp. 84-86).

The final step in Tyler's model is evaluation. Evaluation is based upon the educational objectives that specified the behavioral change desired. Specifically, it is "the process of determining the degree to which these changes in behavior are actually taking place" (p. 106). According to Tyler, evaluation must be based upon overt behavior since that is the only way one "can tell whether students have acquired given types of behavior" (p. 111). Methods of evaluation can be varied, however, including tests (written and oral), questionnaires, observations, and samplings of a student's work. Evaluations should be used for both individual and program assessments. Tyler points out that curriculum planning is a continuous process in which evaluation leads to replanning and redevelopment (p. 123).

Tyler's behavioral model has had a significant impact on adult education. Houle (1972) notes that, although the system has been expanded and criticized, "the fundamental way of thought which Tyler suggested still remains intact, underlying the discussion and practice of most education today" (p. 15).

Tyler's thought can be readily seen in most program planning models in adult education. Houle, whose philosophical orientation draws from several schools of thought, credits Tyler with having the primary influence on his system for planning and implementing adult education programs (Houle, 1972). Houle's "fundamental system" begins by identifying an educational activity and deciding to proceed. General and specific objectives are identified and refined. Once objectives are put into some hierarchy, the most suitable learning format and its accompanying activities are designed for carrying out the objectives. The program is then put into effect. Finally, the results are measured and appraised. Ideally, the evaluation influences future planning. Similarities between Houle's "fundamental system" and Tyler's principles of curriculum design are obvious. Objectives, a measurable form of evaluation, and manipulation of environmental factors to carry out a program are important components in Houle's model.

Although Malcolm Knowles clearly identifies with humanistic psychological principles when proposing an andragogical approach to adult education (1970), his program planning model nevertheless reflects Tyler's influence. His model begins with a needs assessment. Sources of identifying needs are adult learners themselves, organizations, and communities. Tyler, it might be remembered, suggests identifying "purposes" from learners, contemporary life and specialists. Purposes for Tyler become objectives after considering them in terms of philosophy and psychologically based learning theories. Needs in Knowles' scheme become objectives once they are filtered through institutional purposes and philosophies, and feasibility, which, Knowles notes, includes "the psychology of learning" (p. 125) and the interests of the clientele.

Knowles divides objectives into operational—things to be done to improve the quality of resources for meeting needs, and educational—"the kinds of behavioral outcomes that participants are to be invited to seek in specific areas of content" (p. 126). Knowles' model proceeds to the selection of a learning format "that will most effectively accomplish the objectives of the program" (p. 133). Implementation and evaluation are the final steps in the model.

Numerous other program planning models (Boyle and Jahns, 1970; Boone, et al. 1971; Spikes, 1978; Knox, 1971) draw from Tyler's design for curriculum and instruction. That is not to say that the authors of various models are behaviorist adult educators. Rather, some of the basic concepts of behavioral psychology are particularly appropriate to situations where a person or agency wants to bring about certain behaviors. Thus, behavioral terminology has found expression in the design and implementation of educational activities ranging from a single unit of instruction to more comprehensive programs.

Instructional Methods

Behaviorism's impact on education has resulted in the development of several specific instructional methodologies. Competency-based education can be viewed as an instructional method as well as a concept. So too can criterion-referenced instruction. Other methods associated with behaviorism are programmed instruction, computer based or computer assisted instruction, mastery learning, teaching machines, contract learning, Personalized System of Instruction (PSI), Individually Guided Education (IGE), and Individually Prescribed Instruction (IPI). Whatever the method, the responsibility for learning lies primarily with the learner. Herman (1977) notes several other commonalities:

> All of these programs are based on the principles of operant conditioning and on the assumption that learning is acquired through repeated reinforcement of behavior. They all define learning in *behavioral terms*, and almost all shape the student's behavior through a *gradual progression* toward the goal. They provide for *constant and immediate feedback*, *liberal positive reinforcement*, and *self-pacing* insures that no student must fail just because he learns less quickly than others. [Herman, 1977, p. 93]

Building upon the work of Sidney Pressey, B. F. Skinner is accredited with developing programmed instruction. Programmed instruction, via teaching machines and now usually in book or computerized form, is simply a "device which arranges contingencies of reinforcement" (Skinner, 1965, p. 65). According to Skinner (1968), there are four types of programming designed either to (1) generate new patterns of behavior, (2) alter properties of behavior, (3) bring behavior under control of stimuli, or (4) maintain behavior under infrequent reinforcement. Programs can be linear in which material is broken into small units leading towards a final goal, or branching, which allows students to explore wrong answers and skip sections already understood. As with other aspects of behavioral education, programmed instruction has its advocates and its opponents. The controversy centers on two points—student satisfaction with the method, and acquisition and retention of material. Research in both areas has thus far failed to establish either the superiority or inferiority of programmed instruction (Herman, 1977).

Various methods for individualizing instruction such as the Keller Plan or Personalized System of Instruction (PSI), Individually Prescribed Instruction (IPI), and Individually Guided Education (IGE), employ behavioral learning principles. Several systems of individualized instruction make use of programmed materials and/or learning contracts. Homme and Csanyi (1968) have developed a training program for bringing about self-directed learning behavior. Called "contingency contracting," the first phase has the behavior manager or teacher determine the tasks to be performed and the type of reinforcement offered. In phase 2, called "transitional contracting," both the teacher and student determine the terms of the contract. In phase 3, the student contracts with him or herself, determines the behavior to be performed and the consequences or reinforcement that will follow. This program thus moves from teacher-directed to learner-directed behavior.

Many adult educators would like to see more emphasis on educational activities that foster self-directed learning. Knowles' *Self Directed Learning* (1975) advocates a process most akin to phase 3 of Homme and Csanyi's model—that is, the student him or herself determines the behavior to be performed and criteria and mechanisms for evaluation. In reality, formal instruction in adult education is more likely to be 'individualized' through joint teacher-student contracting or teacher determined tasks. In an analysis of individualized instruction, Herman (1977) has delineated the following steps by which educators and learners at all levels can utilize principles of behaviorism for designing individualized instruction:

Step 1: Specify Behavioral Goals.
Step 2: Analyze the Learning Task—sequence material in a logical progression.
Step 3: Assess Entry Behavior—identify what your students or you already know.
Step 4: Plan Presentation—provide cues, feedback, reinforcement, and self-pacing.
Step 5: Evaluate, record, and adjust. [Herman, 1977, pp. 126-128]

Individualized learning systems and programmed instruction are more likely to supplement rather than replace the more traditional group instruction and teacher-directed activities. The behavioral concepts of operant conditioning, reward, reinforcement, pacing and feedback, however, permeate instruction and the arrangement of activities for learners from pre-school through adult education.

Conclusion

Estimating the extent of behaviorism's impact upon adult education has been a difficult undertaking. Aside from B. F. Skinner who has attempted to transfer psychological concepts into educational practice, there is no adult educator or specific educational program that espouses a philosophy drawn exclusively from behavioral psychology. Rather, one must look to policies, programs, and practices in education and in adult education in particular to detect behaviorism's influence. Behavioral objectives and accountability are two concepts soundly based in behaviorism and permeating all levels of education. Competency-based education has become popular in adult vocational education, continuing education, and adult basic education, especially through the Adult Performance Level study. Program planning and instructional methods in adult and continuing education also contain concepts from behavioral psychology. The diverse and wide-spread manifestations of behaviorism in education perhaps speak to the desire on the part of all educators to know better the nature of the impact one has in the learning process.

REFERENCES

Adult Performance Level Staff. *Adult Functional Competency: A Summary.* Austin, Texas: University of Texas, March 1975.

Barro, Stephen M. "An Approach to Developing Accountability Measures for the Public Schools." Julia DeCarlo and Constant Madon (eds.), *Innovations in Education for the Seventies: Selected Readings.* New York: Behavioral Publications, 1973.

Boone, Edward J. and others. *Programming in the Cooperative Extension Service: A Conceptual Scheme.* Raleigh: The North Carolina Agricultural Extension Service. Misc. Extension Publication 73, 1971.

Boyle, Patrick and Irwin Jahns. "Program Development and Evaluation." In Robert M. Smith, George F. Aker, and J. R. Kidd (eds.), *Handbook of Adult Education.* New York: MacMillan Co., 1970.

Competency-Based Vocational Education: Participants Guide for Inservice Teaching. Richmond, VA: Division of Vocational Education, VA State Department of Education, 1977.

Fischer, Joan K. "A Review of Competency-Based Adult Education," *Report of the USOE Invitational Workshop in Adult Competency Education.* Washington, D.C.: U.S. Government Printing Office, 1978.

Gagne, Robert M. "Behavioral Objectives? Yes!" In Julia DeCarlo and Constant Madon (eds.), *Innovatives in Education for the Seventies: Selected Readings.* New York: Behavioral Publications, 1973.

Griffith, William S. and Ronald M. Cervero. "The Adult Performance Level Program: A Serious and Deliberate Examination," *Adult Education.* 1977, 27, 209-224.

Herman, Therese M. *Creating Learning Environments: The Behavioral Approach to Education.* Boston: Allyn and Bacon, Inc., 1977.

Homme, L. W. and A. P. Csanyi. *Contingency Contracting: A System for Motivation Management in Education.* Albuquerque, NM: Southwestern Cooperating Training Laboratories, 1968.

Houle, Cyril. *The Design of Education.* San Francisco: Jossey-Bass, Inc., 1972.

Karen, Robert L. *An Introduction to Behavior Theory and its Application.* New York: Harper and Row, 1974.

Keller, Fred. "Behaviorism." *Collier's Encyclopedia* (Vol. 4). New York: MacMillan Educational Corporation, Inc., 1977.

Kinkade, Kathleen. *A Walden Two Experiment: The First Five Years of Twin Oaks Community.* New York: William Morrow, 1972.

Knowles, Malcolm. *The Modern Practice of Adult Education.* Tallahassee: The Florida State University Adult Research Information Processing Center, 1971.

Knowles, Malcolm. *Self Directed Learning.* Chicago: Associated Press, Follett Publishing Co., 1975.

Kolesnik, Walter B. *Humanism and/or Behaviorism in Education.* Boston: Allyn and Bacon, Inc., 1975.

Londoner, Carroll A. "The Systems Approach as an Administrative and Program Planning Tool for Continuing Education," *Educational Technology.* August 1972, 24-30.

Lusterman, Seymour. "Education in Industry," *Lifelong Learning: The Adult Years,* 1978, *1,* 8-9, 38-39.

Nye, Robert D. *Three Views of Man.* Monterey, California: Brooks/Cole Publishing Company, 1975.

Popham, W. James. "Probing the Validity of Arguments Against Behavioral Goals," In Miriam B. Kapter (ed.), *Behavioral Objectives in Curriculum Development.* Englewood Cliffs, NJ: Educational Technology Publications, 1971.

Popham, W. James. "The New World of Accountability: In the Classroom," In Julia DeCarlo and Constant Mason (eds.), *Innovations in Education for the Seventies: Selected Readings.* New York: Behavioral Publications, 1973.

Ryle, Gilbert. *The Concept of Mind.* New York: Barnes and Noble, 1943.

Skinner, Burrhus F. *About Behaviorism.* New York: Alfred A. Knopf, 1974.

Skinner, Burrhus F. *Beyond Freedom and Dignity.* New York: Alfred A. Knopf, 1971.

Skinner, Burrhus F. *The Technology of Teaching.* New York: Appleton-Century-Crofts, 1968.

Spikes, Frank. "A Multidimensional Program Planning Model for Continuing Nursing Education," *Lifelong Learning: The Adult Years,* 1978, *1,* 4-8.

Thorndike, Edward L. *The Fundamentals of Learning.* New York: Teachers College, Columbia University, 1932.

"Tuition-Aid Concepts at Kimberly-Clark Show Dramatic Results," *Training and Development Journal.* December 1977, 8-10.

Tyler, Ralph. *Basic Principles of Curriculum and Instruction.* Chicago: The University of Chicago Press, 1949.

Verdium, John Jr., G. Miller, and C. Greer. *Adults Teaching Adults.* Austin, TX: Learning Concepts, 1977.

CHAPTER V

HUMANISTIC ADULT EDUCATION

Humanism is a broad philosophical point of view that holds sacred the dignity and autonomy of human beings. As a philosophy, humanism is as old as human civilization and as modern as the twentieth century. Its roots can be traced back to classical China, Greece, and Rome; historically it has found expression in religion, education, and psychology.

Humanistic adult education draws from some of the same sources as liberal adult education. The emphasis of the humanistic educator, however, is not upon the works of the past and the values these possess, but upon the freedom and dignity of the individual person that is highlighted in this tradition. Humanistic adult educators are concerned with the development of the whole person with a special emphasis upon the emotional and affective dimensions of the personality. In this particular stance, humanistic adult educators are more closely allied with a number of contemporary existentialist thinkers.

This chapter will first follow the threads of humanism as it has surfaced at various points and in various contexts through history. Second, the general principles gleaned from humanism's many expressions and which most humanists would ascribe to will be presented and discussed. A third section will be devoted to an exploration of humanism as it manifests itself in modern general and adult education. The chapter concludes with a discussion and analysis of humanistic adult education, its major proponents and applications.

Humanism in an Historical Context

Humanism as a philosophy can be traced back to Confucius and Greco-Roman thinkers, especially Aristotle. The Italian Renaissance, however, is most often pointed to as the first full expression of this philosophy. The term itself derives from the 15th century Italian *humanista,* meaning teacher of the humanities. In its strictest sense, humanism referred to a Renaissance literary cult that spearheaded an awakened interest in studying Greek and Roman literature. Studying such works for their own sake, it was believed, would develop autonomous and responsible individuals. The so-called "New Learning" movement was a revolt against the stultifying authority of a church-dominated world in which the Classics were read for the edification of Christianity. The emergence of humanism in Renaissance Italy as a revolt against a dehumanizing force begins a pattern repeated several times.

Italian humanism, despite repression from the Church, introduced the study of Greek, translated Plato's writings in Latin, and produced work in historiography. A belief that man had great potential and an innate ethical sense is clearly reflected in their writings. Not so clear is their image of man. Castiglione's *Courtier,* for example, presents a worldly, cultured gentleman which contrasts with Machiavelli's evil, though rational, *Prince.*

The influence of Italian humanism was pervasive. It eventually molded the world view of many Europeans and resulted in diminishing the powerful grip of the Church. The humanists' fascination with Classical scholarship was equaled by an interest in Hebrew and Christian writings. Erasmus, the best known of the Christian Humanists, propounded a resolute faith in reason, popularized the new learning of the humanist tradition, and worked for reform from within the Church. In retrospect, the Renaissance humanists left a legacy of principles adopted by humanists from then on: the revolt against a force such as the church which tries to control knowledge; emphasis on intellectual capabilities; the ideal of a gentleman-scholar; and the promotion of a good-life for all humanity.

Humanism was identified to some extent with the Enlightenment of the 18th century. The Enlightenment's interest in works of antiquity, confidence in human intellect and reason, and an appetite for learning were endeavors highly compatible with a humanistic world view. An even greater resurgence in humanism occurred in the late 19th and early 20th centuries. As with Renaissance humanism, modern humanism developed as a protest against forces viewed as threatening to humanity—the industrial revolution with its pursuit of wealth and material goods, the advance of natural science which had given vogue some felt "to a mechanistic philosophy or destroyed the philosophical pursuit altogether," and the spread of communism which had promoted atheism and materialism (Perry, 1956, p. 5). In more recent years, humanism has been a protest against behavioristic psychology and the dehumanizing potential of nuclear power.

Humanists' reactions to these forces have taken many forms. To deal with the problem of science, Scientific Humanism evolved which proposes using science to enhance human life. Christian Humanism rejects traditional concepts of God and devotes its attention to promoting the well-being of humanity. A myriad of other movements and philosophies have espoused a humanistic component—Marxism existentialism, pragmatism, etc.

Existentialism is a contemporary expression of humanistic thought that has had great influence on a number of adult educators, especially Carl Rogers. Existentialism is a broad term that embraces the thought of a rather diverse group of thinkers: Kierkegaard, Nietzsche, Heidegger, Jaspers, Camus, Marcel, Tillich, Buber, and Sartre. This philosophical movement is deeply concerned with the freedom and integrity of the individual in the face of increased bureaucratization in society and its institutions as well as the gamut of human relations. Existentialists stress awareness, consciousness, perception, the total meaning-structure of the individual, his vision of life and death, his word choices, and other aspects of his relating to life.

Pratte (1971) briefly summarizes a number of common philosophic themes in existentialism that have some influence upon existential and humanistic educational theory. Existentialists contend that existence precedes essence in the sense that the person is not ready-made but is rather the designer of his own being or essence. Second, essence is contingent or superfluous for, in the words of Sartre (1949), "every existing being is born without reason, prolongs life out of weakness, and dies by chance"

(p. 18). Third, human existence is fundamentally absurd or irrational for no reason can be given for a thing being one way rather than another. Fourth, persons are destined to choose and bear responsibility for their choices. Fifth, meaningful human relations are the very substance of human life.

As a means of obtaining its goals of developing the individual and promoting the well-being of humanity, humanists have always placed great value upon education. Although the process of education proposed by Aristotle would hardly be humanistic by today's standards, much from his philosophy can be construed in a humanistic light. For Aristotle, the goal of all human striving is the attainment of the highest or supreme good which is often synonomous with happiness. Moral and political action and intellectual activities were the best ways to achieve the ultimate goal. Striving for this goal is a self-actualizing activity. The mediate goal of education, Aristotle felt, was "to cultivate the disposition that will lead people to be ready, able, and willing to engage in the excellent activities that constitute or which lead to happiness" (Patterson, 1973, p. 34).

The humanists of the Renaissance taught in schools and universities as well as actively participated in affairs of state, thus exemplifying the well-rounded educated person. Erasmus, already mentioned as an influential humanist who sought to reform the Catholic church, wrote a work called "The Education of a Christian Prince." In it he recommends that virtue be the highest quality to be obtained. Montaigne, another Renaissance scholar, thought a youth should see learning "not so much for external advantages as for his own good, to enrich and furnish himself within," and that a tutor should be selected for character and intelligence (Montaigne, 1972, p. 72).

Humanistic values underlie the educational thought of such important thinkers as Comenius, Rousseau, and Pestalozzi. Comenius in his book *The Great Didactic* (1657) set forth a methodology of teaching for leading the learner toward a maximum attainment in knowledge, virtue, and piety. In keeping with the Renaissance ideal of the well-rounded citizen, Comenius proposed a system of education that would enhance social, emotional, spiritual, and intellectual development.

Rousseau's *Emile* (1762) is perhaps one of the best known treatises on education. Written to a parent who was concerned about her son's education, Rousseau describes the ideal education of a fictitious boy, Emile. Believing in the natural goodness of human nature and deploring the corrupting forces of society and its institutions, Rousseau felt education should strive to preserve the naturalness of man. The humane and sensitive teacher would allow the learner to become self-sufficient, to develop all his/her potentialities, and to learn naturally. Rousseau is quite modern in his advocacy of the learner as starting point, of problem-posing and discovery techniques, and of a warm and relaxed teacher-student relationship (Noll and Kelly, 1970).

Like Comenius and Rousseau, Pestalozzi emphasized the total development of the learner and the need for education to be as natural as possible. The growth and development of learners was to be brought out by love in a loving environment. The result of the educative process would be a humanist—a man who was emotionally secure, intellectually alive, and socially active.

Thus, the basic and essential principles of humanistic education have been enunciated by thinkers since Aristotle. Patterson (1973, p. 44) identifies two major principles inherited from earlier educators: "(1) the purpose of education is to develop the potentials—all the potentials—of man as a whole; (2) the essential method for achieving this is the providing of a good human relationship between the teacher and the student."

In the past two decades a number of educational theorists have attempted to apply various themes of existential philosophy to the traditional components of educational philosophy (Kneller, 1958; Morris, 1966; Greene, 1973). The overly pessimistic themes of some existentialists have in these writings been abandoned, with emphasis being placed upon the educational task of assisting a feeling, suffering, rejoicing free person to fashion an essence or character. The primary task of the existentialist educator is defined as assisting in the development of responsible selfhood in the face of the complexities and problems of modern life.

Humanistic psychology has also had a significant impact upon educational theory and practice. As with the earlier humanist "revolts," humanistic psychology developed from a reaction to behaviorism, the predominant psychological orientation of the first half of the century. Commonly referred to as the "third force" in psychology, humanism rejected the view of man espoused by both behaviorists and Freudian psychologists. While humanists could accept Freudian and behaviorists' contributions to understanding human nature, and behaviorists' efforts to make psychology an exact science, they were distressed by the lack of concern these two positions had for the complexity of human beings. What was lacking, they felt, was a recognition of man's individuality, potentialities, creativity, and freedom.

The common point of reference for all behaviorists, as was discussed earlier in this text, is their attempt to explain behavior in terms of the connection between stimuli and observable responses. This largely mechanistic and piecemeal approach to human behavior and learning was first challenged by the introduction of Gestalt psychology to America in the 1930's. Gestalt theorists proposed looking at the whole rather than individual parts and at the total structure of learning rather than one incident. The major proponents of Gestalt psychology, Koehler, Koffka, and Wertheimer, broadened the investigation of learning to include notions of understanding, insight, and problem-solving. The individual, however, was still primarily at the mercy of a configuration of external forces. Not until the mid-1950's with the writings of Maslow, Rogers, Buhler, and Bugental was a humanistic psychological position clearly delineated. Bugental succintly stated the difference between the behaviorist and humanist view of human nature. According to Bugental (1967), the behaviorists see man as

> an object acted upon from the outside by various forces or driven from within by other forces which are to be characterized by their relation to the outside (e.g., thirst, hunger, sexual appetite). The regularities in man thus most attract the mechanomorph: instincts, reflexes, conditional responses, habits, learning. [p. 8]

In the humanistic psychologists' model of man,

> man is viewed as a subject in the midst of his own living, acting on the world, changing himself and all about him. While man's reactiveness is certainly recognized, the humanistic psychologist regards this as less distinctive of the human

experience and tends to look to those ways in which humans distinguish themselves from objects, from lower animals and from one another. [p. 8]

An understanding of the humanistic orientation toward human nature can be gleaned from noting the general differences with respect to research between behaviorists and humanists:

1) scientific versus intuitive: behaviorists use rigorous scientific methods and precise language in their experimentation; humanists are more concerned with intuition, understanding and subjective experience than objectification.
2) means versus ends: behaviorists are more concerned with the means of changing behavior; humanists emphasize the ends toward which change should be directed.
3) external behavior versus internal emotion: behaviorists are concerned with observable external behavior of man as opposed to internal and often not clearly discerned emotions.
4) behavior change versus insight: in learning situations as well as in therapeutic treatment, behaviorists look for changes in overt behavior whereas humanists aim for achieving insight into problem-solving.
5) manipulation versus humanization: behaviorists manipulate people or the environment to produce an effect; humanists "attempt to sensitize people to their uniquely human characteristics and possibilities." [Wandersman, 1976, p. 24]

Other dichotomies that have been used to characterize their differences in approach to humans include pessimistic versus optimistic, reductionist versus wholistic, objective versus subjective.

The humanistic psychologists have done much to establish humanism as a major philosophical system in the United States. In a later section of this chapter the humanistic psychologists' impact upon educational theory and practice will be discussed. Modern humanists, whether they identify themselves as psychologists, philosophers, or theologians, share certain fundamental beliefs and values. The following discussion elucidates these basic tenets.

Basic Assumptions of Humanistic Philosophy

Humanism is a philosophy broad enough to encompass many individual variations and manifestations. Each age has sought to define what its basic values are, what it holds as irreducible, what it seeks to accomplish. In 1933, thirty-four humanists in the United States met for the purpose of defining humanism's fundamental principles. The result of their meeting was the *Humanist Manifesto I.* In this short document, any notion of a dogmatic or deterministic control over human beings is firmly rejected. Instead, man himself is held responsible for bettering the state of human affairs: "the quest for the good life is still the central task of mankind. Man is at last becoming aware that he alone is responsible for the realization of the world of his dreams, that he has within himself the power for its achievement. He must set intelligence and will to the task" (*Humanist Manifestos I and II,* 1973, p. 10).

In 1973, forty years after *Humanist Manifesto I* appeared, a second and more comprehensive document was written and signed by 114 prominent individuals. Since 1973, the document has been endorsed worldwide by countless others representing many disciplines. As with the earlier version, the starting point for *Humanist Manifesto II* is the preservation and enhancement of all things human. The document then addresses itself to religion and ethics as well as the issues of civil liberties, equality, democracy, the survival of human kind, world economic growth, population and ecological control, war and peace, and the building of a world community. The statement presents a vision of faith in the human potentiality of each person and in humanity as a whole.

As was noted earlier, the humanistic psychologists have had a great influence on the establishment of humanism in the United States. The Association for Humanistic Psychology lists four characteristics with which most humanists would agree. These tenets, when considered in conjunction with *Humanist Manifestos I and II,* provide a foundation for uncovering the basic assumptions of humanism. Protagonists of humanistic psychology would agree to

> A centering of attention on the experiencing *person* and thus a focus on experience as the primary phenomenon in the study of man. Both theoretical explanations and overt behavior are considered secondary to experience itself and to its meaning to the person.

An emphasis on such distinctively human qualities as choice, creativity, valuation, and self-realization, as opposed to thinking about human beings in mechanistic and reductionistic terms.

An allegiance to meaningfulness in the selection of problems for study and of research procedures, and an opposition to a primary emphasis on objectivity at the expense of significance.

An ultimate concern with and valuing of the dignity and worth of man and an interest in the development of the potential inherent in every person. Central in this view is the person as he discovers his own being and relates to other persons and to social groups. [Misiak, 1973, p. 116]

These common elements of humanism that psychologists propose and the underlying assumptions of the *Manifestos* are complementary to one another. These documents as well as other humanistic writings are predicated upon the following principles of humanism. These presented are not meant to be exclusive; major points have been selected for discussion.

Human Nature is Naturally Good. Many humanists believe that man is naturally, inherently good. Given a loving environment and freedom to develop, human beings will grow in a manner beneficial to themselves and to society in general. It is partly due to this assumption that humanists are considered by some to be romantics. Humanists, however, support this view by pointing out that man and societies have continually striven toward a better and more ideal society. "If there were not an inherent drive toward good in man," they argue, "it is difficult to understand how the human race could have continued to survive; men would long ago have killed each other off" (Patterson, 1973, p. 65).

The view that human nature is inherently good corresponds to many humanists' rejection of a religious force that has power over the lives of men and women. Most religions are predicated upon the depravity of man. Hence, man is in need of a god to save himself from destruction and annihilation. In believing that man is naturally good and therefore not automatically doomed, there is little need to ascribe to a traditional theism. Faith is not placed in a force outside the individual but within the individual him/herself.

Not all humanists and existentialists see an incompatibility between affirming the autonomy and dignity of man and the existence of God. A group of religious existentialists that includes Marcel, Jaspers, Buber, and Tillich have attempted to develop a concept of God that is consonant with and not contradictory to full human autonomy and integrity. Their religious philosophies downplay the traditional emphasis on human depravity and put stress on the basic goodness and power of man as God's creature to cooperate with God in fashioning a more perfect human society.

The humanistic view of human nature stands in contrast to both the Freudian and behaviorist view. Freud portrays the majority of individuals as anti-social, destructive and hostile. The id, or core of one's personality, has instinctive tendencies toward gratification, aggression, destruction, and death. These impulses are to be checked by the ego and superego, but they nevertheless constitute the essence of human nature.

The behaviorists do not see humans as either inherently good or bad. For them, all behavior is learned. Humans are controlled by forces in the environment and are in essence programmed to respond in predetermined ways. It might be recalled that the humanistic psychology movement was begun as a protest against both the Freudian and behaviorist positions.

Freedom and Autonomy. Again in contrast to the behaviorist position that "free inner man . . . is only a prescientific substitute for the kinds of causes which are discovered in the course of scientific analysis" (Skinner in Rogers, 1965, p. 396), humanists believe that man is truly a free creature. A person's behavior is not determined by external forces or internal urges. Behavior is the consequence of human choice which individuals can freely exercise.

This notion of freedom and autonomy does not mean that behavior is totally random, uncontrolled, and unaffected by heredity or environment. Rather, human beings are capable of making significant personal choices within the constraints imposed by heredity, personal history, and environment. Not all is predetermined. Man can be proactive rather than reactive and, in so being, exert an influence on his situation. The force of the person who is free to act can bring about change for the betterment of one's life and humanity in general.

Individuality and Potentiality. In humanistic philosophy the individuality or uniqueness of each person is recognized and valued. Behavior, then, is not as predictable as some would desire. Likewise, it is important to promote one's individuality by nurturing each person's special talents and skills. The potentiality each person possesses for growth and development is unlimited.

Humanism places unlimited faith in man and believes that human beings possess the power or potentiality for achieving the good life, for solving one's own problems, and for developing into the best person possible. Reason and intelligence are the most effective tools man has in this process, but they are not to be depended upon solely. Intuition and emotions are important components of the whole person. As expressed in *Manifesto II* (1973, p. 18), "critical intelligence, infused by a sense of human caring, is the best method humanity has for solving problems. Reason should be balanced with compassion and empathy and the whole person fulfilled."

Self-Concept and The Self. Humanism has been criticized on occasion as devoting too much time to the self. The humanistic emphasis on the self does not mean to promulgate, however, a self-centeredness that excludes others. In fact, an important assumption of humanistic philosophy is one's responsibility to others and working for the good of humanity in general. For humanists, the self is the heart of the person, the enhancement of which is possible through actualizing individual potentialities.

As defined by humanists, the self consists of the sum total of everything that distinguishes one person from another—attitudes, body, values, feelings, intellect, etc. This brings one back to the humanists' emphasis on the uniqueness of each individual, for each "self" is like no other.

The notion of self-concept is also fundamental to the humanistic position, especially the psychologist's. Briefly defined, the self-concept is a person's subjective evaluation of who he or she is. The self is what a person really is; the self-concept is a determiner of behavior and has a great influence on one's ability to grow and develop.

Self Actualization. Growth, self-actualization, or self-transcendence are innate human characteristics according to humanistic philosophy and psychology. Men and women continuously strive toward personal growth and toward realizing tneir unique potentialities. Although a number of humanistic psychologists have written of man's stiving for self-actualization, Abraham Maslow's *Motivation and Personality* first published in 1954, popularized the term. In this work Maslow offers a theory of human motivation based on a hierarchy of needs. The needs at the lowest level of the hierarchy are physiological, such as hunger and thirst and must be attended to before a person can cope with safety needs—those related to security, protection, etc. The next three levels on Maslow's hierarchy are belongingness, love needs, and esteem needs—to feel that one is useful and one's life has worth— and finally, the need for self-actualization. The needs are hierarchical but at the same time "people who are normal are partially satisfied in all their basic needs and partially unsatisfied at the same time" (Maslow, 1954, p. 94). Self-actualization manifests itself in a desire for self-fulfillment, for becoming what one has the potentiality to become.

Perception. Another important concept of humanism is that behavior is the result of selective perception. The world is known and stimuli, external and internal, are reacted to as a result of one's individual perception. The same seemingly objective stimuli can be perceived differently by different persons. It is at this juncture that the philosophy of phenomenology intersects with humanism. For both phenomenologists and humanists, reality is what one believes it to be, not necessarily what actually exists.

Perception is a key concept in humanism for it explains behavior. A person's overt behavior as well as attitudes, feelings, beliefs, and values are all a product of personal perceptions. In order to understand another's behavior one must enter that person's world. An empathic identification with other human situations lays the foundation for the humanist goal of promoting a better world for all of humanity.

Responsibility and Humanity. Humanism's emphasis upon the self, the individual, and the free autonomous person carries with it a strong sense of responsibility both to the self and to other people. Individuals are charged with the task of developing their potentialities to the fullest, of striving toward self-actualization. In becoming a better person, individuals contribute to the betterment of humanity.

Interaction with others is essential because man is not only by nature a social being, but needs others in order to satisfy drives for love, recognition, esteem, etc. The growth of self does not occur in isolation from others; neither is the welfare of humanity advanced by ignoring the humanness of all peoples. While each person is unique, the humanist vision is predicated upon the recognition of the common humanity of all people. Much of the 1973 *Manifesto* is devoted to promoting a world community and an ideal vision of human potentiality.

Delineating "basic assumptions" of any philosophy leaves one open to criticisms of omission and selectivity. The ones that have been presented here represent a synthesis of humanistic philosophical and psychological position statements. They are also logical derivations from the historical evolution of humanistic thought. A faith in man's basic goodness, for example, underlies Rousseau's *Emile*. Individual freedom in lieu of obedience to an oppressive religion was embraced by Italian Renaissance humanists. And the importance of perception, self-concept, and self-actualization have been emphasized by twentieth century psychologists. Many of these same assumptions can be traced in the application of humanism to an educational setting.

General and Adult Humanistic Education

Education in the United States has been affected by humanistic philosophy and psychology. Since the mid-twentieth century, humanistic education has exerted an influence comparable to that of behavioristic education. All levels of education, from pre-school through adult, have modified both theory and practice in accordance with humanistic principles.

Historically, the purpose of education has been the transmission of cultural heritage and the perpetuation of existing society. This concept is based upon the assumptions that society will remain pretty much the same from generation to generation and that society's elders know what knowledge and skills are necessary for maintaining the cultural status quo. This view also assumes that there is an identifiable body of knowledge that can be packaged and passed on to new learners. Even in the area of adult education, it has been assumed that adults need to know certain basic skills for functioning in society (Adult Basic Education), and need to acquire certain values and attitudes (Americanization Education, Schools for the Foreign Born) if they had somehow missed them in earlier schooling. There is much that can be said in support of the transmission of cultural heritage to a society's new learners, and humanists would not exclude this as an outcome of the educative process. However, humanistic educators see the purpose of education as being considerably broader, not limited to a particular culture or historical pattern.

Simply stated, the goal of humanistic education is the development of persons—persons who are open to change and continued learning, persons who strive for self-actualization, and persons who can live together as fully-functioning individuals. As such, the whole focus of humanistic education is upon the individual learner rather than a body of information. That is not to say that humanistic education lacks substance. It is the approach to material and persons within the educative process that is emphasized. Patterson (1973) noted that there are really two aspects of humanistic education: "The first is that of teaching subject matter in a more human way, that is, facilitating subject matter learning by students. The second is that of educating the non-intellectual or affective aspects of the student, that is, developing persons who understand themselves, who understand others, and who can relate to others" (p. x).

Several components of humanistic education find expression in both general and adult education. In both educative settings, the student is the center of the process, the teacher is a facilitator, and learning is by discovery.

Student-Centered. Humanistic education is student centered. In this orientation the teacher does not necessarily know best, especially when working with adult learners. Philosophical assumptions of individual freedom, responsibility, and natural goodness underpin the student-centered emphasis in humanistic education. Arbitrary curriculum and methodological decisions violate the student's ability to identify his or her own learning needs. Humanistic education places the responsibility for learning with the student—the student is free to learn what he or she wants to learn and in a manner desired by the learner. A teacher can guide or facilitate the process, but the emphasis is upon learning rather than teaching and the student rather than the instructor.

Humanistic education is student-centered not only with regard to the responsibility for learning but in terms of the self-development of each learner. The student is viewed as a unique individual in which all aspects of the person must be allowed to grow in the educative process. Emotions, attitudes, physical aspects are as important as intellectual development. The whole personality, all the dimensions of humanness that differentiate human beings from animals, is deemed the important area of development in humanistic education. Education's assistance in the development of persons leads to a better society—one of the philosophical goals of humanism. A society of self-actualizing or fully-functioning, thinking, feeling, active individuals will result, humanists feel, in the betterment of humanity as a whole.

Both Abraham Maslow and Carl Rogers see education as a means of fostering self-actualizing and fully-functioning individuals. The goal of education according to Maslow is self-actualization, or "helping the person to become the best that he is able to become." Educationists should think in terms of bringing about intrinsic rather than extrinsic learning—"that is, learning to be a human being in general, and second, learning to be *this* particular human being" (Maslow, 1976, pp. 120-121). While Maslow felt that self-actualization did not occur in young people, education at all levels could assist in bringing about its development. Given that being a self-actualized person is an adult phenomenon, however, a humanistic approach to adult education would seem to be essential. It was, in fact, Maslow's study of extraordinary adults such as Lincoln, Beethoven, and Schweitzer which led to the following personality characteristics of the self-actualized person:

- they are realistically oriented
- they accept themselves, other people, and the natural world for what they are
- they are spontaneous in thinking, emotions, and behavior

— they are problem-centered rather than self-centered in the sense of being able to devote their attention to a task, duty, or mission that seems cut out for them

— they have a need for privacy and even seek it out on occasion, needing it for periods of intense concentration on subjects of interest to them

— they are autonomous, independent, and able to remain true to themselves in the face of rejection or unpopularity

— they have a continuous freshness of appreciation and capacity to stand in awe again and again of the basic goods of life, a sunset, a flower, a baby, a melody, a person.

— they have frequent "mystic" or "oceanic" experiences, although not necessarily religious in character

— they feel a sense of identification with mankind as a whole in the sense of being concerned not only with the lot of their own immediate families, but with the welfare of the world as a whole

— their intimate relationships with a few specifically loved people tend to be profound and deeply emotional rather than superficial

— they have democratic character structures in the sense of judging people and being friendly not on the basis of race, status, religion, but rather on the basis of who other people are as individuals

— they have a highly developed sense of ethics

— they resist total conformity to culture. [Maslow, 1954, pp. 203-208]

Similar to Maslow's self-actualizing person is Rogers' fully-functioning individual, the goal of the educative process. The emphasis upon the student is obvious in Rogers' question, "If education were as complete as we could wish it to be in promoting personal growth and development, what sort of person would emerge?" His answer is the person who

is able to experience all of his feelings, and is afraid of none of his feelings; he is his own sifter of evidence, but is open to evidence from all sources; he is completely engaged in the process of being and becoming himself, and thus discovers that he is soundly and realistically social; he lives completely in this moment, but learns that this is the soundest living for all time. He is a fully functioning organism, and because of the awareness of himself which flows freely in and through his experiences, he is a fully functioning person. [Rogers, 1969, p. 288]

For Rogers, the emphasis upon the student in the learning process is essential. It is also a principle that can be applied to any student in any setting. In *Freedom to Learn* (1969), for example, Rogers shows how humanistic student-centered education has been employed in a sixth grade, a college psychology course, and a graduate seminar. For humanists, a student-centered approach is more than taking into account the individual learning style, needs, and interests of students. Rather, these formulate "the starting point and guiding principles of the entire educational process" (Kolesnik, 1975, p. 55).

Teacher as Facilitator. The role of the teacher in a humanistic setting is that of facilitator, helper, and partner in the learning process. The teacher does not simply provide information; it is the teacher's role to create the conditions within which learning can take place. In order to be a facilitator one must trust students to assume responsibility for their learning. This is a most difficult stance for the traditional teacher for it necessitates abdicating the authority generally ascribed to the teacher role. The truly humanistic teacher respects and utilizes the experiences and potentialities of students. Ideally, the humanistic teacher is a self-actualized or fully-functioning individual. That this applies to an adult educational setting as well as any other is obvious. An adult instructor dealing with adult students can hardly ignore the wealth and variety of individual experiences as a foundation for facilitating learning.

Carl Rogers has worked extensively with adults in both counseling and educational settings, and has set forth guidelines characterizing the qualities and methods of a facilitator. These guidelines reflect many of the philosophical assumptions underlying humanism presented earlier in this chapter:

1. The facilitator sets the initial mood or climate of the group or class experience.
2. He/she helps to elicit and clarify the purposes of the individuals in the class as well as the more general purposes of the group. Diversity of purpose is permitted to exist.

3. The facilitator relies upon the desire of each student to implement those purposes which have meaning for him, as the motivational force behind significant learning.

4. He endeavors to organize and make easily available the widest possible range of resources for learning.

5. He regards himself as a flexible resource to be utilized by the group.

6. In responding to expressions in the classroom group, he accepts both the intellectual content and the emotionalized attitudes, endeavoring to give each aspect the approximate degree of emphasis which it has for the individual or group.

7. As the acceptant classroom climate becomes established, the facilitator is able increasingly to become a participant learner, a member of the group, expressing his views as those of one individual only.

8. He takes the initiative in sharing himself with the group--his feelings as well as his thoughts.

9. Throughout the classroom experience, he remains alert to the expressions indicative of deep or strong feelings.

10. In his functioning as a facilitator of learning, the leader endeavors to recognize and accept his own limitations. [Rogers, 1969, pp. 164-166]

The Act of Learning. Humanistic educators view the act of learning as a highly personal endeavor. As mentioned earlier, perception is an important concept in humanistic thought and it bears upon the notion of learning. One perceives selectively which accounts for individual behavior; it also accounts for differences in what is "learned" in an educational setting. A student "learns" what he or she perceives to be necessary, important, or meaningful. The meaning one gleans from a subject depends upon personal goals, interests, attitudes, beliefs, etc. The importance of self-concept also has a bearing on learning. A positive or negative self-concept can promote or inhibit learning respectively. Rogers also feels that there is a real and an ideal self, that which the person would like to be. The discrepancy between the two can provide a stimulus for learning.

Individuals differ; therefore perception is selective and self-concepts vary. Because of this, the most effective learning takes place in discovery. Learners are encouraged to bring all their uniqueness to a situation or problem, grapple with it, and in so doing discover or learn whatever is most meaningful. Learning through experimentation and discovery is that learning which will become a part of the person. Information and knowledge that is given to a student in a traditional instructional situation (called the "banking concept" by Paulo Freire) may be meaningful to a teacher, but will not necessarily be perceived as such by a learner.

In the humanistic learning process, motivation is intrinsic rather than extrinsic. As one writer put it, it is learning "from the inside out" (Weinberg, 1972, p. 123). For humanists, motivation is not something put upon learners, it emanates from the learner. A facilitator need only provide a number of options from which a student might choose. Perhaps more than any other characteristic of humanist education, intrinsic motivation characterizes adult learners. In most adult educational settings, the adult learners are there, not because they have to be, but because they want to be. Most adult students engage in learning activities under no compulsion except that which is generated from within.

Evaluation is an integral part of the learning process. For humanists, self-evaluation is the only meaningful test of whether learning has taken place. Students themselves are thought to be the best judges of whether learning has met their needs and interests. Educators have experimented with various methods of self-evaluation including student reporting, learning by student designed objectives, pass-fail grading, and concept mastery learning.

Thus, self-evaluation, intrinsic motivation, self-concept, perception, and discovery are all important components in the learning process for learners of any age. Rogers calls meaningful learning "experiential" and sums up the process in the following principles of learning:

> 1) personal involvement—the affective and cognitive aspects of a person should be involved in the learning event;
> 2) self-initiated—a sense of discovery needs to come from within;
> 3) pervasive—the learning makes impact on the behavior, attitudes or personality of the learner;
> 4) evaluated by the learner—the learner can best evaluate if the experience is meeting a need;

5. essence is meaning—when experiential learning takes place its meaning to the learner becomes incorporated into his total experience. [Rogers, 1969, p. 5]

Curriculum

The goal of humanistic education is the development of self-actualizing persons. The selection of content is subsumed under the goal of assisting learners to grow and develop in accordance with their needs and interests. Humanistic education is a process. It is a stance assumed by the teacher which respects learners as unique individuals, motivated to learn and anxious to grow. Curriculum becomes a vehicle, not an end in itself for achieving humanistic goals.

Historically, the classical humanistic curriculum consisted of the study of Greek and Roman literature and later Judaeo-Christian works. Through the centuries the term "humanities" has been broadened to include philosophy, literature, history, ethics, language, and social sciences. The humanities as a curriculum is compatible with humanistic education, for the humanists "have traditionally been concerned with the person—the individual—and the eternal, existential questions of relationships among persons, universes, gods and dreams" (Simpson and Gray, 1976, p. 6).

Modern humanistic education includes much more than the humanities. While studying the social, political, religious, and philosophical values of other ages and cultures might contribute to the development of the self, an equally valued source of curriculum is the examination of one's *own* values, attitudes, and emotions. With youth this emphasis finds expression in the evaluation of moral dilemmas and in courses designed to develop empathic attitudes toward others. Adult education has embraced this emphasis through values clarification workshops, encounter groups, transactional analysis, and human potential workshops.

Teaching a curriculum, then, is not the goal of humanistic educators. The curriculum functions as a vehicle which, if creatively employed, can promote the real goal of humanistic education—the development of self-actualizing individuals.

Cooperation and Groups

Humanists strive for self-actualization. But self-development and growth do not occur in an individual isolated from others. Growth is best fostered in a cooperative, supportive environment. In an educational setting, humanists attempt to attend to the affective and emotional dimensions of a learner as well as the intellectual. This is best achieved through improving interpersonal relationships in a cooperative, oftentimes group learning experience. Humanists thus stand in opposition to the notion of competition as a motivating force in education.

First, if one adopts the humanistic assumption that motivation is intrinsic to the learner, then one need not construct an artificial motivating force such as competition. Second, competition is threatening; learning that is threatening tends to be resisted (Rogers, 1969). Combs (1971) notes the negative relationship between competition and threat:

> Competition has motivating force only for those persons who believe they have a chance of winning. . . . Persons who are forced to compete and who do not believe they have a chance of success, are not motivated by the experience; they are threatened by it. . . . When competition becomes too important, any means become justified to achieve the ends. [pp. 110-111]

One of the best ways to foster growth and cooperation amongst learners is through groups. Discussions, small group projects, committees, and teams as instructional techniques are not new to education. Dewey and other progressive educators, including adult educators Lindeman and Bergevin, gave their support to group activities as a means of promoting learning and preserving democratic ideals. Groups as an outgrowth of the humanistic psychological movement of the mid-twentieth century took on a meaning different from the progressive education movement. The primary purpose of the encounter groups, training groups (T-groups), or sensitivity groups of the 1960's was to foster personal growth and development through an experiential process. The goal of what Rogers called a "basic encounter group" was to "enable the participants to become experiencing persons capable of choice, creativity, valuation, and self-actualization" (Misiak and Sexton, 1973, p. 121).

It is interesting to note that the encounter group movement has been a largely adult activity. Since the 1960's large numbers of educators, businesspeople, executives, criminals, housewives, single and married men and women have met in homes, churches, business, and growth centers (such as the Esalen Institute in Big Sur, California) for the purpose of experiencing and interacting with other people. What one learns in an encounter group varies. Overall, it is a direct approach to promoting affective growth, an important component of a humanistic education. One writer has delineated the possible learning outcomes of an encounter group experience:

> to listen to others
> to accept and respect others
> to understand others
> to identify and become aware of feelings
> to express one's own feelings
> to become aware of the feelings of others
> to experience being listened to by others
> to experience being accepted and respected by others
> to experience being understood by others
> to recognize the basic commonalities of human experience
> to explore oneself
> to develop greater awareness of oneself
> to be oneself
> to change onself in the direction of being more the self
> one wants to be. [Patterson, 1973, p. 195]

The commercialization and sensationalization of personal growth groups have resulted in a cautious use of them in educational settings. Rogers, considered to be the founder of encounter groups, pointed out the possible disadvantages: behavior changes if they occurred in the group were not necessarily lasting; a person may "become deeply involved in revealing himself and then be left with problems which are not worked through"; the surfacing of marital tensions; and complications related to liaisons which develop between group members (Rogers, 1967, pp. 272-274). These criticisms notwithstanding, encounter-type groups have filtered into more liberal, less tradition-bound school systems and they continue to be employed by counselors and adult educators in a variety of settings. From continued professional training to academic settings to human potential seminars in business and industry, groups remain a major manifestation of adult humanistic education.

Humanistic Adult Educators

Humanistic adult educators share the basic tenets of humanistic education explored in the foregoing section of this chapter. As discussed, they are, for the most part, a logical application of humanistic philosophy and psychology to an educational setting. As the major theoretician and spokesperson for humanistic education, Carl Rogers articulated and popularized many of the practical applications of a humanistic philosophy to education. His emphasis upon self-initiated learning that is relevant to the learner, student participation in planning and evaluation, the teacher as facilitator, and group methods has served as a model for adult educators.

That a humanistic orientation is particularly suited to the education of adults has been espoused by Malcolm Knowles. Considered to be one of the most influential adult educators in the United States, Malcolm Knowles has attempted to translate humanistic goals into a theoretical framework for adult educators. Calling for a technology for teaching adults that is distinguishable from teaching children, Knowles proposes using the word *andragogy* to characterize the education of adults. Knowles feels that andragogy, the art and science of helping adults learn, can be contrasted to pedagogy, the education of children.

While trying to propose andragogy as a rubric for adult education, Knowles admits that it means more than helping adults learn. "It means," he says, "helping human beings learn, and . . . it therefore has implications for the education of children and youth" (Knowles, 1970, pp. 38-39). With its emphasis upon the learner and the development of human beings, andragogy is basically a humanistic theoretical framework applied primarily to adult education. An examination of what Knowles considers to be the four underlying assumptions of andragogy reveals the humanistic foundations of this "new technology."

The first assumption centers on the notion of self-concept,

a basic emphasis in humanistic psychology. Knowles notes that as persons mature, their self concepts move from being dependent personalities toward being self-directed human beings. Learning that is most meaningful capitalizes upon the self-directed, autonomous nature of adults. Assuming that adults are self-directed has implications for educational practice. The learning climate must be supportive, cooperative, informal, and in general, cause adults to feel accepted and respected. Because adults are self-directed they are able to, and do, determine their own educational needs. Self-diagnosis of learning needs and self-evaluation of the learning that has taken place are important components of adult educational practice based upon the self-concept assumption of andragogy.

The self-concept of adults with regard to learning, Knowles feels, is a particularly delicate matter. Adults who have experienced failure in earlier schooling and who have little confidence in their ability to learn will find their negative self-concept a barrier to success in adult education.

This first assumption of andragogy, then, incorporates many of the basic principles of humanistic educational thought such as the importance of self-concept, self-diagnosed learning and evaluation, a cooperative rather than competitive atmosphere, and the necessity for respecting and trusting the adult learner.

The second assumption underlying andragogy is that the adult defines him or herself in terms of the accumulation of a unique set of life experiences. While children also have had experiences, an adult has had many more which have had more time to become integrated and internalized into a unique personality. Respect for an individual's uniqueness and experiences is a basic humanistic concept. Knowles proposes using the adult's experiences as resources for learning and advocates an emphasis upon experiential, participatory learning. In particular, Knowles recommends sensitivity or human relations training, at least in the early phases of an educational activity. Reflecting his own humanistic orientation, he states:

> one of the almost universal initial needs of adults is to learn
> how to take responsibility for their own learning through
> self-directed inquiry, how to learn collaboratively with the
> help of colleagues rather than to compete with them, and

especially, how to learn by analyzing one's own experience. Since this is the essence of the human relations laboratory, it is coming to be used increasingly as an orientation activity in a long-run program of adult education. [Knowles, 1970, p. 45]

The third and fourth assumptions upon which andragogy is based place the emphasis in the learning process where humanistic educators believe it should be—with the learners themselves. The third assumption holds that an adult's readiness to learn is linked to developmental tasks unique to a stage in life. The implication of this assumption is that adults will not learn what is not relevant to their stage in life. What is relevant depends upon their particular stage in life which generates needs and interests. These needs and interests give rise to an intrinsic motivation to learn. And as all humanistic educators believe, intrinsic rather than extrinsic motivation is an integral part of the learning process.

The last assumption—that adults desire an immediate application of knowledge as contrasted to postponed application of much youth learning, has implications for a curriculum that is decidedly humanistic. Knowles advocates an adult educational curriculum that subsumes specific subject content under general problem areas. The real and immediate needs of adult learners are more effectively met through problem-solving group techniques in which traditional curriculum content is a by-product.

Andragogy represents an attempt by one adult educator to define what is unique about the education of adults. Adult educators have debated the extent to which the assumptions of andragogy are truly different from those that underlie pedagogy. It is not within the scope of this chapter to enter this debate. Rather, andragogy has been explored in light of its humanistic characteristics.

Malcolm Knowles is indeed a humanistic adult educator. For him, the learning process involves the whole person, emotional, psychological, and intellectual. It is the mission of adult educators to assist adults in developing their full potential in becoming self-actualized and mature adults. Andragogy is a methodology for bringing about these humanistic ideals.

Knowles' philosophy of adult education also incorporates

134 / Philosophical Foundations of Adult Education

elements of the humanistic revolt against a behavioristic, deterministic view of human nature and education. His "democratic philosophy" of education is characterized

> by a concern for the development of persons, a deep conviction as to the work of every individual, and faith that people will make the right decisions for themselves if given the necessary information and support. It gives precedence to growth of *people* over the accomplishment of *things* when these two values are in conflict. It emphasizes the release of human potential over the control of human behavior. [Knowles, 1970, p. 60]

It is interesting to note that research on adult learning tends to support humanistic and andragogical notions that adult learners are self-directed and intrinsically motivated. Allen Tough (1971), an adult educator, studied individual adult learners and discovered that 90 per cent of the adult population conducted at least one major learning effort per year, and 73 per cent of the projects were self-planned. Especially intriguing in Tough's work are the "high learners"—those who spend perhaps two thousand hours a year at learning and complete fifteen or twenty projects in one year. "In their lives," Tough says, "learning is a central activity; such individuals are marked by extraordinary growth" (Tough, 1971, p. 28). These "high learners" exhibit characteristics similar to Rogers' fully functioning individuals or Maslow's self-actualizing adults.

The most recent attempt to present a philosophical framework for the field of adult education has been made by Leon McKenzie (1978). His vision, which he hopes will give meaning to adult educational practice, draws from both humanism and existentialism. McKenzie feels that adult education should foster a courageous spirit among individual learners. Prometheus, who defied Zeus by stealing fire and giving it to humanity, is the prototype of the adult to be produced through education. McKenzie proposes seven principles of adult education, most of which are humanistic. Education, for example, should facilitate in adults a rejection of a deterministic, behavioristic world view. It should also facilitate the development of proactive, self-directed adults who will be responsible for evolving a more enlightened human existence. It is the adult educator's role to foster a concern for human welfare, a spirit of interdependence and cooperation, and courage among adult learners. In discussing the "how" of putting the principles into practice, McKenzie advocates such humanistic educational techniques as self-directed learning in group situations guided by a facilitator.

Rogers, Knowles, and McKenzie are three educators who have delineated for the field of adult education humanistic paradigms which have guided much adult educational practice. The student as center of the experience, the teacher as facilitator, the notion of learning as a personal, internal process, and the value of group activities all lead to the ultimate goal of humanistic education— the fully developed person.

An Assessment of Adult Humanistic Education

Principles from humanistic philosophy and psychology have permeated the field of adult education. While Friere's radical pedagogy perhaps vies with Knowles' andragogy for theoretical popularity, educational practices grounded in humanistic philosophy far exceed the number of radical programs in the United States.

One of the reasons for the popularity of humanistic adult education is humanism's compatibility with democratic values. Education for maintaining a democratic political system becomes translated under humanism to education for the development of better individuals who will then promote a better life for all humanity. The humanistic emphasis upon the individual person as the center of the educational process also reflects democracy's spirit of individualism. Humanism also promotes cooperation and communication among individuals as a vehicle for interpersonal growth; cooperation is a necessity for making democracy work.

A second reason for humanism's hold in adult education is that unlike other levels of education, nearly all adult education is voluntary. Educational activities *must* meet the needs of adult learners in order to survive. Practical considerations thus necessitate an emphasis upon individual needs and interests.

Indirectly, at least, humanistic adult education takes into account adult development. Humanists want to assist individuals to grow and develop toward self-actualization and toward becoming fully-functioning persons. The notion of growth, development, and change is integral to much of the psychological literature on adult development. Adults are no longer viewed as finished products at the age of 16, 18, or 21. Rather, adulthood is a period of change, psychologically, socially, and physiologically. Adult educators are beginning to respond with activities designed to take into account adult development. As was noted earlier, one of the assumptions underlying andragogy related to meeting the needs of adults at the moment. And many of these needs are the direct outgrowth of the developmental tasks salient to the various changing stages of adulthood.

Assessing the impact of humanism on adult education is not an easy task, partly because its emphasis is less in programs than in psychological growth. That is, humanism is a stance or philosophical orientation toward the place of human beings in the scheme of things. Many adult educators have adopted the spirit of humanism in their approach to adult learners. The valuing of individuals, the commitment to educating the whole person— these are not readily measurable. Nevertheless, at least two programmatic components of humanistic education can be identified as important additions to adult education: (1) human development or human potential seminars, as found in the training programs of many businesses and industries, and (2) encounter-type groups and cooperative activities in settings as diverse as libraries, hospitals, factories, and schools.

Thus modern adult education programs in the United States testify to the impact humanistic philosophy and psychology have had on educational theory and practice. The basic principles of humanism with their primary focus upon the development of the person corresponds closely to the society and cultural values of twentieth-century America. Adult education programs that center on the needs and interests of the learners are indebted to a philosophy dedicated to the development of individual human beings.

REFERENCES

Bugental, James F. T. *Challenges of Humanistic Psychology.* New York: McGraw Hill, 1967.

Combs, Arthur W., Donald L. Avila, and William W. Purkey. *Helping Relationships: Basic Concepts for the Helping Professions.* Boston: Allyn and Bacon, 1971.

Greene, Maxine. *Teacher as Stranger: Educational Philosophy for the Modern Age.* Belmont, CA: Wadsworth, 1973.

Kneller, George. *Existentialism and Education.* New York: Wiley, 1958.

Knowles, Malcolm S. *The Modern Practice of Adult Education: Andragogy Versus Pedagogy.* New York: Association Press, 1970.

Kolesnik, Walter B. *Humanism and/or Behaviorism in Education.* Boston: Allyn and Bacon, 1975.

Maslow, Abraham. *Motivation and Personality.* New York: Harper and Row, 1954.

Maslow, Abraham. "Education and Peak Experience," *The Person in Education: A Humanistic Approach,* Courtney D. Schlosser (ed.), New York: Macmillan, 1976.

McKenzie, Leon. *Adult Education and the Burden of the Future.* Washington, D.C.: University Press of America, 1978.

Misiak, Henryk and Virginia Standt Sexton. *Phenomenological, Existential, and Humanistic Psychologies: A Historical Survey.* New York: Grune and Stratton, 1973.

Montaigne, Michel de. *Essays. Foundations of Education in America: An Anthology of Major Thoughts and Significant Actions,* J. W. Noll and Sam P. Kelly (eds.), New York: Harper and Row, 1970.

Morris, Van Cleve. *Existentialism in Education.* New York: Harper and Row, 1966.

Noll, J. W. and Sam P. Kelly. *Foundations of Education in America: An Anthology of Major Thoughts and Significant Actions.* New York: Harper and Row, 1970.

Patterson, C. H. *Humanistic Education.* Englewood Cliffs, NJ: Prentice-Hall, 1973.

Perry, Ralph Barton. *The Humanity of Man.* New York: George Braziller, 1956.

Pratte, Richard. *Contemporary Theories of Education.* Scranton, PA: Intext Educational Publishers, 1971.

Rogers, Carl R. "The Place of the Person in the New World of the Behavioral Sciences," *Humanistic Viewpoints in Psychology.* Frank T. Severin (ed.), New York: McGraw-Hill, 1965.

Rogers, Carl R. "The Process of the Basic Encounter Group," *Challenges of Humanistic Psychology,* James F. T. Bugental (ed.), New York: McGraw-Hill, 1967.

Rogers, Carl R. *Freedom to Learn.* Columbus, OH: Charles E. Merrill, 1969.

Sartre, John Paul. *Nausea.* Lloyd Alexander (translator), Paulton (Somerset and London): Purnell and Sons, 1949.

Simpson, Elizabeth Leonie and Mary Ann Gray. *Humanistic Education: An Interpretation.* Cambridge, MA: Ballinger, 1976.

Tough, Allen. *The Adult's Learning Projects.* Toronto: Ontario Institute for Studies in Education, 1971.

Wandersman, Abraham, Paul J. Poppen, and David F. Ricks (eds.). *Humanism and Behaviorism: Dialogue and Growth.* Oxford: Pergamon Press, 1976.

Weinberg, Carl (ed.). *Humanistic Foundations of Education.* Englewood Cliffs, NJ: Prentice-Hall, 1972.

CHAPTER VI

RADICAL ADULT EDUCATION

In the early 1970's a Latin American adult educator propounded a revolutionary philosophy for adult educators throughout the world. Paulo Freire, an exiled Brazilian educator, described in his *Pedagogy of the Oppressed* (1970) a radical theory of conscientization or political consciousness-raising and action. Though this philosophy of education is closely tied to a situation of political, social, and economic oppression in parts of Latin America, adult educators in many countries have examined it and attempted to utilize its radical thrust in educational efforts in other cultural situations.

Freire's philosophy of adult education is an example of a radical philosophy of adult education. The theory is radical in the political sense of utilizing education to bring about social, political, and economic changes in society. Though radical educational philosophies have not been common in the history of education, Freire's philosophy has historical roots in 18th, 19th, and 20th century thinkers. The social context in which these theorists worked was similar to the Latin American situation in which Freire's radical philosophy developed.

After first presenting the historical background of radical thought, this chapter will analyze Freire's philosophy of education; it will also explore the philosophy's relevance for the theory and practice of adult education.

Historical Roots of Radical Adult Education

Radical educational thought stands outside the mainstream of educational philosophy. Most educational philosophies accept the given societal values and attempt to propound educational philosophies within these value structures. While progressives and humanists attempt to utilize education to reform society, it is only the radical critics that propose profound changes in society.

Radical educational thought flows from at least three sources. The anarchist tradition developing in the 18th century and continuing in the 19th and 20th centuries has consistently opposed public schooling as destructive of individual autonomy. The Marxist tradition has criticized schooling as a form of alienation in the modern industrial world. It sees the overcoming of alienation as the first step in radical change. Freire stands in this tradition with his theory of conscientization. The third tradition is represented by the Freudian Left and includes such people as Wilhelm Reich and A. S. Neill. This tradition places its main emphasis on changing personality traits, family structures, and child-rearing practices as the first step in radical education.

Though the main concern of radicals in all three traditions has been with public schooling, many of their criticisms and proposals are applicable to adult education. The ever increasing institutionalization of adult education is a target for anarchist educators. Freire's indebtedness to the Marxist tradition has been mentioned and will be more fully explored in this chapter. Adult educators need also to consider the proposals of the radical Freudians with regard to family structures and the freedom of the individual from repressive influences in society.

The Anarchist Tradition

The anarchist tradition in education has been examined by Spring (1973, 1975). As a social and political philosophy anarchism has raised fundamental questions about the role and nature of authority in society, and since the 18th century it has questioned the very existence of state systems of schooling and the possibility of non-authoritarian forms of education. Contemporary educators influenced by this tradition include Paul Goodman, Ivan Illich, and John Ohliger.

Anarchism opposes national systems of education because of its conviction that education in the hands of the state would serve the political interests of those in control. The central concern of this tradition is to preserve as much as possible personal autonomy. Francisco Ferrer, a Spanish anarchist, criticized educational systems for conditioning students for obedience and docility (1913). An educational system, in his view, expounded political dogmas and attempted to shape the individual into a useful citizen by removing personal autonomy and setting limits to the power of individuals. Max Sterner contended that knowledge should not be taught because the process of absorbing knowledge turns the individual into a learner rather than a creative person (1967). The heart of education according to the anarchist is the development of individuals able to choose, free of dogmas and prejudices, their own goals and purposes. The tradition also maintains that it is impossible to do this in government sponsored educational systems.

One of the best known proponents of radical educational philosophy was Leo Tolstoi, the Russian Christian anarchist. Tolstoi made a distinction between culture and education. Culture represented the unconscious and nondeliberate transmission of knowledge and values that shaped the individual; education was the conscious and deliberate shaping of individual character and implied some form of objectionable compulsion. Tolstoi's concept of noncompulsory education was one without a planned program, where teachers would teach what they wished and their courses would be regulated by the demands of the students (1967).

Certain ideas from the anarchist tradition surfaced in the educational reform movements in the 1960's and early 1970's. The emphasis on freedom and autonomy of the learner, the development of free schools, opposition to compulsory education, and the de-schooling movement were, to varying degrees, inspired by anarchist principles of freedom and opposition to state control of education. As will be discussed later in this chapter, Ivan Illich's proposals for education in a convivial society and John Ohliger's opposition to compulsory adult education have connections with this anarchist tradition.

Marxist-Socialist Tradition

While the anarchist attempts to promote personal freedom and autonomy by removing education from state control, the Marxist-socialist tradition in education attempts to produce the free and autonomous person through a revolutionary change from a capitalistic political economy to a socialist form of government and economy. Marx himself did not give education an important role in the making of the socialist revolution, for he considered it too closely tied to the interests of the dominant class. But such radical educators as George Counts, Theodore Brameld, and Paulo Freire have utilized Marxist ideas such as false consciousness, alienation, class struggle, and political revolution in developing a radical philosophy of education.

The first American educator who advocated a radical approach to education inspired by Marxist principles was George Counts, Professor of Education at Columbia University. In 1932, in the midst of the Depression, Counts challenged American educators to reach for political power and to lead the nation to socialism. In a famous speech before the Progressive Education Association he gave a Marxist analysis of the causes of the depression and the social ills of the country and proposed using the schools as a means of curing these ills. To achieve these goals he urged that it was necessary to indoctrinate students about the evils of capitalism and the social values upon which it rests. For the next few years Counts' ideas were debated in journals and at conferences by outstanding American educators including John Dewey, Merle Curti, Sidney Hook, and Eduard Lindeman.

Although a number of American educators accepted Counts' analysis of the situation, they did not share his optimism that the schools could be an important force in bringing about the socialist society. To most educators, Counts' advocacy of indoctrination was a contradiction to the essential freedom that they desired in the educational process. Most educators shared the viewpoint of journalist Agnes de Lima (1932):

> ... to expect teachers to lead us out of our morass is fantastic indeed. ... A class long trained to social docility and economically protected by life tenure of office—on good behavior—is unlikely to challenge unduly the status quo. [p. 317]

An American educator who has consistently maintained the Marxist-socialist position in educational philosophy is Theodore Brameld, Professor Emeritus at Boston University. In a number of works Brameld has developed a reconstructionist philosophy of education. Throughout the years Brameld has remained confident that education can make a significant contribution to bringing about a socialist society, though he has rejected the methods of indoctrination espoused by Counts. Brameld also separates himself from the progressive position on the role of the teacher for he advocates a more committed position on the part of the teacher.

In the 1960's and 1970's a number of educators, historians and social critics have analyzed the American educational system according to Marxist and socialist principles. Michael Katz (1968) showed how the various educational reform movements in the history of this country have failed to bring about the necessary radical changes. Educational reform according to his analysis is an attempt to avoid radical change by imposing moderate changes in structures or methods of teaching. Samuel Bowles and Herbert Gintis (1975) have presented an analysis of the relationships between the school system and the capitalist society that it serves. The social criticism of Jonathan Kozol (1975) echoes a number of Marxist themes: class struggle, alienation, and revolutionary praxis. Kozol considers himself a disciple of the Christian Marxist, Paulo Freire.

The adult educator whose ideas are greatly formed by the Marxist tradition of radical criticism is Freire. As will be seen later in this chapter, Freire began ideologically as a Christian social democrat, and in later writings he embraced the fundamental principles of Marxist social philosophy. To this philosophy of Marxism, Freire has added a revolutionary pedagogy and philosophy of education.

The Freudian Left

One of the basic problems of the Marxist-socialist approach to educational change is its assumption that once people become aware of what they view as evil social structures, they will be able to bring about the necessary changes. The Freudian Left addresses itself to the problems inherent in this assumption. It points out that many persons are prevented from acting in their own self interests because of a structure of authoritarianism that is imposed from the earliest stages of child development. The solutions that the Freudian Left advocate lie in the areas of sexual freedom, changes in family organization, and libertarian methods of child-rearing and education.

The Freudian Left, represented especially by Wilhelm Reich, was critical of Freud for his conservative social philosophy. Reich felt that the result of Freudian psychoanalysis was to accommodate people to accept the given societal structures even if these were oppressive. Changes were to be made in individual consciousness and not in societal structures and values. Reich's interest in Marxist social thought led him to reject this position. He wanted psychology to be concerned with changing political and social structures. Reich also found a weakness in Marxist social analysis which he attempted to remedy. Marx did not adequately explain why exploited workers failed to strike out against their exploiters. For Reich the reason was psychological; a character structure of repression and authoritarianism prevented this necessary reaction, even though individuals saw their state of oppression. Character structures would have to be changed through different forms of child-rearing and a different type of education. Reich analyzed the working class acceptance of fascism in Europe according to these principles.

Though he had arrived at his philosophy of freedom before he met Reich, A. S. Neill, the founder of the famous British free school Summerhill, found a kindred spirit when he came to know Reich. Neill saw the source of the world's problems in the repressions of children's drives. He permitted no religious or moral education in his school. Students were encouraged to have their own sexual lives. They were free to attend class or not. The school was run by the students. For Neill no man was good enough to give another his own ideals. Freedom alone was the cure for the problem child. He advocated the free family in which children were released from the internalized constraints that come from moral discipline (1960).

The ideas of the Freudian Left are not influential ideas in adult education today; yet it is important for these ideas to be examined for they raise important questions for the philosophical position of the radical adult educator. Radical educators such as Freire are rather optimistic in presuming the close connection between knowing and acting. An analysis of psychological factors can shed some light upon people's failure to act in what appears to be their best interests. Reich and Neill's analyses offer, however, one possible explanation for explaining such failures to act.

This brief description of the radical tradition in education does not do justice to the richness and diversity of ideas that radicals have offered in the past three centuries. It does, however, present the necessary intellectual background for understanding present day radical educational thought. This dissenting tradition has been strongest in time of social and political unrest, as in the Depression and the late 1960's. In times of crisis explanations are called for and new visions are needed. The radicals are strong in both criticism and visions. In making its criticisms and presenting its visions the radical tradition questions the basic values, structures, and practices of society. Every area of societal life is touched by the radical theorists: family, schooling, work, religion, economic and political systems. While few educators have espoused the radical tradition, none can afford to ignore the questions that it raises for contemporary society and education.

Paulo Freire's Theory of Radical Conscientization

The most prominent philosopher of adult education in the radical tradition is the exiled Brazilian educator, Paulo Freire. An exposition and evaluation of his philosophy of education provides the example of an educator who advocates a revolutionary pedagogy for both Third World and industrialized countries. The treatment of this revolutionary pedagogy includes the historical context of Freire's philosophy, an exposition and evaluation of his philosophy of adult education, the educational practice of Freire's literacy program, and a discussion of the relevance of this philosophy and practice for contemporary adult educational efforts.

Freire's Life and Works

Paulo Freire's initial education was in philosophy and law. It was while he worked as a labor union lawyer among the people of the slums in Northeast Brazil that he became interested in literacy training. He quickly became dissatisfied with traditional literacy methods because of the paternalism and authoritarianism that they involved. In 1959, Freire was appointed a Professor of the History and Philosophy of Education at the University of Pernambuco in Recife, Brazil. In this capacity he continued his literacy work among the poor and was able to involve many students in his project. In the early 1960's democratic reform centering on the Popular Culture Movement developed in the Northeast. The members of this movement, to which Freire belonged, conducted many discussions with the masses. In these discussions visual aids were used to dramatize various social issues. So satisfactory were the results, that Freire decided to use the same types of methods in his literacy training.

From all accounts the Freire Method was successful in the few years of its operation in Brazil. In the city of Angicos three hundred workers learned to read and write in 45 days. In June 1963, the literacy program was extended in principle to the entire nation, and between June 1963 and March 1964 training programs were developed in almost all the state capitols. The 1964 plan was to establish twenty thousand discussion groups which would be equipped to teach twenty million illiterates. Widespread opposition began to develop in Brazilian conservative circles, however, and Freire was accused of using his literacy method to spread subversive and revolutionary ideas.

Freire's literacy work in Brazil was brought to an abrupt end in April 1964. A military coup toppled the Goulart government and along with many other leaders of leftist groups, Freire was jailed. He spent seventy days in jail, was stripped of his rights of citizenship and forced into exile. With his wife and five children, he went to Santiago, Chile, where he worked as a UNESCO consultant and with the Agrarian Reform Training and Research Institute.

Toward the end of the 1960's, Freire left Latin America and came to the United States where he was Visiting Professor at Harvard's Center for Studies in Education. Since 1971 Freire has made his home in Geneva where he serves as Special Educational Consultant to the World Council of Churches. He also serves as chairman of the *Institut d'Action Culterelle* (IDAC). This institute attempts to spread Freire's ideas on conscientization and publishes documents promoting his ideas and applying them in different cultural situations.

While in prison, Freire began to write an account of his literacy method and develop his philosophy of education. He finished his first book, *Educacao Como Pratica da Liberdade* (1967), in Chile where it was extensively used. The work has appeared in English as the first part of *Education for Critical Consciousness* (1973). Freire has also written numerous articles and two additional books on his educational philosophy: *Pedagogy of the Oppressed* (1970) and *Cultural Action for Freedom* (1970).

An analysis of Freire's writings reveals an interesting philosophical journey. In his earliest works he is strongly influenced by a strong Christian personalism that emphasized the place of the individual in the face of a growing technological and scientific culture. These works also exhibit many existentialist themes: freedom, intersubjectivity, authenticity, and dialogue. *Pedagogy of the Oppressed* marks a turning point in his thought. To previous ideas he attempts to assimilate phenomenology—an examination of consciousness and its various states—and Marxist thought. His writing from this time becomes more analytical and dialectical. A revolutionary rhetoric characterizes writings from this period as he moves from the advocacy of social democracy to a plea for the Marxist socialist revolution in oppressed countries. Freire's more recent writings attempt to wed Marxist thought with radical Christian theology. He calls for the radicalization of Christian theology and practice in Latin American countries as well as the acceptance of key Marxist ideas.

Freire's Basic Philosophical Principles

Freire's theory of pedagogy cannot be understood apart from his philosophical principles. He claims that his

> pedagogy cannot do without a vision of man and of the world. It formulates a scientific humanist conception which finds its expression in a dialogical praxis in which the teachers and learners together, in the act of analyzing a dehumanizing reality, denounce it while announcing its transformation in the name of the liberation of man. [1970, p. 4]

Many important elements in Freire's general and educational philosophy are indicated with these words: vision of man and world, dialogue praxis, teacher-learner relationship, analysis, the liberation of man, and the Marxist concept of denouncing and announcing world views and consciousness.

Freire's philosophy begins with a *philosophy or vision of man.* Freire contrasts at some length in his writings the consciousness and the action of man with the consciousness and action of animals. Man is not immersed in reality in some determined manner. Human persons know that they know and know that they are able to change their situation and environments. Because persons can do these things, they are subjects rather than objects. For Freire persons can lift themselves to a higher level of consciousness and become subjects to the extent of their intervention in society, their reflection on this intervention and their commitment to this engagement in society.

Persons differ from animals also in their capacity to create both culture and history. In the context in which Freire worked it was important for him to make learners cognizant of their ability to change the material and social conditions of their lives. Freire utilized various philosophical traditions to emphasize the freedom and autonomy of individuals. Christian personalism stressed the strength of the human person to choose even in a dehumanizing technological society. Existential thought made the important distinction between merely existing and really living. From Marxist/existentialist thought Freire has adopted the concept of the human person as unfinished and always in the process of becoming. Marxist thought also provides the critical concept of human existence as a task of praxis: persons give meaning to history and culture, indeed create history and culture, by combining reflective activity with actions.

Freire's philosophy of man, though idealist and utopian, has certain weaknesses. Freire rarely gets beyond generalities or pieties in developing this philosophy. Though in his literacy work he was involved with real men and women, Freire produces only abstraction when he writes about the human person. In his writings the person lives often in no historical time; has no body, passions, emotions. He knows neither relativism nor pluralism. He is not faced with compromises; he never has to choose between evil alternatives. He lives in a world where things are clearly right or wrong. The dark side of man is not found in this vision and as Heilbroner points out this is one of the deepest weaknesses of the Marxist and utopian vision of man. The utopian vision

> has failed to formulate a conception of human behavior in all its historical, sociological, sexual, and ideational complexity, a conception that would present man as being at once biologic as well as social, tragic as well as heroic, limited as well as plastic. [1970, p. 105]

Freire's vision of the human person, though in some ways a faulty one, is powerful in its optimism. Few philosophers have presented as forceful an image in modern times. True humanization takes place in the world only when each person becomes conscious of the social forces working upon him or her, reflects upon these forces, and becomes capable of transforming the world. To be human is to be an actor in the world and to seek to guide one's own destiny. To be free, to be an actor in the world, means knowing one's identity and realizing how one has been shaped in one's social world and environment.

For Freire the opposite of humanization is dehumanization or oppression. The condition of oppression is what Freire calls the culture of silence. The culture of silence can come from either ignorance or education. The Brazilian peasants were in a culture of silence because they were kept in ignorance of the true conditions of their poverty. For Freire assimilating the peasants into the social system that produces poverty is a form of oppressive education.

Since the concept of oppression is an important concept in Freire's social philosophy, it is unfortunate that he does not give a more adequate treatment of it. Oppression for Freire is "any situation in which 'A' objectivity exploits 'B' or hinders his pursuit of self affirmation as a responsible person" (*Pedagogy*, p. 40). This explanation is somewhat tautological since no criteria are given for judging what objective exploitation would be or what a responsible person would be. Freire certainly labored in situations in Brazil that one would term oppressive; yet he has not adequately analyzed these situations when he divides Brazilian society into the oppressors and the oppressed.

In discussing Freire's concept of humanization and oppression, we have moved from Freire's philosophy of man to his *philosophy and vision of the world.* Freire's view of social reality is decidedly Marxist. Social reality is in dialectical historical process. Human persons are part of this process and can bring about significant changes in the world by the exercise of praxis, action with reflection. In man's relationship to the world, the world appears as filled with problems or contradictions. Man's task is to break through these problems and to act to change the social reality in which he lives.

Freire's (1970b) analysis of the problems that exist in a particular historical epoch is somewhat complex. For him

> An epoch is characterized by a complex of ideas, concepts, hopes, values, and challenges in dialectical interaction with their opposites, striving toward plenitude. The concrete representation of many of these ideas, values, concepts, and hopes, as well as the obstacles which impede man's full humanization, constitute the themes of that epoch. These themes imply others which are opposing or even antithetical; they also indicate tasks to be carried out and fulfilled. [p. 91]

Freire's analysis of the Third World concluded that it was characterized by social, political, and economic oppression. These ideas and values are in conflict or contradiction with freedom, responsibility, and true humanization. The various forms of oppression constitute the concrete problems or contradictions that are the task of his revolutionary pedagogy.

Though Freire's analysis of social reality is both abstract and theoretical, his educational process does bring the themes of the particular historical epoch out in concrete fashion. The circles of culture discuss such issues as work, salary, family, prostitution, and slums as part of the general themes of oppression. In many ways Freire's theory of conscientization is a highly theoretical explanation of an educational process that is both simple and concrete. In the discussion of the Freire method this basic simplicity will be made clear.

A third area in Freire's basic philosophical position is his *theory of human knowing or consciousness.* Freire's indebtedness to phenomenological and Marxist thought is very strong in this aspect of his philosophy. Thinking and knowing are dependent upon history and culture. The social reality in which we live shapes our ideas and our thinking. Knowledge for Freire is the process through which individuals become aware of objective reality and of their own knowledge of this reality. He contends that true knowledge of reality, which he terms conscientization, penetrates to what reality really is because it is connected with praxis or reflective activity. Freire is true to the phenomenological position in attempting to avoid both materialism and idealism:

> In reality consciousness is not just a copy of the Real, nor is the Real only a capricious construction of consciousness. It is only by way of an understanding of the dialectical unity, in which we find solidarity between subjectivity and objectivity, that we can get away from the subjectivist error as well as the mechanical error. And then we must take into account the role of consciousness or of the "conscious being" in the transformation of reality. [1972, p. 5]

Freire's discussion of his theory of knowledge is not just an exercise in epistemology, for it has for him political and educational implications. In these spheres the objectivist or materialist error leads to treating persons as things or objects. The subjectivist or idealist error leads to the assumption that the future will change when individuals change their consciousness. What both of these errors miss, according to Freire, is the transforming role of human reflection and action.

The Marxist influence on Freire's theory of conscientization is most evident in his demonstration of the relationships between levels of individual consciousness and levels of development and social organization. Individual liberation and societal liberation are closely tied together in his theory.

Freire (1973) employs an analogy for grammer (transivity) to describe states of human and social consciousness. The lowest level of consciousness is intransitive consciousness. This is the culture of silence in the peasant societies of the Third World. At this level individuals are preoccupied with meeting their most elementary needs. They are characterized by the near absence of historical consciousness. Immersed in a one-dimensional oppressive present, the peasants cannot comprehend the forces that have shaped their lives. Individuals at this level ascribe their plight to self-blame or to supernatural causes. Societies in which this consciousness is present are closed and oppressive.

Semi-intransitivity or magical consciousness is the second level of consciousness. It is a prevalent consciousness in the emerging societies of the Third World. Self-depreciation is a common characteristic of this consciousness, for individuals have internalized the negative values that the dominant culture ascribes to them. This consciousness is also marked by excessive emotional dependency. To be is to be under someone, to depend on him. This form of consciousness often expresses itself in defensive and therapeutic magic.

Freire calls his third level of consciousness naive-transitiveness. It is transitive because people begin to experience reality as a problem. This consciousness has not fully emerged from the culture of silence. Pressure and criticism begin to be applied to the dominant groups in society. Nevertheless it remains an oppressed consciousness and susceptible to populist manipulation. Power elites can manipulate this consciousness by force, propaganda, slogans, or dehumanizing utilization of technology. The advantage of this level of consciousness is that individuals begin to sense that they have some control over their lives. The danger is that they are still able to be pacified by receiving certain political and economic privileges.

The highest level of consciousness for Freire is critical consciousness, achieved through the process of conscientization. This level is marked by depth in the interpretation of problems, self confidence in discussions, receptiveness, and refusal to shirk responsibility. The quality of discourse is dialogical. At this level as the person scrutinizes his own thoughts, he sees the proper causal and circumstantial correlations. Conscientization means a radical denunciation of dehumanizing structures, accompanied by an announcement of a new reality to be created by men. It entails a rigorous and rational critique of the ideology that supports these structures. Critical consciousness is brought about not through intellectual efforts but through praxis, the authentic union of action and reflection.

Conscientization for Freire is a social activity. Humanistic acts of knowing imply communication through dialogue with others to determine how they experience reality. For Freire (1970c):

to know, which is always a process, implies a dialogical situation. There is not, strictly speaking, "I think," but "we think." It is not "I think" which constitutes "we think," but on the contrary, it is "we think" that makes it possible for me to think. [p. 1]

This concept of knowing or conscientization will have implications for Freire's theory of pedagogy where dialogue and social activity are essential to the learning process.

Though Freire's theory of conscientization is impressive, it still suffers from a number of weaknesses. Freire has valiantly attempted to avoid the idealist position, but it appears that he does not succeed. His theory of conscientization depends on some sort of transcendent view of reality through which individuals come to see what is real and authentic. There appears to be little room in his view for the painful struggling with different views and opposing viewpoints. It all comes down to the dominant classes with their distorted view of reality and conscientized individuals with their view of the reality that really is. Casting social reality in black and white terms is more the characteristic of the simplistic religious preacher than the critical philosopher of knowledge and education.

Freire's idealist view of knowledge is also apparent where the connection between thought and action becomes blurred. Freire seems to say that people involved in the circles of culture will fashion a new reality that will replace the old reality that they have come to denounce. He seems to assume that a person's knowledge of his true interests guarantees his participation in activity to achieve these interests. As Horowitz rightly points out:

The line between action and interests is far from straight. Even if we ignore the dilemmas arising out of a direct correlation of actions and interests, there is a policy issue involved; namely, the degree of social unrest necessary to stimulate a person to think along developmental lines without creating complete revolutionary upheaval. [1966, p. 265]

There is also the real possibility that people involved in conscientization efforts might even become more entrenched in their thinking once they realize the full impact of oppression in their lives.

The final major area of Freire's general philosophy is his *theory of values*. A treatment of these values makes explicit themes that are already implicit in the other areas of Freire's general philosophy that have been discussed. The highest human goal is humanization through a process of liberation. This goal is a social goal and thus to be achieved in cooperation with others. Authentic human liberation entails the permanent transformation of social structures of a given society. Freire advocates revolutionary political action to bring about these changes. He advocates the overthrow of capitalist regimes but does not give clear details of the type of social structures that he would advocate, beyond some sort of vague socialism.

The means of achieving personal and social liberation for Freire are dialogue and praxis. The role of dialogue in politics, social change, and education is expounded again and again in his writings. Dialogue demands the attitudes of trust, faith, humility, willingness to risk, and love. The authentic praxis that Freire advocates implies a commitment to Utopia. By this Freire seems to mean an orientation to change and a commitment to the future that demands a rigorous investigation of the ideological myths that undergird present ideologies and social structures. He puts great faith in science as a force in demythologizing religious, political, and economic myths, but does not greatly develop how science accomplishes this.

In his later writings, as has been noted in this chapter, Freire puts increasing emphasis on the value of religion as a force in the liberation of man from oppressive social structures. As a believing and committed Christian, he expounds a view of God that attempts to refute Marxist criticism of religion as a reactionary and oppressive force in society. He places himself in the prophetic religious tradition that denounces evil social structures and calls believers to work for change in human society. In Latin America where Freire's ideas took root, left wing Catholics have reached ideological agreements with Marxists on many areas relating to social and political action. Freire identifies himself with a Latin American theology of liberation that is attempting to emphasize the prophetic and activist elements in the Christian tradition. Freire aligns himself with such theologians of liberation as Guttierrez (1971) who claims that

In Latin America the church must realize that it exists in a continent undergoing revolution, where violence is present in different ways. The world in which the Christian community is called to live . . . is one in social revolution. Its mission must be achieved keeping that in account. The church has no alternative. Only a total break with the unjust order to which it is bound in a thousand conscious or unconscious ways, and a forthright commitment to a new society, will make men in Latin America believe the message of love it bears. [p. 60]

Freire's Educational Principles

Freire is a radical critic of traditional education. For Freire, traditional education equals banking education in which students receive, file, and store deposits. Knowledge in this view is seen as a gift bestowed on students by the teacher. This type of education, according to Freire, offends the freedom and autonomy of the students. Banking education domesticates students, for it emphasizes the transfer of existing knowledge to passive objects who must memorize and repeat this knowledge. This type of education is a form of violence, for in imposing curricula, ideas, and values, it submerges the consciousness of the students. This produces alienated consciousness as students are not involved in a real act of knowing, but are given a ready-made view of social reality.

The Marxist concept of alienation illuminates the full meaning of Freire's criticism of banking education. For Marx, alienation meant that work or life activity is not an object for human fulfillment; rather, the individual becomes a mere object for production. Marx (in Fromm, 1960) wrote that

The alienation of the worker in his product means not only that his labor becomes an object, assumes an external existence, but that it exists independently, outside himself, and alien to him, and that it stands opposed to him as an autonomous power. [p. 109]

Similarly in banking education the learner's self becomes an object of the educational process, worked upon to achieve goals external to itself. The object of this education is not to understand the self but to change the individual according to alien goals.

In place of the traditional banking form of education, Freire offers a *libertarian, dialogic, and problem-posing education.* Cultural action for freedom is the expression that Freire uses to designate the educational process. This action is one in which a group of persons, through dialogue, come to realize the concrete situation in which they live, the reasons for this situation, and the possible solutions. In order for action to be authentic, the participants must be free to create the curriculum along with the teacher. Freire's problem posing education is based upon respect, communication, and solidarity.

Freire's dialogic education is problem posing in that it begins with an investigation of the cultural situation of the learners. This cultural situation provides the curriculum of problems that are to be discussed in the educational process. As the result of dialogue on these problems, teachers and learners alike are to arrive at a decision to become involved in concrete actions to solve these problems. The investigation of the culture of the learners includes discovering how their history and culture are conditioned by ideas, beliefs, myths, art, science, manners, tastes, and political preferences.

Though Freire emphasizes the importance of dialogue and equality between teacher and learners, he does give a positive *role to the teacher* in the educational process. Notwithstanding this role, Freire insists that teachers must also be students and that students can also be teachers. The teacher can present material for consideration so long as he or she is open to clarifications and modifications. Teachers can suggest but not determine the themes that serve to organize the content of the dialogues. The Freire method utilizes expert knowledge of various social science disciplines in various stages of the educational process. Freire is thus not opposed to the presentation of views by teachers and experts. He is more interested that this not be done in a purely didactic manner and that the heart of the curricular process begins and continues along lines of the problems that learners raise in their own situation.

For Freire authentic education is unquestionably *political action.* For him there is no such thing as neutral education. Education is either for domestication or for liberation. A theory of education that is subordinated to social and political purposes opens itself to the charge of indoctrination and manipulation. The situation in which Freire worked in Brazil made him sensitive to these charges, at least to the degree of avoiding conflict with conservatives. Freire answers the charges of indoctrination by contending that his goal is to get people to learn by having them challenge the concrete reality of their lives as presented in their own words and in pictorial codifications of these words. Another view of social reality is not imposed on them, but through discussing a problematic situation they are led to see the true condition under which they live. Through discussion they also begin to see that the present situation is not determined but can be changed.

The danger of indoctrination and manipulation is present in all forms of education. It is especially present in various forms of political education where there are conflicting political positions and ideologies. Given Freire's tendency to see reality in black and white, and given his lack of critical examination of his own presuppositions and ideologies, there is a real danger that this method can be indoctrinative. Freire presents too little information about the quality of the dialogues in the educational process to determine how conflicting views were handled in his literacy efforts. For certain, skilled teachers are needed in this highly politicized form of education in order to satisfy the demands for objectivity and appeal to rational argument.

Freire's educational philosophy is not only political but it is also a revolutionary pedagogy. Freire considers that his main contribution to a theory of revolution is his emphasis on the dialogical nature of revolutionary action, believing that leaders should be in constant dialogue with the people at all points of the revolution. He wrote *Pedagogy* (1970b) to defend the eminently pedagogical nature of the revolutionary action. He contends that

> Critical and liberating dialogue, which presupposes action, must be carried on with the oppressed at whatever stage of their struggle for liberation. The content of that dialogue can and should vary in accordance with historical situations and the level at which they can perceive reality. [p. 52]

Though Freire advocates dialogic education as part of revolutionary action, he is realistic enough to make a number of exceptions. Freire has great difficulty making his hero, Che Guevara, an advocate of dialogical revolutionary action. He quotes the revolutionary leader's words:

> Mistrust: at the beginning, do not trust your own shadow, never trust friendly peasants, informers, guides, or contact men. Do not trust anything or anybody until a zone is completely liberated. [1970b, p. 169]

Freire also denies the revolutionaries' need to dialogue with the former oppressors. He agrees with Guevara's admonition to punish the deserter from the revolutionary group for reasons of cohesion and discipline of the group. He also agrees with the guerilla leader in his nontolerance of those who are not ready to accept the conclusion that the revolution is essential. Freire's effort to maintain the essentially dialogical and educational aspect of revolutionary action has to be pronounced a failure in light of these exceptions and others.

Theory and Practice in Radical Adult Education: Paulo Freire Method

Freire developed his educational method or practice for the purpose of teaching literacy. In later writings he extended the use of this method to post-literacy or political education. The best description of this method is found in *Education for Critical Consciousness* (1973), a work that Freire wrote while in prison and in the early years of his exile.

Phase One Literacy Campaign

Stage I: The Study of the Context

An interdisciplinary team studies the context in which the people live in order to determine the common vocabulary and the problems that confront the people in that area. A maximum amount of participation by the people is sought at this level. The thinking, aspirations, and problems of the people are discussed through informal conversations. The team faithfully records the words and the language of the people. Since Freire's method is deeply contextual, he developed different lists of words and problems for rural and urban people; and, after his move to Chile, he had to develop new lists of words.

Freire decided to elicit words from the people themselves because he was against the practice of supplying primers that utilized common words. Freire contends that words should come from the people and not be imposed on them. Educators who teach reading in urban areas have come to the same awareness that Freire arrived at in his literacy work.

Stage II: The Selection of Words from the Discovered Vocabulary

From the words suggested, the team chooses words that are most charged with existential and relevant meaning for the people. Freire was interested not only in the typical expressions of the people but also in words that had major emotional content for them. He called these words *generative* because of their power to generate other words for the students.

Freire has various criteria for his choice of generative words for his literacy training. The first criterion is the capacity of the words to include the basic sounds of the Portuguese or Spanish language. The words of these languages are based on syllables with little variation in vocalic sounds and with a minimum of combinations of syllables. Freire discovered that sixteen to twenty words sufficed to cover all the sounds of the language.

The second criterion for the choice of generative words is that the vocabulary, when organized, would enable the student to move from simple letters and sounds to more complex ones. Freire in this way ensures success for the method by providing a sense of accomplishment at the earlier stages of the training. With the basic words as a point of departure, the student could discover syllables, letters, and specific difficulties with syllables in his own idiom. The words chosen, if truly generative, should thus serve as starting points for the discovery of new words.

The third and most important criterion for a word to be chosen as a generative word is its capacity to confront the social, cultural, and political reality in which the people live. For Freire the words have to suggest and mean something important for the people;

they must provide both mental and emotional stimulation for the students. For example, some of the words chosen for use in the state of Rio de Janeiro were: *favela*—slum; *terreno*—plot of land; *trabatho*—work; *salario*—salary; *governo*—government; *manque*— swamp (also the zone of prostitution in Rio); and *riquezza*— wealth. Such words brought up in the discussions pressing problems in the lives of the people: poverty, property rights, and distribution, the meaning and value of work, just wages, the power of government over their lives, the evils of prostitution on a personal and social level, and inequities in the distribution of wealth.

Stage III: The Actual Process of Literary Training

1. *Motivation Sessions.* Literacy training in Brazil was preceded by at least three sessions of motivation in which the students analyzed the concept on culture. (In Chile Freire incorporated these sessions into the literacy training itself for he found that the Chileans were not interested in this type of discussion.) In these sessions the group coordinator showed pictures without words. The purpose of doing this was to provoke among the people some sort of a debate and discussion about the notions of man, world, nature, nature and culture, man and animals, human culture, and patterns of human behavior. A further purpose was the development of a group consciousness where illiterates would see themselves in the process of learning and reflecting. The process of conscientization began with these sessions. It is to be noted that the topics for discussion included the basic concepts of Freire's general philosophy of man and the world.

2. *Development of Teaching Materials.* The interdisciplinary team develops materials appropriate to each situation. These are of two types. There is a set of cards or slides that show the breaking down of words into their parts. The second type of materials is a set of cards that depict situations related to the words and designed to impress various images upon the students. These pictures are designed to stimulate thinking about the situations that the words imply. Freire refers to this process

of developing images of concrete realities as codification. Through various pictures, situations in the lives of the people, such as poverty, are codified or presented in pictorial form.

Freire has given certain guidelines for these codifications. They must be neither too clear nor too vague. If they are too clear, there would be the danger of imposing particular views on the students. If they are too vague, they serve not as stimulations for thought but as puzzles or enigmas to be solved. This creative use of images or codifications is a distinctive aspect of Freire's method. They are not just aids in the teaching process; they are at the heart of the educational process because they initiate and stimulate the process of critical thinking.

3. *Literacy Training (Decodification)*. Each session is built around words and pictures. For example, the word *favela*—slum—is printed with a picture of a slum in the background. The class begins to break down the codified whole, both word and picture. They discuss the existential situation of the slum and the relationship between the word *favela* and the reality it signifies. Then a slide is projected with only the word *favela*, which as a generative word is now separated into its syllables: fa-ve-la. The family of the first syllable is shown: *fa, fe, fi, fo, fu*. This is done with the remaining syllables. The students are then led to create other words using these syllables and their families. When the second generative-word is shown, the students create other words using syllables from both words. From knowing five or six words, the students can begin to write brief notes. At the same time they continue to discuss and analyze critically the real context represented in the codifications.

Phase II: Post Literacy Campaign

While he was still director of the National Literacy Program in Brazil, Freire was planning a post-literacy campaign for those who had already passed through the first stage of literacy training. He was never able to institute this program because of the military coup. Freire utilized this part of his method in Chile. *Pedagogy* (1970b) is a further development of this post-literacy phase.

Stage I: Investigation of Themes

In the past literacy campaign, an interdisciplinary team investigates themes that are prevalent in the lives of the people. These themes are found in the tape recordings and notes of the literacy process. The generative themes indicate the aspirations of the people. The people themselves are involved in the selection and development of these themes. Freire gives a number of themes that might be investigated in Third World countries: development and underdevelopment, dependency, domination, liberation, propaganda, advertising, and education. Freire suggests that the various themes be classified according to the various social sciences. Thus the theme of development can be looked at from the vantage point of economics, political science, sociology, religion, and anthropology. (It should be noted that in his literacy work Freire was able to utilize the assistance of a university staff of anthropologists, psychologists and educators.)

Stage II: Codification of Themes

As in the literacy process, various types of representations are used to concretize and draw attention to the themes for discussion and dialogue. Both sketches and photographs are employed. The codifications must represent situations with which the people are familiar. Like the generative words, they must not be too explicit or too enigmatic. They should be organized as some sort of a fan. Certain themes should open up to other themes. The themes should be presented in such a way that the people are led to see certain contradictions in their lives.

Once the team has developed a number of codifications of various themes, they return to the groups to initiate dialogue with the people on these themes. This material is taped for further study. The coordinator of the group both listens to the people and challenges them by posing certain problems. A true dialogue takes place between the coordinator and the people.

After the initial dialogues, the team makes an interdisciplinary study of the findings from this preliminary use of the chosen codifications and themes. The themes are then broken down into various parts. Certain themes may be added by the team, called hinged themes, to make clear the connections between two or more themes. Not only the professionals but also the students involved in the process are free to add these hinged themes to the discussions. Codifications are then chosen for all the themes that will be used in the post-literacy program.

Stage III: Post Literacy Education

Now that the themes have been chosen, dialogue on them takes place between the coordinators of the groups and the people. Freire suggests various methods of carrying out this dialogue and education: reading and discussion of magazine articles, newspapers and books, as well as the use of instruction manuals. But the primary emphasis is on the dialogues and discussions that take place. The people must feel that they are listened to and that their ideas are important.

This detailed description of the Freire Method of conscientization is clearly an emphasis of this chapter. Extensive treatment has been given to this method because it makes explicit and direct connections between philosophical principles and educational practice. The Freire method demonstrates most dramatically the close connection that should exist between theory and practice in education. This extensive treatment is also useful, for the Freire method has implications for various types of adult education: literacy education, consciousness raising, and social action program.

Paulo Freire and Adult Education

The educational philosophy and method of Paulo Freire arose in concrete historical circumstances. As has been indicated in this chapter, it is a philosophy and method for bringing oppressed people to both literacy and political consciousness. It is also an attempt to democratize the culture of Brazil and later of Chile. The method presents both a theory and a method for cultural and political change.

At first sight it would appear that there is little in common between Paulo Freire teaching adult illiterates in Latin America and an adult educator in North America. The two cultural situations are so diverse. The culture of the one is rather primitive, at least with regard to the people among whom Freire worked; the culture of the latter is considered advanced technologically. A second look, however, reveals a number of similarities in the two cultural situations.

First of all, illiteracy is a problem that is not restricted to the countries of the Third World. Many adults in American society do not learn to read and write. The use of Freire's method in literacy education adds some new dimensions to this form of education. Literacy education begins with the words, language, and idioms of the students. Literacy education is closely connected with the cultural and political life of the students. Since illiterates in American society belong predominantly to the lower classes, the cultural and political dimensions of Freire's literacy education are applicable in this culture.

Freire calls his educational theory and method a "pedagogy of the oppressed." Is this type pedagogy needed in this country at this time? Is the method so attached to the realities of oppression and political consciousness in Third World situations that it can be used only in situations that are similar? Are there forms of oppression in American society that prevent persons from being truly subjects and not objects? Is Freire's method of conscientization applicable in these situations? Questions like these form the basis for a discussion of the relevance of the Freire method for this culture.

It would be hard to deny the existence of real oppression in this society, though it might not take the precise form that it does in some Third World countries. Richard Shaull (1970), in his foreword to the English edition of *Pedagogy of the Oppressed*, commented that

> if we take a closer look, we may discover that Freire's methodology, as well as his educational philosophy are as important for us as for the dispossessed in Latin America. Their struggle to become free subjects and to participate in the transformation of their society is similar, in many ways, to the struggle not only of the blacks and Mexican-Americans but also of middle class people in this country. The sharpness and intensity of that struggle in the developing world may well provide us with new insights, new models, and new hope as we face our own situation. [p. 10]

Freire's philosophy and methodology has relevance for any group that is concerned with such issues as oppression, liberation, consciousness raising, and community political and social action. Freire's Institute in Geneva has, for example, attempted to apply the principles of conscientization to the woman's liberation movement in two booklets, *Liberation of Women: To Change the World and Re-Invent Life* (1974), and *Toward a Woman's World* (1975).

Besides its relevance for literacy education and the education of the oppressed in our society, the real relevance of Freire's philosophy and methodology lies in its questioning of two basic educational assumptions. The first of these assumptions is the presumed neutrality of education. In Western educational thought education is often regarded as the public transmission of neutral bits of information about the world. What is taught is viewed as devoid of any ideological content. In Freire's analysis of the relationship between education and culture, it is culture that produces education and uses it for its own self-perpetuation because the assumptions of the culture are contained in the educational process. Education is clearly non-neutral and value laden. A recent American example of this non-neutrality of education is our "discovery" of the treatment of blacks, women, and Indians as part of our past. These groups were excluded from historical accounts as a selective educational practice to serve particular values and goals.

The second assumption against which Freire struggled is the relative status of teacher and student and the psychological effects that existing methods have on students. His criticism of traditional education as banking education is an attempt to handle this problem. Knowledge for Freire is power, something political. In getting a person to know or learn what the teacher wants him to learn, the teacher exercises power and control over the student. Education and other forms of socialization have been used to indoctrinate groups of people into specific attitudes and behavior: women accept an inferior role; the poor blame themselves for their poverty; the unemployed see themselves as deficient; masses of people accept arbitrary religious authorities; and masses of people accept the need to produce and consume. When education is thus domesticating, people are prevented from thinking their own thoughts, arriving at their own decisions, having the consciousness that change is possible.

166 / Philosophical Foundations of Adult Education

It is Freire's contention that education can be for liberation only if an equality is established between teachers and students in the educational process. The lives, experiences, insights, questions, and problems of students must form the center of the educational process. Freire does not call for a reversal of roles between teachers and students but rather advocates teachers and students together initiating and sustaining the process of dialogue on issues that are real in the lives of both. Education in this sense is liberating not only in the sense of consciousness raising but also because of its connection with action; knowing, for Freire, is inseparable from deciding to do something in reference to the knowledge. To preserve, to change, to destroy, to fully experience are possible actions one might take as a result of knowing something.

The Deschooling Movement and Adult Education: Illich and Ohliger

The late 1960's and early 1970's saw the emergence of a radical approach to educational reform, based somewhat on anarchist principles. The intellectual leader of this movement was Ivan Illich, the founder of the Center for Intercultural Documentation (CIDOC), in Cuernavaca, Mexico. In numerous articles and books Illich has proposed the elimination of schools from society as the necessary condition for freeing people from their addiction to manipulative and oppressive institutions. Illich's criticism and rejection of schooling is based not so much on its failures as on its central position in maintaining overindustrialized and over-consumerized society. Illich's ideas have been extended into the field of adult education by John Ohliger, visiting Professor of Education at the University of Wisconsin.

Though Illich is foremost a radical social critic, his philosophical views on education and learning are at the heart of his thinking. The type of learning that Illich espouses is one that promotes human freedom, equality, and close personal relationships. True learning is learning in which a person freely consents to participate. For Illich no one has the right to interfere in the learning of another without his consent. He contends, in addition, that most learning is not the result of teaching, but rather is gathered incidentally as one participates in life. The learnings that a person cannot gather incidentally from life and things, he can easily appropriate from a skill master, a peer, or from books and other learning instruments.

For Illich, then, the fundamental aspect of learning is that it is freely-chosen learning from life, both from things and from persons. Compulsory learning is always harmful for the individual and for society. Illich makes rather extensive claims for the freedom to learn which he espouses. He contends that educational research has demonstrated that children learn most of what teachers pretend to teach them from peer groups, chance observations, and comics (*Deschooling*, 1970, p. 29). Freedom to learn will result in immeasurable re-creation among people who share an issue that for them is socially important. Free learning will enable people to be spontaneous, independent, and interrelated to one another (DS. p. 52). This type of learning will increase a person's poetic ability, his power to endow the world with personal meaning, and his creative energies (1973, pp. 60 ff).

In rejecting schools as a form of education, Illich does not fail to provide alternative arrangements for the convivial society that he envisions. He has proposed the establishment of four classes of learning networks in *Deschooling Society*. The first network provides access to educational *objects* such as books, radios, microscopes and television. A second network is a *skill exchange* wherein students who wish to master a skill could contact a master who would demonstrate it for the learner. The third network is *peer matching* on the basis of common interests. This peer matching would be done through a computer. The fourth and final network is a *system of independent educators* who would pursue jointly determined, but difficult, tasks.

Illich's purpose in proposing these networks is to present alternatives to schools as we now know them. He contends that these networks will avoid institutionalizing the value of learning and at the same time will make learning both free and incidental. Though Illich's description of his networks shows imagination and boldness, there also appears to be a certain simplicity in his expectations for these networks. He makes the education of all persons sound rather simple when he describes it in terms of access to things and people. Illich is no doubt right in arguing for a breakdown of the excessive bureaucratization of education. But his concrete proposals are mere skeletons with a minimum of muscle.

Illich's proposals have been widely debated in this decade. The criticism of Jonathon Kozol is significant for in many ways he is sympathetic to Illich's ideas and has visited Cuernavaca on a number of occasions. Kozol (1972) confesses that on returning to the Boston ghetto, he is less impressed with Illich's views. He writes that

> It is a luxury at 2,000 miles distance to consider an educational experience that does not involve credentials or curriculum, or long term sequential learning. In immediate terms, in cities such as Boston and New York, it is unwise and perhaps destructive to do so. Instead, we must face up to the hard truth that these credentials and measured areas of expertise and certified ability constitute the irreducible framework of our labor and struggle. [p. 33]

Kozol's main point is that millions of people in the cities of the United States are without the survival skills that Illich has contended are picked up incidentally. Kozol has learned from experience that these survival skills are desperately needed by adults and children in our society.

"A voice crying in the wilderness" might be the best way to describe the efforts of professor John Ohliger to apply the ideas of Freire and Illich to adult education in the United States. In numerous articles and talks Ohliger has alleged that more and more adult education institutions define people as inadequate, insufficient, lacking, and incomplete. Over the years he has kept a careful watch over the number of courses that adults are required to take by law, regulation, or pressure. His enumeration of the groups now involved in compulsory adult education is extensive:

> traffic offenders and judges; parents of delinquents and public school teachers; illiterates on welfare; nurses; pharmacists; physicians; optometrists; nursing home administrators; firemen; policemen, dentists, psychiatrists; dieticians; podiatrists; preachers; veterinarians; many municipal, state provincial, and federal civil servants; employees of all types pressured into taking courses, classes, joining sensitivity

training or organizational development groups; and of course the military, where most, if not all adult education is compulsory. [1974, p. 2]

The institutionalization of adult education is the chief target of Ohliger's criticism. Compulsory adult education has become pervasive in the health professions. Adult education has become more imbedded into the structure of the schooling establishment. Adult degrees, external degrees, and open learning for adults are ways that the educational establishment has developed for making education a commodity for thousands of adults. Ohliger views the UNESCO book *Learning To Be* as dangerous in preferring official knowledge or learning over the personal or experiential learning that a person gains incidentally through mere living. Ohliger closely echoes Illich when he asks

> As we seem to be moving toward a society in which adults are told more and more that they must consume official knowledge in lifelong learning, is it any wonder that we say that adult education is becoming an oppressive force that is taking over people's lives? [p. 9]

In his proposals for the practice of adult education, Ohliger again shows his indebtedness to both Freire and Illich. He briefly describes three types of adult education that educators have to choose from. The first form takes place within institutions of adult education. Here the task is to loosen and resist the economic and bureaucratic controls that stifle educators. A second form of adult education takes place outside the establishment, or at its fringes. Here Freire's approach can be helpful in working with individuals and groups that are moving toward awareness of political and economic oppression. The third path is cultural, and it involves

> living/learning as individuals, in small groups, or new communities as examples of, or as seeds for, a future society in which what is now called less will be recognized as more. Here is where the ideas of Ivan Illich's American colleague Everett Reimer, would be worthwhile for adult educators. [1974, p. 10]

The ideas of Illich and Ohliger, though intriguing, have not found many adherents among adult educators. The reason for this will become clearer in the overall evaluation of the impact of radical adult education on the discipline and field of adult education in this country.

Radical Adult Education: An Assessment

It should be an obvious fact that radical adult education has not had any great impact on the practice of adult education in this country. This is equally true of the impact of other forms of radicalism in American culture. Radicalism has been a minor force in the American tradition. Its ideas have received a serious hearing from large numbers of people only in the 1930's and 1960's when, in the face of various crises, radicalism, together with other reform proposals, was discussed openly in books, articles, and journals of thought. Radical educational thought has had its strongest appeal in precisely these decades of crisis.

There are a number of particular reasons for the unreceptivity of adult educators to educational radicalism. Adult education in this country is conducted within institutions that are basically conservative of traditional values and societal structures: public schools, religious institutions, business and industry, governmental and military institutions. Though adult educators have often expressed criticisms and reservations about the values and structures of these institutions, they maintain strong commitments to the institutions within which they work. If they advocate measures of change, these are most often moderate and such that will reform the institutions.

Any concern for change among adult educators usually focuses upon personal and individual change and not radical social or political change. In this characteristic adult educators differ little from other educators. It is the rare American professional who espouses or proposes radical measures of social and political change for dealing with individual and personal needs. The popularity of a humanistic philosophy of education, such as that espoused by Carl Rogers, is more consonant with the ideological outlook of the vast majority of American professionals in the helping professions.

Though it is true that radical thought has not greatly influenced the practice of adult education, there are a number of advantages in a serious examination of this tradition, some of which have been presented in this chapter. Radical thought is a good antidote to complacency. Radicals are strong on societal criticism and equally strong on presenting alternative and utopian futures. Adult educators engaged in direct work with individuals for short term purposes can easily lose sight of societal ills and long term visions. Connection with the radical tradition can make adult educators more critical and reflective in their work and also provide visions of alternative or future possibilities.

In presenting a view of the nature of man and society, radical adult education challenges the traditional view of the primary function of education as transmitting the culture and its societal structures from generation to generation. Radicalism prefers not to transmit but to change the culture and its structures, for it believes that these are, in the present situation, destructive to human freedom and oppressive to human dignity. There is enough truth in the radical's contention that education must be the *creator* rather than the *creature* of the social order to make adult educators question the basic thrusts of their efforts.

Though radical adult education has a number of contributions to make to theorizing about the nature and functions of adult education, as a unifying philosophy of education it must be considered inadequate. Its major weakness is its failure to take into account the pluralistic nature of most cultures. American pluralism strongly militates against the adoption of a monolithic-utopian educational philosophy, such as is proposed by radical adult educational philosophy, such as that proposed by radical adult succinctly analyzed by Randall (1943) in his definition of the spirit of American philosophy:

> The roots of this pluralistic attitude lie deep in American experience. There is first the fact that American thinkers have always been able to enjoy a certain perspective on the various cultures of Europe. They have been bound to no single intellectual tradition.... Secondly, the fact that America is a continent and not a nation has long led to an emphasis on regionalism, on the wide differences between the various sections of our country. Thirdly, there is the deep-seated and traditional religious pluralism of American life.... Long accustomed to this diversity of faiths in the most important matters, Americans have found other

diversities equally natural. Finally there is the historical pluralism fostered by the extraordinary changes in American life. [p. 126]

REFERENCES

Bowles, Samuel and Herbert Gintis. *Schooling in a Capitalist Society.* New York: Basic Books, 1975.

De Lima, Agnes. "Education for What?" *The New Republic. LXXI,* 922 (August 3, 1932).

Ferrer, Francisco. *The Origin and Ideals of the Modern School.* New York: Putnam, 1913.

Freire, Paulo. *Educacao como Pratica da Libertade.* Rio de Janeiro: Paz e Terra, 1967.

Freire, Paulo. *Cultural Action for Freedom.* Harvard Educational Review and Center for the Study of Development and Social Change, Cambridge, MA: 1970. (a)

Freire, Paulo. *Pedagogy of the Oppressed.* New York: Herder and Herder, 1970. (b)

Freire, Paulo. "The Political Literacy Process—An Introduction." Mimeographed manuscript prepared for publication in *Lutherische Monatshefte.* Hanover, Germany, 1970. (c)

Freire, Paulo. *Conscientization and Liberation.* Geneva: Institute of Cultural Action, 1972.

Freire, Paulo. *Education for Critical Consciousness.* New York: Seabury, 1973.

Guttierrez, Gustavo. "A Latin American Perception of a Theology of Liberation. In Louis Colonnese (ed.), *Conscientization for Liberation.* Washington, D.C: United States Catholic Conference, 1971.

Heilbroner, Robert. *Between Capitalism and Socialism.* New York: Random House, 1972.

Horowitz, Louis. *Three Worlds of Development.* New York: Oxford University Press, 1966.

Illich, Ivan. *Deschooling Society.* New York: Harper and Row, 1970.

Illich, Ivan. *Tools for Conviviality.* New York: Harper and Row, 1973.

Institute for Cultural Action. *Liberation of Woman: To Change the World and Re-Invent Life.* Geneva: Institute for Cultural Action, 1974.

Institute for Cultural Action. *Toward a Woman's World.* Geneva: Institute for Cultural Action, 1975.

Katz, Michael. *The Irony of Early School Reform.* Boston: Beacon, 1968.

Kozol, Jonathan. *Free Schools.* Boston: Houghton Mifflin, 1972.

Kozol, Jonathan. *The Night is Dark and I am Far from Home.* New York: Bantam Books, 1975.

Marx, Karl. *Economic and Philosophic Manuscripts.* In Erich Fromm's *Marx's Concept of Man.* New York: Frederick Ungar, 1961.

Neil, A. S. *Summerhill.* New York: Hart Publishing Co., 1960.

Ohliger, John. "Is Lifelong Adult Education a Guarantee of Permanent Inadequacy:" Public lecture at Saskatoon, Saskatchewan, March 1974. Available from John Ohliger, University of Wisconsin.

Randall, John Herman, Jr. "The Spirit of American Philosophy. In F. Ernest Johnson's (ed.), *Wellsprings of the American Spirit.* New York: Harper and Row, 1948.

Shaull, Richard. A foreword to Paulo Freire's *Pedagogy of the Oppressed.* New York: Herder and Herder, 1970.

Silberman, Charles. *Crisis in the Classroom.* New York: Random House, 1970.

Spring, Joel. "Anarchism and Education: A Dissenting Tradition." In *Roots of Crisis: American Education in the Twentieth Century,* Clarence Karier, Paul Violas, Joel Spring. Chicago: Rand McNally, 1973.

Spring, Joel. *A Primer of Libertarian Education.* New York: Free Life Editions, Inc., 1975.

Stirner, Max. *The False Principle of Education.* Translated by Robert Beebe. Colorado Springs: Ralph Myles, 1967.

Tolstoy, Leo. *Tolstoy on Education.* Translated by Leo Wierner. Chicago: University of Chicago Press, 1967.

CHAPTER VII

ANALYTIC PHILOSOPHY
OF ADULT EDUCATION

In the past twenty years a predominant force in educational philosophy in English-speaking countries has been the work of analytic philosophers of education who have utilized the various methods of analytic philosophy. This approach to educational theory has tended to avoid systems building in philosophy in order to concentrate on the careful analysis of educational concepts, arguments, slogans, and policy statements. Analytic philosophers in education have attempted to build a solid philosophical foundation through careful analysis and argumentation. The contributions of this approach to educational philosophy have been substantial. Numerous books, articles, and journals have presented the results of this newest philosophical approach.

Though analytic philosophers of education have been writing for at least twenty years, it is only in the past half decade that works of an analytic nature have appeared in the area of adult education. Two British philosophers, Paterson and Lawson, and one American educator, Monette, have written books and articles that are clearly influenced by this philosophic orientation.

Since analytic philosophy has become such a prevalent form of philosophy in education, it is certain that the field of adult education will receive more extensive analytic treatment in the future. This approach to philosophy may provide for some the long-awaited philosophical foundation that adult educators have contended that the field needs (Merriam, 1977, p. 196). Not all adult educators, however, will be pleased with this approach since even in its beginnings it has questioned some of the basic principles generally accepted by adult educators in this country.

The task of introducing the analytic approach to adult education is not an easy one. We will attempt to do this by first seeing
the historical development of the various forms of analytic philosophy. Second, the basic procedures and techniques of this
approach will be presented. Third, some of the key contributions of this approach in adult education will be examined and
critiqued. Finally, an assessment will be made of the impact of
this approach for the field of adult education.

Historical Background for Analytic Philosophy
of Adult Education

In a certain sense, all philosophers have been engaged in the
analysis of language. Plato's dialogues all include the careful
analysis of such concepts as virtue, justice, the good person, and
the good society. In the *Meno*, for example, Plato poses the
question: Can virtue be taught or is it something inherent in
an individual? He attempts to answer the question by presenting a skillful dialogue on the meaning of virtue and of teaching.
Aristotle, Plato's disciple, continued in this analytic tradition in
his analysis of such concepts as happiness, habits, voluntary and
involuntary actions, truth, goodness, and beauty.

In medieval times the scholastic philosophers, Thomas Aquinas,
Duns Scotus, Peter Abelard, and William of Ockham used careful
analysis and argumentation to present both philosophical and
religious views. One of the chief problems of medieval philosophy
concerned the reference point of such universal or abstract terms
as justice, goodness, and beauty. For some scholastics, abstract
words were mere words without objective reference points. For
other medieval philosophers they had some basis in reality either
in ideal forms or essences, or in concrete objects from which they
were abstracted.

Although the clarification of concepts in philosophy goes back
to the very beginnings of philosophy, it is only in the past century
that a distinctive analytic approach has emerged. This philosophy
differs from the past in abandoning metaphysical statements
about the nature of the world, God, reality, human persons, and
instead concentrates upon the analysis of language as the exclusive
function of philosophy. In its anti-metaphysical posture, this

philosophy has created a revolution in philosophy, the impact of which has been widely debated.

It is important at this point to note that the term analytic philosophy includes a number of different forms of philosophy, only one of which, conceptual analysis, has become prominent in educational philosophy. Analytic philosophy is commonly divided into four parts in its historical development: Scientific Realism, Logical Analysis or Logical Atomism, Logical Positivism, and Linguistic, Ordinary Language, or Conceptual Analysis (Weitz, 1966, p. 1). A brief description of each of these branches of analytic philosophy affords the best perspective from which to view the work of conceptual analysis in education.

The beginnings of modern analytic philosophy took place in the development of Scientific Realism, found in the early writings of Moore (1903) and Russell (1912). This theory asserted that matter was not reducible to mind and that universal ideas were not reducible to particular ideas. Presented in opposition to the Idealism of Hegel and the English philosopher Bradley, this form of Idealism blurred the distinctions between matter and mind, universals and particulars.

Scientific Realism also had other teachings. On the nature of truth it contended that there was truth when there was a correspondence between what was in the mind and what existed in reality. Belief was also viewed as a correspondence between a subjective state and an external situation. Also, value was considered a real property of an object or situation, no less real than the material qualities of objects.

The position of Scientific Realism was not one that Moore and Russell maintained throughout their lives. Yet it was a position that forced both men to focus on the nature of language and the reality to which language corresponded. Moore later developed a Philosophy of Common Sense and Russell became more interested in science, mathematics, and in Logical Analysis as an approach to philosophy. While Moore accused philosophers of abusing language when they used it differently from common, ordinary language, Russell developed a more influential stand in philosophy in his procedure of Logical Analysis.

Russell's Logical Analysis is the second phase in the development of analytic philosophy. Other descriptions of this approach to philosophy include the analysis of denoting phrases, the clarification of unclear symbols, the method of dispensing with abstractions, and logical constructionism. For Russell, all of these denoted a set of techniques for the replacement of defective symbols or words (Weitz, 1966, p. 4). Through logical analysis Russell attempted to give philosophy the exactness that mathematics and science had in his time. Thus to determine the meaning of a sentence, it had to be broken down into its molecular parts. Sentences in language are true if the parts refer to what actually exists. In this analytic approach, Russell reduced each problem into its parts, then examined each part to pick out its essential features. He saw the task of philosophy not in arriving at great answers or in making grand syntheses, but in working out careful analyses. This approach was reductive in breaking down all propositions to their smallest components; it was also empirical, for each aspect had to correspond with some part of reality.

The basic ideas of Russell's Logical Analysis were accepted and extended in the early philosophical work of Wittgenstein. In his *Tractatus Logico-Philosophicus* (1921), Wittgenstein discussed the nature and function of language, mathematics, scientific laws, and the relation between language and the world. As will be seen shortly, Wittgenstein repudiated much of this earlier view. Yet, this earlier work, which was rather close to Russell's position, has had a great influence in the history of analytic philosophy.

The basic themes of the *Tractatus* are clear, though the book is notoriously difficult in its details. Wittgenstein contended that philosophical problems are the result of misunderstandings in language and logic. He asserted that these difficulties can be solved or avoided by creating and using an ideal language. This new language must be exactly representative of the reality to which it points. Thus only statements that represent reality in some way have meaning.

According to the *Tractatus*, the purpose of logical analysis is to make every statement an adequate picture of the reality it represents. Analysis is thus the process of reducing statements to their atomic and constituent parts. The view of knowledge that is implied in this theory is that knowing is really a relationship between reality and language, not between the knower and the known.

The implications of this form of analytic philosophy are extensive. It renders all statements meaningless that are not based on sensory knowledge or logic. Religious statements, traditional philosophical statements about the world, statements expressing appreciation, and values are all meaningless propositions in that they reveal nothing about the world in which we live. They may tell us something about the person making the statements, but they tell us nothing about the world or objective reality outside the mind of the speaker. The further implications of this philosophical viewpoint are found in Logical Positivism, the third form of philosophical analysis.

Logical Positivism was a dominant form of philosophy from the 1920's to the beginning of the Second World War. Among the doctrines of this approach are

> The verifiability theory of meaning, the rejection of metaphysics, the emotive theory of moral judgment, the unity of science, the conception of language as a calculus, the conventionalistic interpretation of logic and mathematics, and the claim that legitimate philosophy consists solely of logical analysis. [Weitz, 1966, p. 8]

The principle of verification is the chief teaching of this approach to philosophy. According to this principle, propositions have meaning only if they can be empirically or logically verified. Logic, mathematics, and the sciences have meaning since their statements can be verified through empirical data or logic. All other assertions are considered meaningless.

The most influential proponent of Logical Positivism in the English-speaking world has been A. J. Ayer (1959). The task for philosophy, according to Ayer, is to classify language, distinguish true propositions from false ones, explain the meaning and justification of statements. Using the verification principle, Ayer has attempted to show that religious, evaluative, and metaphysical statements are meaningless statements.

The position of the logical positivist has not prevailed in analytic philosophy. Especially after the Second World War, but beginning before it, the major propositions of Logical Positivism have been rejected by such influential analysts as Wittgenstein in his *Philosophical Investigations* (1953), Gilbert Ryle in his *Concept of Mind* (1949), and John Wisdom in his *Other Minds* (1953). All three of these philosophers have attacked the verification principle and ushered in the fourth stage of analytic philosophy called Conceptual Analysis, Ordinary Language Philsophy, or Linguistic Analysis. It is this fourth phase of analytic philosophy that has greatly influenced contemporary analytic philosophers of education.

One of the earliest proponents of conceptual analysis was John Wisdom, Professor of Philosophy at Cambridge University. In an essay "Philosophical Perplexity" (1936), he attempted to provide a general account of the many puzzles and paradoxes of traditional philosophy. Wisdom proposed the notion that the task of philosophy was the resolution of puzzles and not the answering of problems. Wisdom thus reduced philosophical questions to language questions and philosophical answers to recommendations for proper language use.

Wisdom's work has a strong parallel in the writings of Gilbert Ryle. Ryle's book called *Concept of Mind* (1943) is a classic work in contemporary philosophy of conceptual analysis. In this work, Ryle argues that the mind can be reduced to the mental behaviors of the person. The mind is not an extra being, a "Ghost in the Machine," but a person's abilities, liabilities, and limitations. Ryle's work is basically an argument for metaphysical behaviorism. But what is of interest here is more his methodology, that of arriving at his basic theses through an analysis of the words and concepts used in ordinary language. Ryle has also contributed directly to education by his careful analysis of such concepts as teaching, training, and education (1967, pp. 105-119).

Though Ryle, Wisdom, and others have made important contributions to conceptual analysis, it is the later work of Wittgenstein that has been most influential in shaping language philosophy in the past two decades. In *Philosophical Investigations* (1953), Wittgenstein abandoned the narrowly framed vertification principle for the position that the meaning of language is in its use. To understand a word is to be able to use it in accord with custom and social practice. Thus there is no need to construct a new language, as the logical positivists attempted.

Rather, attention could be directed to determining the correct usages that words had in ordinary language.

Language thus became something that could be used to suit one's purpose. Language in this view was a social phenomenon, a cooperative achievement. To determine what language meant one looked not only to its reference in the real world, but also to what the person intended the language to mean or to do.

The role of the philosopher, according to the conceptual analysts, is not to construct explanations about reality but to eliminate language confusions. Philosophy is a method of investigation that results in pure description. In this theory no language, no matter how abstract, metaphysical, or theological, is to be dismissed. The philosopher's task is to determine what the language means for the persons and groups that use it. Words have only the meaning that people give to them. Philosophy's task is to attempt to clarify these usages of language. In this role, the language philosopher is more like the social scientist who attempts to maintain a value-neutral position about the references of the language that people utilize to express themselves.

Language, according to ordinary language philosophers, has many tasks and many levels; it may or may not be used to describe the world. The task of the philosopher is to find out on each occasion what is being intended by the language used without the preconception that one type of language is basic and the others are reducible to it. This was the position of the logical positivists, who took the language of science and mathematics as normative to what language should be. In describing the use of language to achieve many purposes, Wittgenstein used the analogy of playing games. Both games and the use of language are governed by rules. To understand someone's language, we must understand the rules by which they use language. To understand some language games like poetry and technical writing may demand intensive training. To read the books of scientists, philosophers, statisticians, and poets, one must know and understand the rules of the language being used.

Wittgenstein has presented a list of some of the different things that people do with language:

> Give orders and obey them; describe the appearance of an object or give its measurement; construct an object from a

description; report an event; form and test a hypothesis; present the result of an experiment in tables and diagrams; make up a story and read a story; playacting; sing catches; guess riddles; make jokes. . . . Ask, think, curse, greet, pray. [Wittgenstein, 1953, p. 23]

An examination of this list shows the complexity that is involved in determining how language functions. It is to this complexity that language philosophers have directed their attention.

This brief summary of the more significant developments in twentieth century language philosophy should provide a background for understanding the analytic approach to educational philosophy that is presented in this chapter. The next task is to examine the nature, purposes, methods, and limitations of linguistic or conceptual analysis.

Philosophy as Conceptual or Linguistic Analysis

As we have seen in the last section of this chapter, conceptual analysts view the task of philosophy differently from traditional philosophers. Traditional philosophy is concerned with developing a system of thought about all aspects of the world: God, human persons, nature, knowledge, values, and beauty. Scheffler (1960) has indicated how linguistic analysis differs from this approach:

Philosophical analysis, in substantially its current forms, got under way interested fundamentally in the clarification of basic notions and modes of argument rather than in synthesizing available beliefs into some total outlook, in thoroughly appraising root ideas rather than in painting suggestive but vague portraits of the universe. [Scheffler, 1960, p. 7]

Conceptual analysis then is concerned with the analysis of concepts and the grounds for knowledge, beliefs, actions, and activities that make up human life. All areas of human activity can be subjected to this form of philosophical analysis.

Another way to make the distinction between conceptual analysis and traditional philosophy is to use the distinction that Frankena proposes. Frankena (1970) distinguishes between *analytic philosophy* with its emphasis on the analysis of concepts, arguments, slogans, and statements and *normative philosophy* which makes normative or descriptive statements about the world, human persons, and human actions. Applied to education, the distinction is between analyzing the concept of education, teaching, or learning, and prescribing what education and schools should or should not do with regard to aims, content, methods, and evaluation (Frankena, 1970, pp. 15-22).

Conceptual analysis achieves its task of clarifying language through the use of various techniques, tools, and methods. Analysts first of all use the tools of logic that have been in use in philosophy since the writings of Aristotle. These involve the use of definitions, deductive and inductive reasoning, the pointing out of logical fallacies, and establishing criteria for determining the truth or falsity of ideas. At first sight, many analytical books and articles appear to be exercises in logical reasoning.

In their work of analysis, however, contemporary analysts have developed a number of methods that go beyond the traditional logical tools of traditional philosophy. A consideration of a number of these tools with some examples may give a clearer idea of how conceptual analysts proceed.

Analysts distinguish three types of questions: questions of fact, questions of value, and questions of concept. A question of fact is: How extensively has democracy spread over the entire world? A question of value is: Is democracy a desirable form of government? A question of concept is: Is democracy compatible with communism? It is the final question, the question of concept, that the language philosopher is most concerned with, though the first two questions are not ignored. To answer the first two questions one must first of all arrive at an accepted concept of democracy to test its factual extent or judge its value.

Questions of concept, for example, entail examining ways in which such words as "democracy" and "communism" are used. Analysis involves making a cognitive map of the ways in which the two concepts are used in order to see the similarities and dissimilarities between the terms. Another way of phrasing a question of concept is to ask whether the one can exist without the other. If the one can exist without the other, then the two concepts are distinct. Questions of concept are answered not by merely giving definitions of the terms but by examining the ways in which the terms are used. We can adequately analyze concepts by comparing and contrasting them to concepts with which they are similar. As will be seen later, a proper analysis of adult education demands a comparable analysis of adult training, adult indoctrination, and other allied concepts.

Conceptual analysts recognize that there are not usually right answers when it comes to the analysis of concepts. For example, the concept of education has a variety of meanings or usages in ordinary language. These usages are not totally arbitrary. The concept of education is more appropriately applied to persons than to animals or plants. We usually distinguish education from training and indoctrination. Thus, there are some usages of the term that are nearer to the heart of the concept than others. It is getting to the heart of the concept as it is ordinarily used that is one of the principal tasks of the conceptual analyst.

Besides isolating questions of concept and avoiding the search for *the* right meaning of a concept, conceptual analysts use a number of other techniques. Analysts look for *model cases* in which the concept is used in such a way that everyone would agree that this is a good use of the concept. We will see in a later section of this chapter that some liberal adult educators present liberal adult education as a model case for adult education. They examine the key characteristics of this liberal adult education and compare other forms with it. They have also made the rather debatable point of advocating that the term education in adult education be restricted only to liberal adult education. This position will be examined later.

Besides model cases, analysts examine concepts through the use of *contrary cases*, cases in which the term clearly cannot be appropriately used. Thus one cannot speak of a stone being educated. This indicates that some form of life or ability to change from within is needed for an educational process. Contrary cases have value in conceptual analysis especially in the preliminary stages when one is first setting out to form a cognitive map of usages of the concept.

As has been mentioned above, analysis of concepts is most often applied to a group of related or allied concepts. Various terms are analyzed in order to become clearer about their meanings: teaching, learning, training, conditioning, indoctrination, explanation, development, and personal relationships. Through the analysis of related concepts one comes closer to a clearer understanding of the concept one is considering, and those features of it that separate it from other concepts. If we know the essential features of a concept, we will more likely use the concept in a proper manner and thus avoid conceptual and linguistic confusion.

Many concepts that we use in ordinary language are what analysts refer to as borderline usages or cases. These are also called odd or queer cases because although the usage of the concept is legitimate, it is a somewhat strained use of the concept. A possible borderline use of education is in the concept of self-education. There is something a bit strange about speaking of someone educating himself or herself. Self learning is less odd, for we readily accept that persons can learn on their own. But the term education in its ordinary usage usually implies some kind of encounter with another person. This is not present in the case of self-education. The value of looking at odd or borderline cases is to determine the missing element that makes the usage odd. This gives us a better handle on the essential qualities of the concept.

An important distinction that analysts make is between concepts that are *ambiguous* and those that are *vague*. A concept is ambiguous if it can bear more than one meaning. The cause of the ambiguity may lie in the concept itself. The word trunk, for example, is ambiguous for it can refer to baggage, a part of a tree, or a part of an elephant. The context makes it clear what the meaning of the concept is. Yet some concepts remain ambiguous even in a context. If we were to say that Aristotle's teaching was terrible, we could not show whether the reference was to the manner of teaching, or to the content of teaching. Thus the term is ambiguous even in its content.

Ambiguity is one thing, but vagueness is another. Concepts are vague if they refer to a quality that things have in different degrees. Large and small are vague words; baldness is a vague word. How large, small, or bald does a person have to be to possess this quality? Rationality is also a quality that is vague because different people, children, adolescents, and adults possess it in various degrees. Adulthood or maturity is often a vague concept. It refers to qualities that persons have in varying degrees.

The distinction between ambiguity and vagueness of concepts is an important one in conceptual analysis. It is especially vague and ambiguous concepts that produce much of the language confusion that exists in talk about education and other areas. The attempt of the analysts is to remove ambiguity and to make vague usages more precise.

From an examination of these various techniques that conceptual analysts use, it is clear that analysts are searching for definitions or criteria by which concepts are correctly used. Analysts have recognized, however, that the very concept of *definition* needs some clarification. Scheffler has pointed out three meanings of the concept of definition (1960, ch. 1). At times a definition is *stipulative*, as when authors give a meaning to a term according to the way that they will use it. The stipulative definition is usually somewhat different from the common usage, or it is an attempt to choose one out of numerous possible meanings of a concept. A person may determine to use the term culture as referring only to artistic achievements in a work, recognizing that in common usage the term has much broader usages.

A definition is *descriptive* when it proposes to describe what is being defined. Descriptive definitions answer the question What does the term generally mean in common usage? Dictionaries give some descriptive definitions, but they do not give all the possible meanings or usages that a concept may have, together with distinctions from allied concepts. In a later section of this chapter we will examine the concept of "needs" to discover the various descriptive usages of this term. Distinctions exist, for example, between real and felt needs, ascribed or prescribed needs. A full analysis of such a basic concept in adult education has been presented in the work of Monette (1977, 1979). Much of conceptual analysis is an attempt to arrive at the full range of descriptive usages of a concept in order to be clear about how the concept is being used in particular cases.

The third type of definition proposed by Scheffler is the *programmatic definition*, which tells overtly or implicitly what should be done rather than what is done. For example, when we say that education is the process for developing critical abilities in individuals we are giving a programmatic rather than a descriptive definition of the concept. We are not telling what actually happens but are prescribing what should happen in an educational process. It is difficult in describing such value-laden concepts as education not to include prescriptive or programmatic elements in our definitions. Thus the definitions we usually use are often a combination of descriptive and programmatic elements. In our examination of proposed definitions of adult education we will see that many such definitions have strong programmatic features, especially those definitions that want to restrict the term to mean liberal adult education.

In traditional philosophy it has usually been the case that discussion begins with a definition of terms. In analytic philosophy this process is reversed. The purpose of analysis is to arrive at definitions of concepts that can then be used in developing philosophical statements or policies. The quest for clarity need not begin with a consensus on definitions. Some general agreement is important at the beginning, but the lack of full agreement at the start is not necessary, and in fact may cut off fruitful discussion in philosophy.

Besides clarifying our usage of definitions, analysts have also given great attention to the *examination of metaphors* that are used in the field of education. Metaphors are used to explain more clearly what we mean. The unknown is made clear by a comparison to the known. Various metaphors have been used to elucidate the meaning of education: growth, development, personal encounter, transmission, social reconstruction, and behavioral modification. Each theory of education examined in this book has a basic metaphor by which it attempts to describe the fundamental process of education, together with its aims and objectives. Even the word analysis is a metaphor taken from the realm of chemistry. Each of these metaphors is helpful in explaining some aspect of what education is. Metaphors are constructive when they make clear something about the concept being explained. Thus when Dewey referred to education as growth, he emphasized that in education there is necessarily involved a process of change and development, similar to biological evolution.

Analysts have been careful to point out the limitations involved in dealing with metaphors, similies, and analogies. All metaphors eventually break down because they cannot explain all aspects of the reality in question. Education as growth explains the development or change aspect involved in education, but it does not adequately lend itself to treating the human factor involved in educational processes. Human growth through education is not the orderly process that it is in the sphere of animals and plants. Though education might be compared to an artist forming a work of art out of some material, the analogy breaks down because of the lack of responsiveness of human persons in the educational process. Education is certainly similar to shaping, but the analogy limps when we consider what power human persons have in determining the directions in which they will be shaped.

Analysts such as Scheffler (1960, ch. 3) have performed a useful task in showing both the value and limitations of educational metaphors such as growth, formation, and artistic creation. From his discussion, it is clear that no single metaphor can form an adequate basis for describing such complex processes as education, teaching and learning, explaining and understanding. Educational metaphors aid in organizing thought and in developing theories, but they are not precise descriptions of the processes they attempt to illuminate.

Metaphors are not the only aspect of educational language that have come under analytic scrutiny. Analysts have also directed their attention to the common use and misuse of *slogans* in education. Slogans in education include: We teach children, not subjects; Back to the basics; Andragogy not pedagogy; No teaching without learning. Slogans function in educational discourse more as symbols and rallying cries of movements, ideas, and attitudes. Slogans are not to be pondered as serious educational theory because usually they are oversimplifications of the issues involved. But in some way the slogan capitalizes on a movement, provides it with a symbol, and gains adherents to the movement. Komisar and McClellan (1961) have examined the use of slogans in education and have pointed out how entire systems of thought may be based on slogans, or emotive statements.

What has been presented thus far in this chapter should give some idea of the nature and techniques used in conceptual analysis. What remains in this section is the problem of the *purpose* or *point* of this form of educational philosophy. Analysts do not usually analyze concepts just for the sake of analyzing them.

Conceptual clarity is sought in areas where there is confusion and where this confusion has led to practical difficulties and differences of opinion and policy. Many concepts used in education and in other areas of human endeavor need clarification if there is to be any intelligent discussion of problems and issues. Educational talk about adult education and its aims and objectives often has a certain confusion attached to it. Such language is used as Education should be adapted to the needs and interests of the learners; Education should be learner centered. If these phrases are to have any meaning, there must be some clarity about the meaning of the terms and the way that these expressions are used. Such a popular movement in education as the competency-based teacher education movement suffers from a vagueness in usage of the term competency. The movement will flounder unless there is more conceptual clarity.

As practiced by many analysts, conceptual analysis is a value-free or neutral philosophical activity. Increasingly, however, those who do conceptual analysis have attempted to go beyond the analysis of concepts to make normative proposals about what education should be. Analysts such as R. S. Peters have emphasized that since educating involves questions of value in an important way, philosophers who are involved in it cannot escape the value questions (Peters, 1967a, p. 3). Peters and other British analysts such as Lawson and Paterson often move in their philosophical writings into the area of normative philosophy in taking stands on value questions in education.

Conceptual Analysis in Adult Education

The most serious work in the conceptual analysis of adult education has been done by Lawson (1975) and Paterson (1979). A number of articles have appeared by Maurice Monette which utilize this philosophical approach to some degree in elucidating the concept of needs in adult education (1977, 1979). The purpose of this section is to review some of the conclusions and arguments that have been introduced by these analysts into the field of adult education.

Lawson (1975) makes it clear that his work is one of conceptual analysis. He is concerned about the "lack of impact upon adult education of the growing volume of literature which deals with general educational concepts from the standpoint of linguistic analysis" (p. 7). His work is an effort to redress this balance. Lawson asserts that there are some special concepts in the field of adult education that require analysis, for these concepts are different from those analyzed in general educational theory.

Paterson's work is also clearly in the linguistic analysis that both he and Lawson do, and it is not the value-free analysis that is most common in the field. Both men move from the analysis of concepts to make normative statements about the issues that they examine. The same can be said of Monette who sees his work partly in the analytic tradition as making a case for "the critical examination of the values and assumptions underlying the technology which is advocated by [many contemporary] theorists. It presents a case for philosophizing in adult education" (1979, p. 92). In Monette's view,

> Philosophy of education is basically a justification of the educational endeavor in its various modalities. It is distinguished from educational theorizing or educational research in that it oversees these processes, seeking to clarify, criticize and question them—to integrate them into wholeness and coherence which is one's own. [Monette, 1979, p. 93]

In developing this section of the chapter, we will follow the basic structure of Paterson's work. Into his outline it is easy to place the various issues that Lawson and Monette treat in their works. The four parts of Paterson's work are: *Educational Concepts* (concepts of adult, adult education, and liberal adult education); *Educational Objectives* (communication of knowledge, advancement of reason, and moral education of adults); *Educational Processes* (teaching, learning, and adult maturity); *Adult Education and Society* (educational justice and education for democracy).

The Concept of Adult Education

Paterson begins his work with an analysis of the concept of "adult." He argues that adulthood is a normative concept based on chronological age and status in society. Adults have certain rights in society that are not afforded to children. They also have responsibilities to which they are held by society. Though adults may not be emotionally and morally mature, they are expected to be so (Paterson, 1979, p. 10). The only adequate grounds that can be given for these expectations, according to Paterson, are that adults are older than children. The presumption is that in the passage of time, adults have developed the emotional and moral maturity expected of them.

A second concept analyzed by Paterson and Lawson is adult education. In their analyses, both men depend upon the work of the foremost British philosopher of education, R. S. Peters. For Peters, the concept of education entails a number of requirements: that there is a transmission of what is valuable and worthwhile; that individuals will care about what they learn; that they shall want to achieve the standards associated with what is learned; that there is an awareness of what is learned through a process voluntarily undertaken; that there is a cognitive element and an understanding of principles; that what is learned is cognitively connected with other areas of learning so that each area is seen in relation to other areas; and that what is learned shall be usable (Peters, 1967b).

Given this definition of education it is clear that a person's education is never complete and that lifelong education is a necessity for full human development. Yet if one accepts this definition of education, a number of problems arise with regard to the usage of this concept by American adult educators. Paterson makes a strong case that only liberal adult education can properly be called adult *education* because it alone fulfills all the requirements for an educational enterprise. He distinguishes liberal adult education from what is called vocational education, role education, and education for leisure time. Only in cases where the education in these other forms is broadly liberal would they be classified as adult educational activities.

Lawson (1975, ch. 7) follows the line of reasoning that has been developed by Peters and Paterson. He makes a distinction between the education of adults and adult education. The former would include all kinds of activities where adults are involved in learning. The latter term is a normative one and should be applied only where the strict criteria of an educational process as Peters proposes are met. Both Lawson and Paterson reject the usage of the term adult education as it is used in this country to embrace all kinds of learning activities of adults. They contend this usage is an administrative usage without the necessary normative or evaluative meaning.

Monette (1979) has been directly influenced by Lawson's work. He opposes the service centered orientation that adult education has developed in this country. He prefers an approach to adult education that is based on values which he identifies as humanistic and personal. He feels that adult educators have been too much influenced by the technological model of curriculum theorists, such as Tyler, and have ignored value questions about society, the human person, and the nature of educational methodology.

The efforts of Lawson and Paterson to give some philosophical justification for adult education are well reasoned and demand more careful examination than can be attempted here. A number of weaknesses of this analysis, however, can be noted. The definition of education and the criteria that are presented cannot all be derived so easily from our ordinary usage of the word adult education. What Peters, Lawson, and Paterson are proposing is rather a programmatic definition. Adult education, at least as used in this country, has a broader usage. In restricting the concept adult education to what amounts to liberal adult education, these writers are guilty of a rationalist bias towards cognitive education and a bias against education for training and skill development. In the argument between liberal educators and progressive educators, these particular analysts take the side of the liberal educators. This restriction of terminology will, we feel, serve little purpose in justifying adult education, for it legitimates only a part of what is included under the ordinary usage of the term adult education. To call some things adult education and others the education of adults is to bring a bit of elitism and rationalist bias into the field of adult education which has developed along different lines in this country.

The Objectives of Adult Education

Paterson's treatment of the educational objectives of adult education is an extensive analysis of the curriculum of liberal adult education. Adult education has as its purpose the communication of knowledge by bringing about a deepened awareness or consciousness in persons. Skill learning is included in the range of knowledge only if the skills are instrinsically worth learning and not merely instrumental skills. Little attention is given to skills learning and affective learning in Paterson's discussion of educational objectives. An academic subject matter approach is central to the view of the educational objectives he presents. The subject matter of adult education entails nine different kinds of knowledge:

> namely the kinds of knowledge distinctive of mathematics, the physical sciences, history, the human sciences, languages, the arts, morals, religion and philosophy. [Paterson, 1979, p. 84]

Paterson argues that the objective worth and richness of these disciplines has long been established.

In his treatment of the curriculum for adult education, Paterson faces the problem of how this curriculum differs from that of children and adolescents. He admits the educational objectives remain the same. He does contend, however, that certain aspects of these disciplines are more appropriate for adults because they presume an adult maturity, especially in moral, philosophical, and religious areas (1979, p. 99).

The two other objectives for adult education that Paterson presents are the development of the virtues of reason and the learning of moral values. Developing the virtues of reason gives a person mental autonomy, and learning values gives moral autonomy. Both of these objectives, Paterson feels, can be realized in a particular manner in adults because of their mental and moral maturity. Paterson shows himself sensitive to the problems of what justifies one adult educating other adults in moral values. He is less sensitive to this problem in the case of children and adolescents, where it also needs justification. He concludes that the moral education of adults will be a more indirect education through art, literature, philosophy, etc., where the teacher does not impart values or doctrine but discusses with adults the moral implications of situations found in these sources.

Lawson in discussing the objectives for adult education makes a case for the learning of skills as a legitimate form of knowledge within adult education. Yet his inclusion of craft subjects and skills learning is based on reducing these to a form of knowledge and intelligent behavior. Insofar as the learning of skills demands intelligence, they can be considered adult educational activities. A craft qualifies as education insofar as it is a "system of skills, criteria, values, and cognitive knowledge" (1975, p. 67). Lawson also maintains a distinction between education and training. Training is involved with goals outside the process, goals of a utilitarian nature, while education is involved with values that are intrinsic to the very concept of education (Lawson, 1975, p. 99).

The treatment that the two British analysts give to the educational objectives of adult education is consistent with their analysis of the concept of education. If the cognitive, rational, and intellectual dimension of education are the only dimensions worthy of being called educational, then only those objectives that foster this form of development can be appropriate objectives for adult education. It is not that these analysts believe other objectives and forms of human activity are not worthwhile, it is only that they should not be classified under adult education. They believe that a confusion arises when adult education is used as the umbrella term to embrace all types of learning activities. When it is so used it is difficult in their opinion to give an educational justification for the field of adult education.

One can sympathize with the conceptual analysts in their attempts to give a more precise definition to education and educational objectives, but their excessive concentration on rationality and cognitive understanding has resulted in a narrow view of adult education. Human persons are much more than rational beings. They are emotional, intuitive, and practical. Human persons are parents, friends, workers, citizens, playmates, and activists. To say that what promotes human development in any of these other areas is not education, and to restrict the term to merely what can be reduced to cognitive understanding, is to base the educational enterprise on a narrow and elitist basis. Though it may be difficult to draw the distinction between education and recreation, education and training, education and social service, we feel certain that this distinction should not be based upon a relatively narrow concept of human rationality and understanding.

Educational Processes

Paterson's analysis of the educational processes of adult education includes, first of all, an analysis of the concepts of teaching and learning. He rejects the behaviorist viewpoint that learning is a change in behavior. He considers learning a coming-to-know. Even in the learning of skills, the coming-to-know aspect is fundamental to the concept of learning (1979, p. 161). In the analysis of teaching it is emphasized that

> Teaching is a collaborative process, involving exchanges, outgoings, and interaction between two separate and independent centres of consciousness, and converging on to some objective and accessible reality. . . [Paterson, 1979, p. 172]

Teaching is an intentional activity in which communication is intended. Paterson is interested in separating teaching from indoctrination which leads him to a discussion of the freedom of the student in the teaching-learning process.

Indoctrination is distinguished from teaching in that the former attempts to bring about an uncritical acceptance of beliefs. Paterson contends that there is no contradiction in the concept that adults can be indoctrinated. It is a matter of empirical study whether or not adults are actually indoctrinated. The harm with indoctrination in his view is that it narrows the breadth of vision and awareness of those being instructed (Paterson, 1979, pp. 286-187).

Since Paterson limits his view of education to liberal education, he does not consider the question of mandatory continuing education. This is certainly a limitation on the rights of adults to pursue or not pursue their own education. Complicating this issue, however, is the right of society to demand that persons in certain professions keep abreast of knowledge deemed necessary for the service of others. In the chapter on Radical Adult Education, this question has been considered in the light of Illich's and Ohliger's opposition to mandatory adult education.

From his treatment of the concepts of learning and teaching, Paterson turns to a discussion of the criteria for determining genuine processes of adult education. These criteria are "wittingness, voluntariness, conscious control, interpersonal encounter, and active participation by the educator" (1979, p. 196). There is a general presumption that adults are *witting* or aware recipients of the learning in which they are involved. This is not always the case in the education of children and adolescents. The participation of adults is *voluntary* if they participate for the reason that the educational experience is worth having for its own sake. Paterson contends that adults involved in education will not suffer the harmful effects of schooling because their education is freely chosen, and they can easily remove themselves from it. For an educational process to be genuine, adults must also be in *conscious control* of the process. They must have the power to require instruction from the teacher. This learner control will result only if there is some *encounter between persons* in the educational process. This criterion is more realizable in the case of adults, for they are more likely to act toward one another in such a way as to respect the persons of others. Finally, an educational encounter must involve *active participation* of the learners. Such participation must be in educationally relevant ways. Dialogue through class discussion is the most appropriate form of activity in adult educational processes, and real dialogue includes only those communications that are educationally significant. In Paterson's view, it is only in the education of adults that these criteria can be realized to the highest degree.

Lawson's approach to educational processes in adult education is an argument against a number of popular approaches to adult education proposed in theory and practice. He is critical of the service orientation of adult education which attempts merely to respond to the demands of students. He also argues against student-centered education, which he takes to refer to

> Forms of organization which place the emphasis on the requirements of the learner rather than upon those of the subject to be taught or upon the professional and personal values of teachers. [Lawson, 1975, p. 18]

Lawson critiques student-centered teaching that places emphasis on private thought rather than public knowledge, and reduces the inputs and contribution of the teacher to a minimum (1975, p. 21). He argues against viewing adult education in terms of learning situations rather than teaching situations.

The basis of Lawson's argument against these approaches lies in his analysis of education as a value oriented or normative activity. Lawson views these various student-centered approaches as attempts to shift the responsibility of value judgment about what is educationally worthwhile from the teacher to the student. For Lawson, the task of the teacher in adult education is to make the choices about those things that *are* educationally worthwhile.

The concept of needs assessment in adult education has been analyzed by Monette (1977) who arrives at conclusions similar to those reached by Lawson. Needs, in Monette's view, logically demand some standards or social norms against which they can be measured. Monette concludes that adult education should move from a technological approach to a more humanistic approach in which values and needs are collectively determined by students and teachers together. Monette advocates the Freire approach to needs assessment, and thus his view appears better balanced than the position of Lawson who sees the teacher as the sole determiner of what is valuable in educational activities.

Adult Education and Society

The last set of issues that are examined by Paterson concerns the relationship of adult education to the society in which it takes place. The first issue that Paterson considers is the right and duty of adults to pursue lifelong education. His treatment is thorough and balanced and thus not easily summarized. After analyzing such concepts as justice, rights, and duties, Paterson discusses the right of adults to education. Based upon the individual's right to deepen knowledge and develop personality, Paterson concludes that individuals have both rights and duties in pursuing lifelong education (1979, pp. 234-235). The process of establishing these general principles leads Paterson to a discussion of more precise educational rights.

Paterson discusses the specified share of educational resources to which adults are entitled. In general, every individual adult

> Does have a right to, it seems clear, . . . to some appropriate share, and neither more nor less than that share, of whatever overall resources a society finds that it can reasonably devote to the business of promoting the education of its adult members. [Paterson, 1979, p. 239]

Some preferential treatment should be given to those who through no fault of their own are deprived of educational opportunities before they became adults. The responsibility of societies is limited in these areas, however, by the availability of resources.

Paterson's discussion of these issues is important for clarifying the concepts to be used in public policy arguments about the rights to continuing adult education. The past two decades have seen in this country debates on these issues with regard to educational equality and compensatory education for children and adolescents. No comparable public policy debate has taken place with regard to adult education. Most funding in adult education from Federal government sources is directed toward compensatory education, originating in the social programs of the 1960's. The issues raised by Paterson are cast philosophically, but they have practical implications with regard to funding in adult education.

The second issue that Paterson treats is the social purpose or social relevance of adult education. After an analysis of these terms, Paterson raises the question of what social purposes or goals should adult education address. In keeping with his position on adult education as serving the liberal purposes of education of the mind and reason, Paterson sees no direct social purpose for adult education. He concludes:

> It cannot be part of the purpose of education either to vindicate the status quo or to advocate social change, whether gentle and piecemeal or radical and sweeping. The commitment of education is to knowledge, understanding, insight, in whatever social directions these may happen to point. The commitment of education is always and necessarily to the truth, wherever it may lead. [Paterson, 1979, p. 256]

What education does to promote social progress is to educate persons liberally. In so doing, this education indirectly promotes a democratic society. Education cannot remain education if it allows itself to be used as an instrument for attaining non-educational goals, "however socially necessary or desirable these may often admittedly be" (Paterson, 1979, p. 268).

Paterson's argument for the neutrality of adult education is accepted and reinforced by Lawson. Besides the educational argument, Lawson brings out the practical consideration that if adult education were to become involved in social causes, it would run the risk of not receiving adequate public funds for its management. Another danger is that adult education could become so fluid that it becomes adaptable to every change with regard to social, political, and economic issues.

The position that Paterson and Lawson take on this issue is a well argued one, but it is not one that all adult educators have maintained. In the chapter on radicalism and adult education, the views of Paulo Freire have been examined on this issue. It is his contention that it is impossible for education to be value free when it comes to social purpose and relevance. The position of the two British analysts is also not one that has been accepted by all educators who espouse liberal education. What these analysts are proposing may be a purist concept of education that does not take into account the close connection between education and the society in which it takes place.

Assessment of Analytic Philosophy of Adult Education

There is something challenging about the analytic philosophy of adult education that has appeared thus far. The writings of Lawson and Paterson, and to a lesser extent Monette (lesser because his full length treatment has not yet appeared), are precise and carefully reasoned. There is a conceptual clarity in these analyses that is unrivaled by other philosophical writings in adult education. Arguments and explanations are detailed. Possible objections to the positions taken are foreseen and answered in clear and restrained argumentation.

These philosophical analyses are also a challenge because they introduce the readers to an influential tradition in contemporary philosophy of education. The clear and persuasive positions arrived at by the renown British analyst R. S. Peters are related to adult education. Other analysts in both Britain and the United States have also produced writings of considerable merit. The conceptual analyses presented in this chapter represents a serious attempt to introduce adult educators to this tradition.

Analytic philosophy of education is a challenge to adult educators not only in the clarity and quality of the reasoning, but also because of some of the positions that have been arrived at through this philosophy. This philosophy is critical of some of the loose language and slogans that have prevailed in the writings of adult educators. Lawson's critique of the language of needs, adult education as a service oriented field, and the emphasis on learning situations will serve to sharpen the thinking of many adult educators. Though some of the conclusions that the analysts have arrived at will not be acceptable, it is a useful exercise to have one's thinking challenged by their arguments. To maintain one's views in the face of their criticisms takes a comparable philosophical critique and analysis.

Though analytic philosophy of adult education has already made some contributions to developing a philosophy of adult education, it is not a philosophy without its faults and limitations. Some of these have been pointed out in the course of this chapter. One major limitation or problem with this method is that it may arrive at a false precision which then leads to unwelcome consequences. An example of this is the concept of education that has been adapted by Lawson and Paterson from Peters. This concept brings in a clarity that then eliminates from the concept of education and, consequently, adult education, much of what is ordinarily included by these terms. This leads, as we have seen, to a devaluing of certain forms of education, specifically those that are utilitarian and pragmatic. The introduction of this concept of education into the field of adult education in this country would most likely increase confusion rather than eliminate it.

A second and perhaps more critical weakness of this approach to philosophy is the stance of some analysts in providing a methodology that is value free or neutral. The techniques employed by some analytic philosophers resemble the techniques of the social scientists who attempt to be value free in their inquiry. There is, however, a distinction between holding one's views at abeyance in a philosophical analysis and advocating neutrality in educational decision-making. The arguments of Lawson and Paterson for value free adult education with regard to social purpose and relevance are examples of this confusion. It may be impossible to avoid value decisions in these areas. While analysts often argue for taking neutral positions on social questions, the actual practice of education often makes this impossible.

Perhaps on this point we are asking too much of the analysts. Depth in one area may be achievable only by ignoring other areas of consideration. Perhaps the analysts can achieve language clarity, precision, and vigor only if they separate themselves from political, social, economic, and educational issues in society. This separation is not, we believe, a necessary one, but it is one that has characterized the work of many analysts. If analytic philosophy includes and moves beyond the conceptual analysis to a rational reconstruction of educational enterprise in its full dimension, it may well provide the strongest philosophical basis for contemporary philosophy of adult education.

REFERENCES

Ayer, A. J. "Editor's Introduction," In A. J. Ayer (ed.), *Logical Positivism.* New York: Macmillan, 1959, 3-30.

Frankena, William K. "A Model for Analyzing a Philosophy," In Jane R. Martin (ed.), *Readings in the Philosophy of Education: A Study of Curriculum.* Boston: Allyn and Bacon, 1970.

Komisar, Paul and James McClellan. "The Logic of Slogans," In B. Othanel Smith and Robert H. Ennis (eds.), *Language and Concepts in Education: Analytic Study of Educational Ideas.* Chicago: Rand McNally, 1951, 195-214.

Lawson, K. H. *Philosophical Concepts and Values in Adult Education.* Nottingham, England: Barnes and Humby, Ltd., 1975.

Merriam, Sharan. "Philosophical Perspectives on Adult Education: A Critical Review of the Literature," *Adult Education.* 1977, *27*, 195-208.

Monette, Maurice L. "The Concept of Need: An Analysis of Selected Literature," *Adult Education.* 1977, *27*, 116-127.

Monette, Maurice L. "Need Assessment: A Critique of Philosophical Assumptions," *Adult Education.* 1979, *29*, 83-95.

Moore, George E. *Principia Ethica.* Cambridge: Cambridge University Press, 1903.

Paterson, R. W. K. *Values, Education and the Adult.* Boston: Routledge and Kegan Paul, 1979.

Peters, R. S. *Ethics and Education.* Atlanta: Scott Foresman, 1967a.

Peters, R. S. "What is an Educational Process," In R. S. Peters (ed.), *The Concept of Education.* Boston: Routledge and Kegan Paul, 1967b.

Russell, Bertrand. *The Problem of Philosophy.* London: Home University Press, 1912.

Ryle, Gilbert. *The Concept of Mind.* New York: Barnes and Noble, 1943.

Ryle, Gilbert. "Teaching and Training," In R. S. Peters (ed.), *The Concept of Education.* Boston: Routledge and Kegan Paul, 1967.

Scheffler, Israel. *The Language of Education.* Springfield, IL: Charles Thomas, 1960.

Weitz, Morris. "General Introduction," In Morris Weitz (ed.), *20th-Century Philosophy: The Analytic Tradition.* New York: Macmillan, 1967, 1-12.

Wisdom, John. "Philosophical Perplexity" (1936), In Morris Weitz (ed.), *20th Century Philosophy: The Analytic Tradition.* New York: Macmillan, 1967, 282-296.

Wisdom, John. *Other Minds.* Oxford: Blackwell, 1952.

Wittgenstein, Ludwig. *Tractatus Logico-Philosophicus.* London: Routledge and Kegan Paul, 1921.

Wittgenstein, Ludwig. *Philosophical Investigations.* Oxford: Blackwell, 1953.

CHAPTER VIII

PHILOSOPHY OF ADULT EDUCATION:

RETROSPECT AND PROSPECT

The quest for truth in philosophy is a continuing one. The answers given by one philosopher or system often provide the questions for the next philosopher or system. This quest continues because there is change in human life. People change, societies change, cultures change. These changes call for new explanations, new theories, and often new systems of thought.

Adult education participates in the general philosophical quest. In this search various theoretical positions can be delineated— positions that attempt to develop principles by which adult educators can better understand and exercise their roles. As we have seen in this work, these principles relate to the nature of education, the concept of adulthood and adult education, the teaching-learning process, and the relationship between education and society.

In presenting the various principles of six philosophies of adult education, we have left two issues to the concluding epilogue: how can the relationships among these various theories be clearly and simply understood, and what stance should the adult educator adopt in his or her personal philosophy of adult education? The first question is retrospective as we look back over the various philosophies presented. The second question is prospective, for it involves looking ahead to the future work of adult educators challenged by the philosophical questions raised in this book.

Retrospect

There is a certain logic in the chronological order of development of the six philosophies of adult education treated in this book. Liberal adult education was the predominant philosophy of education from the time of Greek thought to the rise of modern science in the 18th and 19th centuries. The aims, methods, and content of this education were clearly established. Truth was viewed as absolute, and educational values were found in definite disciplines and studies. This educational philosophy corresponded to a static society in which truths, values, and structures were considered authoritative and immutable.

The great challenge to this system came with the rise of modern science and modern philosophy. Change, relativity, and pluralism were introduced into human consciousness. A new educational theory developed to cope with this view of the world. In the progressive thought and writings of John Dewey, the new education found its most eloquent advocate. Progressive adult education became the philosophical position of adult educators in this country.

The richness of progressive adult education is seen in its influence on the other philosophies of adult education. Each of the other philosophies of education can best be understood by viewing its relationship to progressive adult education.

Humanistic adult education is related to the first phase of progressive education which placed an emphasis on the person and learner. Significantly, the foremost contemporary proponent of this theory, Carl Rogers, studied progressive thought at Columbia in the 1930's. Humanistic adult educators have concentrated upon the human potential for growth in both cognitive and affective areas of life. The group work that strongly characterizes humanistic adult education was first brought into prominence by the progressives. Both progressives and humanistic educators are optimistic in their approach to personal and societal change.

Behaviorist adult education is also indebted to progressive thought for some of its basic principles. Progressives placed great emphasis on the scientific method and the importance of experimentation in arriving at truth. Scientific observation, problem-solving, hypothesis testing, and control are features that progressives and behaviorists hold in common. Behaviorism departs from progressive thought, however, in its view of the possibility and desirability of controlling human behavior.

The emphasis on social change so central to radical adult

education can also be traced back to progressive thought. Social reconstructionists like Counts and Brameld accept many basic progressive principles. Even the Brazilian educator, Paulo Freire, has acknowledged his indebtedness to John Dewey. Both progressives and radicals see education as a possible force for bringing about change. The two theories part company when it comes to the explicitness of the vision of the new society and the means to bring about social and political change. Radicals are more willing to adopt utopian visions of society and clearly see education as a legitimate vehicle for reshaping society.

The relationship between analytic philosophy of adult education and progressive adult education is not as clear as in the above three cases. A definite connection does exist, however, in that many of the concepts, slogans, metaphors, and positions of the progressives have been the subject of logical analysis. The conclusions that analysts arrive at on such basic issues as education, learner-centered education, needs and interests, and so on, are often opposed to the views of progressives. Thus, the relationship between these two philosophies is not one of influence, but rather one of opposition.

Finally, in retrospect, a word can be said about the relationship between progressive adult education and liberal adult education. Though progressivism developed in opposition to liberal education, liberal education has been rejuvenated to a degree in its confrontation with progressive thought. Liberal adult education has had to rethink its position on the place of science in the curriculum, the absoluteness of its views of truth and values, and the rigidity of its curriculum of studies. Progressive adult education has also benefited from its battles with liberal adult education. The importance of subject matter, the cultivation of the mind, and the value of tradition emphasized in liberal adult education provide a balance to the pragmatic and vocational thrust of progressive thought.

Prospect

The final question to be considered in this book may ultimately be the most important one: what stance should the adult educator adopt as his or her personal philosophy of adult education?

Whatever the position adopted, it must be held critically. The professional adult educator should be constantly in the process of examining, evaluating and perhaps rejecting or modifying what has been received from the past. A study of philosophies of adult education should produce a professional who questions the theories, practices, institutions, and assumptions of others.

In deciding upon a philosophy of education, one is faced, we believe, with three options. The first option is to choose one of the philosophies, or to determine that one has already espoused, perhaps implicitly, one of the theories discussed in this book. The advantage of this stance is that the educator will have a clearly articulated approach that has a great degree of consistency. In addition, the criticisms offered of the various theories provide the educator with the opportunity to critically examine the assumptions underlying his or her chosen philosophical position.

A second stance is to opt for an eclectic approach to one's philosophy of adult education. In this approach, one chooses certain elements from different theories and operates according to those principles. This alternative has the advantage of flexibility and the possible disadvantage of inconsistency. Yet many persons see themselves as truly eclectic, constantly working toward a synthesis and integration of views.

A third stance is to choose one particular theory as a framework upon which one builds a personal educational philosophy. Within this structure, views from other theories can be incorporated that are not inconsistent with the basic position. This approach gives a certain consistency to one's theory and practice, yet does not close off the possibility of influence from other viewpoints.

Whatever the philosophical stance one adopts, it is important that the continuing philosophical quest is not abandoned. The study of philosophies of adult education is not a means of settling, once and for all, theoretical and practical issues. It is rather a study to enable persons to gain insight into their personal and cultural past and to refine their personal tastes and powers of judgment. The continuing reflection on philosophical issues in adult education should serve to develop methods of critical thinking, aid individuals to ask better questions, and expand the visions of educators beyond their present limits.

CHAPTER IX

PHILOSOPHY OF
ADULT EDUCATION, 1980–1994
A BIBLIOGRAPHIC ESSAY

Philosophy of adult education continues to be a small but lively enterprise within adult education. The past 15 years have witnessed a modest increase in writings of a philosophical or theoretical nature in a field long dominated by practical concerns. Though only a few persons with formal philosophical training are working in the field, adult education has attracted its share of those interested in probing the philosophical or theoretical foundations or in presenting comprehensive visions for adult educators.

The general discipline of philosophy of education is considered by some to be in decline, having lost its place in many teacher education programs to courses in social foundations. The discipline is often attacked for being far removed from educational issues, being irrelevant to teacher and administrative training, engendering skepticism about our ability to know truth and goodness, and fostering radical and destructive ideas. Scholars in the field often experience the dilemma of becoming too theoretical and thus irrelevant to practice or attempting to be relevant at the risk of abandoning philosophic rigor.

While admitting the legitimacy of some of the criticisms, we still contend that the writings reviewed in this essay establish that philosophy of education is not a luxury for adult educators. We maintain that philosophy aids leaders and teachers in becoming more rational and critical in their thinking and acting. Philosophy's emphasis on clarity, purpose, criticism, and legitimation remains important. Philosophy of education at its best presents visions of what persons and society are capable of becoming through involvement in education. The strongest case for this is found in the earlier work of John

Dewey and in the contemporary writings of Paulo Freire, both of whom consider education an essential tool for the reconstruction of both human experience and society.

The value of philosophy of adult education has been addressed in a number of publications. Merriam (1982) has edited a collection which explores ways in which philosophy can be linked to action in adult education. The authors in the collection make the case that since theoretical concerns are implicit in all practical activities, it is advantageous to make these perspectives explicit in order to promote a more reflective form of educational practice. Furthermore, Hiemstra (1988) has given four reasons/advantages for an explicit philosophy of education:

1. A philosophy promotes an understanding of human relationships.
2. A philosophy sensitizes one to the various needs associated with positive human interactions.
3. A philosophy provides a framework for distinguishing, separating, and understanding personal values.
4. A philosophy promotes flexibility and consistency in working with adult learners.

The increasing value of philosophy of adult education has become noticeable especially in the area of ethics. Brockett's (1988) collection contains a number of articles that deal with ethical issues from a philosophical perspective. Here, Brockett (1988) and Hiemstra (1988) explore the importance and relevance of personal value systems in all ethical decision making. Hiemstra explicitly makes connections between these personal systems and individuals' philosophies of education. In the same volume, Cunningham (1988) draws on the ethics of critique developed by some critical theorists to make the case for a greater sense of social responsibility on the part of adult educators. Other chapters deal with ethical issues in program planning, marketing, evaluation, and research.

It is important to recognize that philosophy of education takes many forms (Powers, 1982). Some philosophies tend to be inspirational in presenting utopian ideals, such as Plato's *Republic*, Rousseau's *Emile*, and Skinner's *Walden II*. Other philosophies are normative or prescriptive in offering clear and precise directions for educational practice, such as Hutchins's *Higher Education in Amer-*

ica and Bergevin's *A Philosophy of Adult Education.* A third approach is investigative, examining educational policies and practices with a view to the justification of ideas or the reconstruction of society, such as Dewey's *Democracy and Education* and Lindeman's *The Meaning of Adult Education.* More recent approaches are termed analytic because of their attempts to discover and interpret educational meaning in education, such as Lawson's *Philosophical Concepts and Values in Adult Education.*

Another way of classifying philosophies of adult education is according to function (Broudy, 1981). Philosophy of adult education performs an *educational* function in addressing issues regarding aims, curriculum, organization, teaching and learning, methodology of research, and ethics from a theoretical perspective. In its *analytic* function, philosophy of education clarifies the language and arguments used in educational discourse. Increasingly, attention has been paid to the *critical* function which examines proposals, policies, and underlying ideologies of adult educators. What has been ignored in recent years by philosophers has been the *synthetic* or comprehensive function of providing "a synoptic, systematic, coherent set of beliefs and arguments about education that deals with the educational enterprise as a whole and that makes connection with a philosophy of life" (p. 35).

Historically there has been a close connection between philosophy and religion or theology. The text points out the connection between religion and education especially in the treatment of liberal adult education. Elias (1993) has explored the works of various scholars in the field of religion who have addressed adult education, using the same classifications as found in this book. McKenzie (1982) has applied his humanistic treatment of adult education to religion, showing the strong congruence between the humanistic approach and adult religious education. Thompson (1984) presented five models of adult religious education: enculturation models, needs assessment and participation models, group dynamics models, sociopolitical models, and ecumenical models. Theoretical issues are competently treated in Foltz's (1986) handbook which features a succinct article by McKenzie on a religious philosophy of adult education. Finally, Vogel (1991) in a comprehensive book has provided theoretical models for examining adult religious education.

This review of recent writings considers all of these forms and functions of philosophy to be both valuable and legitimate. In keeping with the introductory nature of this book, this review will present arguments and issues and not take sides in the many debates among contemporary philosophers of education.

This review will address developments within each of the six philosophical positions described in this book. More attention will be given to developments in phenomenology, critical theory, and feminist theory, since much recent work is situated within these genres.

Liberal Adult Education Revisited

The importance of liberal adult education has again been recognized by Adler (1982) in the influential *Paideia Proposal*. Though the manifesto in the main treats schooling, it begins with an important recognition that formal schooling is only part of education; as such, it is incapable of turning out educated men and women because educated persons must pass through many critical trials of adult life. Education is a lifelong process since learning never reaches an end point.

Liberal education in this proposal is presented as threefold: the acquisition of organized knowledge by means of didactic instruction in language, mathematics, and natural sciences; the development of intellectual skills by means of coaching, exercises, and supervised practice in reading, calculating, and exercising critical judgment; and enlarged understanding of ideas and values by means of the maieutic or Socratic method in the discussion of books and involvement in artistic activities.

While the importance of liberal adult education has been recognized, a debate continues over just what should constitute the curriculum. While this debate has, for the most part, been restricted to undergraduate college education, issues involved in this debate are important for liberal adult educators. Bloom (1987) has argued convincingly for the continuing value of the Great Books of Western civilization to provide all of the intellectual nourishment that humans need. The purpose of a liberal education, according to Bloom, is to pose basic questions to students as well as the alternative answers that have been offered over the ages. For him "a liberal education means reading certain generally recognized texts, just reading them, letting them dictate what the questions are and the method of approaching them—not forcing them into categories we make up, not treating them as historical products, but trying to read them as their authors wished them to be read" (p. 344). The classics, in Bloom's view, provide the best education possible for all persons:

> I mean rather that a life based on the Book is closer to the truth, that it provides the material for deeper research in and access to the real nature of things. Without the great revelations, epics and philosophies as part of our natural vision, there is nothing to see out there, and eventually little left inside. The Bible is not the only means to furnish a mind, but without a book of similar gravity, read with the gravity of the potential believer, it will remain unfurnished. (p. 60)

While the university is the focus of attention of Bloom, Hirsch (1987) is concerned with the general issue of cultural literacy, especially the background knowledge necessary for functional literacy, effective national communication, and full citizenship. While his main concern is with the teaching of cultural literacy within the schools, his ideas have relevance for adult liberal educators, especially those involved with educating new immigrants for community life and citizenship. While Bloom seems to assume a single best culture, Hirsch's anthropological theory of education assumes a diversity of cultures in which persons can communicate effectively with one another "only by accumulating shared symbols, and the shared information that the symbols represent" (p. xvii).

Extending Hirsch's provocative ideas into adult education would entail attention to the learning of the national cultural language. This language includes, in his view, the possession of vocabularies which include knowledge of terms used throughout the world, a knowledge of standard English, and information that is special to one's own country. Hirsch finds within this national culture a place for bilingualism and multiculturalism, but contends that these must remain subordinate to the development of a national culture.

These approaches to liberal education and cultural literacy (termed *cultural conservatism* or *neo-conservatism*) have met with much criticism from scholars who advocate a broadening of the liberal curriculum to include works outside the generally established canon accepted in traditional Western education. Bloom and Hirsch along with William Bennett and Saul Bellow have been accused of creating "a narrowly specific cultural capital that will be the normative referent for everyone, but will remain the property of a small and powerful caste that is linguistically and ethnically unified" (Pratt, 1988, p. 15). The following argument against their stand was offered in the now famous debate over undergraduate education at Stanford:

> A "liberal education" for our time should expand beyond the culture-bound, basically colonialist, horizon that relies, albeit subtly, on the myth of the cultural superiority of the West. . . . Does the new integrated vision . . . entail our teaching the Greek Hermes and Prometheus alongside the North American Indian Coyote or the West African Anansi and Legba as paradigms of trickster heroes, or Japanese Noh alongside Greek drama or Indian philosophy alongside Plato? (Pratt, 1988, p. 26)

Some scholars also contest the apparently value-free manner in which Bloom proposes that the classics be approached. Rorty (1988) argues that we always "read books with questions in mind—not questions dictated by the books, but questions we have previously, if vaguely formulated" (p. 32). It is not clear to him that we can totally avoid forcing books into categories we make up. There is, however, no reason to be forced to choose between these two approaches of questioning the text and allowing the text to question us, since both can be used in the educational process. Rorty's point, nevertheless, rightly discourages us from viewing the received texts as some sort of inspired and infallible literature.

Hirsch has also received criticism from many sides, notably on the existence and desirability of education focusing on transmitting a national culture. Smith (1992) argues that this approach to education would actually increase the illiteracy, economic deprivation, social marginalization, and political efficacy that Hirsch wants to eliminate. She argues that the knowledge that Hirsch wants learned belongs to a particular group and would serve to promote their interests at the expense of the interests of other groups in society. What Giroux (1988) finds lacking in cultural conservatism is any notion of education as the critical reconstruction of economic, political, and social life. The call for a critical pedagogy will be explored later in this essay.

The arguments of these liberal and radical critics need to be balanced by the thoughtful responses of those who offer a defense of the basic positions of Bloom and Hirsch relating to the importance of the traditional canon in Western education. Berger (1993) argues for the continued relevance of texts which underlie the intellectual and moral values of Western societies. Schlesinger (1992) both criticizes some of the extreme positions of multiculturalists and reasserts the necessity of focusing upon the value consensus which unites the nation. Gates (1988) makes a case against a particularism which denies the values present in all groups.

The debate over the canon is part of the broader debate over political correctness, which has received extensive coverage in both the popular press and the academic and political communities. The debate is also described as one between those who propose a multicultural curriculum which takes into account ethnicity, class, gender, and sexual orientation and those who maintain that greater emphasis must be placed on transmitting the common culture that Hirsch endorses. While this debate has not engaged widespread attention from adult educators, the work of liberal adult educators necessarily deals with these issues. This may be the opportune time to engage in debates over the Great Books programs which are still fostered in many communities of our nation. Questions should be raised about the goals, content, and methods of these programs.

Progressive Adult Education

When one looks for recent developments in the philosophy of progressive adult education, one encounters an initial sense of disappointment. While progressive is not often used as a category to define a particular philosophical stance in adult education, except among British authors, the ideas of the progressives are still alive in general education, as well as in adult education. Also, there has developed in the past decade a more sophisticated interpretation of progressive education which needs to inform historical thinking about progressive philosophy in adult education.

The history and meaning of progressive education have come under a great deal of discussion. The standard history of progressivism, Cremin's *The Transformation of the Schools* (1957), no longer stands uncontested as a definitive study. Cremin's thesis that progressive education was an enlightened and praiseworthy effort to respond to the problems of American society and education has been criticized by scholars who are critical of both the motives of the re-formers and the effects of their reforms (Lazerson, 1971). Radical revisionists have condemned the movement as one enormous effort aimed at the social control of immigrants and the children of immigrants. (Bowles & Gintis, 1976; Hogan, 1985). Furthermore, writing in an anti-progressive tenor, Ravitch (1982) has challenged the educational and intellectual implications of progressive education.

For a balanced treatment of the philosophy and aims of progressives as well as today's educational issues, Fass's work is relevant. In her view, progressive reformers thought education and schooling:

> were to be at once instruments of remedial socialization and primary agents of culture; they were to connect the democratic potential of an enormously diverse population to the unities of an ancient citizenship; they were to educate for future success but be attentive to present needs. (1989, p. 34)

It took the great faith in the power of education which the progressives possessed, to assign it this paradoxical philosophy.

There is no doubt that the main ideas of Dewey and the progressives (student-centeredness, social reform, scientific method) are still influential today among philosophers of education. Dewey's continued relevance to the issues of developing a public philosophy of education and democracy has been admirably argued by Westbrook (1991). But what has not yet been developed within education is the type of neo-pragmatic philosophizing that is engaged in by Rorty (1988) who sees in the basically optimistic American pragmatic tradition a counteractive force to the excessive pessimism of much of Continental philosophy.

As in general education, there has been some discussion about the meaning of a progressive orientation in adult education. This discussion has been in reference to Knowles's (1980) concept of andragogy. Although primarily humanistic in its grounding, andragogy also rests upon Knowles's firm belief in "the ideals of a democratic citizenship and the belief that civic and democratic virtue would arise out of natural self-fulfillment through adult education" (Pratt, 1993, p. 20). Discussions and critique of the progressive underpinnings of andragogy have been advanced most recently by Pratt (1993), but also by Carlson (1989) and Podeschi (1987).

Behaviorist Adult Education

Behaviorism as a fully articulated philosophy of education is rarely found in adult education. This does not mean, however, that behaviorist or positivist principles have ceased to be important assumptions and guidelines in numerous adult education programs especially in the process of program planning. Many adult educators continue to be influenced by behaviorist philosophy and psychology in treating needs assessment, program design, and evaluation. Specific behavioral objectives and insistence on measurable outcomes are also artifacts of behaviorist philosophy.

The philosophical literature in adult education tends to be highly critical of the assumptions behind behaviorism. This is especially true of those philosophers who make use of critical theory or phenomenology in investigating aspects of adult education (Collins, 1991, Griffin, 1983; Stanage, 1987). Behaviorism has been dismissed as cold, inhumane, devoid of feeling, and ignorant of the subjective, creative, and intuitive dimensions of human behavior. Collins (1991) also points out that often the literature on program planning, design, and evaluation tries to have it both ways by modifying the language of behaviorism with that of humanistic psychology.

One can speculate on the persistence of the behavioral paradigm in adult education, as well as in general education. This paradigm, based as it is on logical empiricist philosophy of science, satisfies the quest for certainty in many educators since it bases education on explicit, scientific-technical procedures. Logical empiricism and behaviorism have devoted great energies toward accounting for method, justification, and procedures of verification (Kaplan, 1964). These philosophies have identified causal elements that might account for, predict, and control human behavior. Furthermore, behaviorism sets before the teachers aims, objectives, and criteria which are standard and fixed.

Probably the most visible articulation of a behaviorist orientation is in the area of human resource development (HRD). This form of adult education is organizationally based, especially in business and industry, where employees are "trained" to enhance their on-the-job performance. Within the last 15 years, a large number of books and monographs have been published reflecting a growing interest in

HRD by both practitioners and academicians. Most reflect a behaviorist perspective.

Jacobs (1987), for example, weaves instructional technology into his concept of HRD, which he renames as human performance technology. This approach uses systems theory "to ensure that the right individuals have the knowledge, skills, motivation, and environmental supports to do their jobs effectively and efficiently" (p. 13). He also presents this very behaviorist definition: "Human performance technology is about engineering human performance. Thus, the technologies involved are based on what is *known* about the principles to change the outcomes of behavior" (p. 19).

In the 1980s, the American Society for Training and Development (ASTD) commissioned two major studies in an attempt to define the field of HRD (McLagan, 1983, 1989). The second study (which sought to update the 1983 study) "summarizes 74 work outputs of HRD, more than 500 quality requirements linked to the outputs, 35 competencies necessary to achieve the outputs, 11 roles that may be enacted by HRD professionals, 5 role clusters that link related roles, and 19 possible uses of the study's results" (Rothwell & Sredl, 1992, p. 87). Several authors, such as Gilley and Eggland (1989) and Rothwell and Kazanas (1989), have drawn heavily from this competency-based model of HRD.

Other recent works in HRD also promote a behaviorist orientation. Carnevale, Gainer, and Villet (1990), whose emphasis is on "the bottom line," present an instructional systems design model derived from the military. They point out that employers are anxious to return to "needs-driven education and training and . . . away from providing a patchwork of unconnected training courses covering topics recognized as 'nice to know' but not immediately germane to the jobs at hand" (p. 31). Finally, Nadler and Nadler (1989), who differentiate among training, education, and development, and who are sensitive to the larger range of philosophical orientations in adult education, also work predominately out of a behaviorist framework.

Humanistic Adult Education

Probably more than any single other orientation, humanistic philosophy and psychology continue to underlie the theory and practice of adult education. Adult educators are generally more concerned with the individual growth and development of their learners than they are with cultural transmission, changing the social order, or an organization's profit margin. Knowles's andragogy is as popular as ever ("adopted by legions of adult educators around the world" [Pratt, 1993, p. 21]), self-directed learning has become a major arena for research and theory-building, and several others have produced major works derived from a largely humanistic philosophy. These developments will be reviewed here.

Andragogy and Self-directed Learning

In 1980, the second edition of Knowles's *The Modern Practice of Adult Education* was published, only this edition's subtitle read, *From Pedagogy to Andragogy*, rather than the 1970 version which read, *Andragogy Versus Pedagogy*. This shift in subtitles reflects the lively debate the field engaged in as to whether andragogy was exclusively for adults, and whether andragogy constituted a theory of adult learning. Knowles became persuaded that andragogy could be seen as being on a continuum with pedagogy at one end, and that each orientation would be at times appropriate for both adults and children, depending upon the instructional situation. Further, most have conceded that rather than a learning theory, andragogy is a set of assumptions that delineate characteristics of adult learners, and thus best functions as a guide to instructional design.

It is in the assumptions underlying andragogy (discussed in this book's Chapter V, Humanistic Adult Education), that Knowles's allegiance to humanism is unabashedly clear. In his autobiographical "journey," Knowles (1989) cites Carl Rogers as a major influence on his thinking, and lists "learning to be authentic" and "learning to make things happen by releasing the energy of others" as two of eight episodes that changed his life. Pratt (1993), in a provocative analysis titled "Andragogy After Twenty-Five Years," concludes that "andragogy is saturated with the ideals of individualism and entrepreneurial democracy" (p. 21). It is also based on five humanistic values including placing the individual at the center of education, believing in the goodness and potency of each person, in each person's potential to grow toward self-actualization, and in autonomy and self-direction as "signposts of adulthood" (p. 21).

As most adult educators are aware, Tough's 1971 book on *The*

Adult's Learning Projects followed by Knowles's *Self-Directed Learning* (1975) inspired a major thrust in adult learning research and theory building. The area of self-directed learning has witnessed a plethora of books, monographs, articles, and conference proceedings over the past 15 years. Much of this literature is reviewed by Caffarella (1993), Merriam and Caffarella (1991), and Candy (1991). Underlying nearly all of this literature is a humanistic philosophy. Caffarella (1993) notes that this is the "predominate" orientation and that

> from this perspective, the focus of learning is on the individual and self-development, with learners expected to assume primary responsibility for their own learning. The process of learning, which is centered on learner need, is seen as more important than the content; therefore, when educators are involved in the learning process, their most important role is to act as facilitators, or guides, as opposed to content experts. (p. 26)

Thus, both andragogy and self-directed learning have had an enormous impact on the field of adult education and both draw from humanistic philosophy going back to Maslow and Rogers in particular (see this book's chapter on Humanistic Adult Education for a discussion of the roots of this philosophy).

In addition to developments in andragogy and self-directed learning, there have been several major additions to the adult education literature, all of which can be loosely categorized under humanistic adult education. To be discussed are Stanage's and others' writing on phenomenology, McKenzie's *Adult Education as Worldview Construction*, Mezirow's work on transformational learning, Brookfield's work on interactive learning, and Jarvis's exploration of the paradoxes of learning.

Phenomenology of Adult Education

Stanage (1987) has provided the field with a difficult and challenging book on the philosophy of adult education. Though he is aware of and makes use of elements of the various philosophical approaches to adult education, he prefers to investigate various phenomena of adult education and learning according to the philosophical methods of Edmund Husserl and other continental philosophers. Stanage also suggests that the works of Dewey, especially *Logic: The Theory of Inquiry*, are particularly useful in examining adult education from a phenomenological perspective.

Stanage offers the reader an introduction to phenomenology (an investigation of human consciousness: feelings, experiences, ideas, hopes, problems, etc.), as well as a phenomenological investigation of the adult world and of the components of adult education (assumptions, goals, means, ends, and methods). He attempts to provide a philosophical understanding that "leads to new programs of learning for the adult learner, adult educators, and the subject matter of adult education, and to a new paradigm of research, new research programs, and the subsequent emergence of new problems" (pp. 2–3). Other analyses pertinent to adult education include a description of feeling, experience, and consciousness, all of which attempt to provide an understanding of the person that should underlie all of adult education.

Stanage's analysis of adult education leads to this provisional definition: "adult education is the enactment of, and the systematic investigation of the phenomena constituting the adult eductions *persons* [feeling, experience, and consciousness], specifically of persons' free and deliberate motives for actions" (p. 37). This knowledge of persons provides us with keen insight into the action of persons, in both private and public spheres.

Stanage's project is a challenging one which has been taken up by a number of doctoral students who have extended this form of analysis into various areas of human consciousness. For Stanage, this approach to adult education constitutes:

> a way through to the theory and practices of adult education conceived as the most rigorous of human sciences. These have as their special subject-matter systematic investigations of the performative enactments of, and the systematic investigation of, the essential structures of the phenomena constituting adult educations of *person*. These phenomena most specifically are of the deliberative liberative actions of consciousing and responsible persons whereby they become transformed and empowered with vital motive for living. (p. 304)

Others have contributed to the expanding understanding of phenomenology of adult education. Spiegelberg (1975), for instance, distinguishes among six forms or phases of phenomenology: descriptive, essential or eidetic, phenomenology of appearances, constitutive, reductive, and hermeneutic. Returning to the philosophical basis of phenomenology, Spiegelberg observes that each of these unique forms is helpful in understanding elements of the social sciences. One, however, is particularly elucidating. Constitutive phenomenology is concerned with the ways in which experience becomes constituted or established in consciousness. This form of phenomenology is especially relevant in the closer examination of the historical or sociocultural phenomena, such as adult education.

Ihde (1977) and Stewart and Mickunas (1974) also suggest that the philosophical foundations of phenomenology offer new and challenging ways to view how we come to learn about, understand, and function in the world around us. Finally, van Manen (1990) recommends phenomenology when one wishes to understand the characteristic and essential themes of a socially significant phenomenon such as adult education.

Adult Education as Worldview Construction

McKenzie (1991) presents a comprehensive or transcendent goal for all of adult education, the construction of a worldview. Worldview construction involves "the ongoing development and maturation of understanding: understanding of the world, of others, of self, of understanding itself" (p. vii). Drawing on the thought of Heidegger, McKenzie presents worldviews as vantage points in time and culture that condition persons' experience of the world and provide an understanding of the self. In this view, the primary goal of adult education is the search for personal meaning.

McKenzie makes use of the work of Gadamer to show how worldview construction is related to tradition. Early socialization provides us with ready-made worldviews. Through education, persons should be led to an understanding of their prejudices, assumptions, and beliefs and to a realization of how these affect interpretations of new experiences of thinking and knowing. Thinking and knowing need to be systematic, that is, balanced, orderly, informed, self-referencing, and productive. Thinking and knowing should lead to understanding, and to "insight that integrates experiences, ideas, judgments, and beliefs into a meaningful whole" (pp. x, xi). All thinking develops in a particular social and cultural context. This analysis is informed by the work of Ludwig Wittgenstein and Bernard Lonergan.

McKenzie, true to his own educational tradition, presents the participation training of Bergevin and McKinley as the best model for promoting worldview construction. He contends, however, that the goal of worldview construction is not incompatible with the ideas of Grundtvig, Lindeman, Apps, and Brookfield.

McKenzie makes a strong case that adult educators have an ethical responsibility to examine their own worldviews so they may avoid imposing them on students. He is strongly critical of how adult educators on the political right and left have imposed their ideologies on their students rather than facilitate the emergence of the learners' own worldviews. While those on the right impose the classic wisdom of the past, those on the left indoctrinate with the political utopias of the future. Although McKenzie argues that adult educators should be impartial in all controversial areas and only attend to the unveiling of the truth, he recognizes that it is often not possible for educators to remain neutral. McKenzie is particularly critical of radical adult educators for their politicizing of the educational process. Informed by the philosophical work of Rorty, he shows a recognition that there are no absolute truths and that the educational process is an ongoing conversation and dialogue in which positions can often change.

McKenzie acknowledges his own philosophical assumptions which are eclectic, drawing as he does on various philosophers. While he remains committed to many Enlightenment prejudices and assumptions, he has come to place higher value on tradition. He remains committed to many of the values of existentialism, phenomenology, and humanistic psychology. What he does not make clear are his own political, social, and economic commitments and how these have influenced his criticisms of radical adult education, liberation theology, and attitudes towards activism among adult educators.

Adult Education as Perspective Transformation

Mezirow (1990, 1991) presents what might be considered a humanistic theory of adult learning. He devotes limited attention, however, to how his theory or perspective transformation might form the basis for a philosophy of adult education.

This theory has its roots in cognitive psychology, psychotherapy, and critical social theory, especially that of the German philosopher, Habermas. While Mezirow has incorporated ideas from a wide variety of sources, a case can be made that humanistic psychology and philosophical humanism are at the basis of the theory.

According to Mezirow (1991), we enter adulthood with a store of meanings, beliefs, and values which are the result of socialization. In adulthood we find many of these inadequate for making meaning out of human experience. In adulthood we are involved in personal meaning making, re-interpreting earlier values, beliefs, and meanings. The process of learning is precisely the construing and appropriating of new meanings to our experiences. Adult learning involves an interpretative process in which we make decisions "that may result in confirmation, rejection, extension, or formulation of a belief or meaning scheme or in finding that belief or scheme presents a problem that requires further examination" (p. 35). Learning also entails assessing reasons and justifications for our meaning schemes.

Mezirow does draw some implications for a philosophy of adult education from his theory of adult learning. The goals of adult education "include helping learners to be self-guided, self-reflective, and rational and helping them to establish communities of discourse in which these qualities are honored and fostered" (p. 224).

Mezirow's theory of transformative learning has been criticized by a number of scholars for a lack of social critique that would identify factors that impede learning, for focusing disproportionately on personal learning, and for not assigning a role to social action for transformative learning and emancipatory adult education (Clark & Wilson, 1991; Collard & Law, 1989; Hart, 1990). He attempts to respond to these criticisms by relating the theory to adult education for social action. Unfortunately, the theoretical bases for the theory do not include an adequate analysis of social structures and functions to buttress a more socially and politically oriented adult education.

A Transactional Approach to Adult Education

Brookfield in a number of writings has argued for a philosophy of practice in adult education which, while grounded in humanistic principles, draws on other philosophical traditions such as critical theory and conceptual analysis. His concept of adult education describes education as:

> a transactional drama in which the personalities, philosophies, and priorities of the chief players (participants and facilitators) interact continuously to influence the nature, direction, and form of the subsequent learning. (1986, p. viii)

To the widely accepted humanistic principles of a respect for participants in the teaching-learning transaction, a commitment to collaboration in program planning, and a recognition of the value of the educational value of life experiences, he adds the dimension of a critical appraisal of alternative values, attitudes, and behaviors.

In presenting his principles for a philosophy of practice, Brookfield stresses the humanistic principles of developing a sense of personal control and autonomy to be realized "in personal relationships, in sociopolitical behavior, and in intellectual judgments" (1986, p. 291). For Brookfield, nothing is more important for advancing the individuals' personal control and autonomy than the capacity to think critically, included in which is the recognition that all knowledge and value systems are culturally constructed (1986, p. 293; 1987).

Central to the philosophy of practice proposed by Brookfield is the principle of critical reflection on practice, derived from the work of John Dewey and Paulo Freire. Brookfield's emphasis on the processes of adult education while staying clear of any distinctive social and political analysis separates his work from that of the critical theorists for whom such analysis is central to the task of adult education. While Brookfield's explicit embrace of critical principles moves him beyond some forms of humanistic education, he remains within the progressive-humanistic tradition for his essential principles.

The Paradoxes of Learning

While he draws on many philosophical and sociological sources for his analysis, Jarvis in *Paradoxes of Learning: On Becoming an Individual in Society* (1992) considers this work as fundamentally humanistic. Influenced by existentialism and critical social theorists such as Habermas, Jarvis explores various paradoxes in human learning: freedom and constraint, certainty and uncertainty, truth and falsehood, joy and sorrow. The social self develops through human learning acquired through paradoxical life and learning in society. The language and culture that we learn both shape our values and free us to shape our own values. From non-reflective learning we move to highly reflective learning which we are able to communicate to others through conscious actions since the purpose of most learning is action in the world. While learning is shaped by our conscious interests, people have the capacity to "reflect back on their society, transcend their social environment, and demonstrate their individuality" (p. 97).

Jarvis develops a more explicit educational philosophy when he discusses how persons grow through lifelong learning. Personal growth takes place through social interaction as described by Marcel and Buber who both noted that it is only in an open relationship with other people that reflective learning and authenticity can be fostered. Jarvis presents as a paradox of learning the contrast between the ideology which states that people are free and autonomous, and the fact that most learning is other directed and other controlled. He writes:

> Self-directed learning is an ideological construct that mirrors much of the current thinking about an open society—but it has become fashionable in a society in which a great deal of public and private space is controlled by others. (p. 142)

In such a situation, humanistic adult education often becomes impossible. Societal constraints also limit the capacity for individuals to achieve meaning and truth in their lives. This control operates in a special way in the world of work and the world of politics. Notwithstanding these constraints, Jarvis holds out the hope for meaningful change and even wisdom in one's life, presumably in the more private spheres of human experience.

While Jarvis's book focuses primarily on learning, it also presents some elements of a philosophy of education. Jarvis raises the ethical issue at the very heart of education, raised by philosophers like Rousseau and Mill: by what right does one impose ideas on others? He believes that educators should frequently raise the question of in whose interests they are teaching. Jarvis concludes as he began on a humanistic note:

> Teaching and reflective learning and human growth and development are all facilitated in the process of genuine human in-

teraction. Teaching is a humanistic enterprise, and only in human relationships is it possible to establish the best conditions for human growth. (p. 245)

Radical Adult Education

Since the publication of our book in 1980, a number of factors have impacted our original conception of radical adult education. The term *radical*, while it reflects the notion of a philosophy that is concerned with challenging the status quo, has not seemed quite broad or powerful enough to capture the liberating, empowering, and transformative aspects that proponents of this orientation espouse. Neither does the term convey the strong critique of taken-for-granted assumptions and power relationships needed in order for social change to occur. The literature has expanded to include in addition to the traditional Marxist analysis, two other orientations—those of critical theory and feminist theory. This section of the essay will review works drawing from a Marxist philosophy, followed by those originating in critical theory, ending with the most recent literature to influence adult education, feminist theory.

From a Marxist Perspective

Paulo Freire continues to be the foremost adult educator who works in part out of a Marxist perspective. In the past 15 years Freire has become the most prominent adult educator in the world. Those desiring a clearer explanation of Freire's actual literacy process will find his *Pedagogy in Process* (1977) a satisfactory introduction. A valuable collection of his political and religious writings is found in *The Politics of Education* (1985). Many of his recent ideas are found in books which reproduce conversations with scholars and practitioners (Freire & Faundez, 1989; Freire & Macedo, 1987; Shor & Freire, 1987). Useful studies on Freire include McClaren (1993, 1994) and Elias (1994).

One of the earliest books in the radical mode was Thompson's (1980) edited collection. Working from a basically Marxist orientation and influenced by the new sociology of education, she argues for a form of adult education committed to a radical reorganization of society. The intellectual resources of the contributors include Marx;

Gramsci, the Italian Marxist; Bourdieu, the French sociologist; Bernstein, a British sociologist; and Freire.

These authors are critical of approaches in adult education which they term liberal progressive and which are associated with Peters, Hirst, Dearden, Lawson, and Patterson, all influential British philosophers of education. This tradition is critiqued for restricting education to purely educational matters and not providing it with a social and political purpose. Liberal progressive education includes liberal adult education which is viewed by the radical educators as of some value but ultimately irrelevant to the lives of many adults in Britain and immaterial to progressive ventures such as education for the disadvantaged, arts workshops, community development, and workers education. The authors raise questions about adult education in Britain with regard to the allocation of resources, its institutional forms, the content, and the processes, as well as the nature of relationships between teachers and students. This essay focuses on the chief theoretical pieces in the collection, which also contains valuable field studies in adult education.

Westwood (1980) proposes "that adult education be reconceptualized as a cultural field in which the cultural competence of the working class is as valid as that of the middle class" (p. 44). This can be done, she argues, by analyzing the role of adult education in relation to advanced capitalism in order to offset the middle-class bias of the field. Keddie (1980) argues that adult education's claim to distinctiveness is based on the ideology of individualism which it shares with initial education. This ideology results from an undue reliance on behaviorist and psychological analyses of teaching and learning. Keddie calls for a critical examination of current adult education practices while asserting that the main problems in the field are not with the adults who do not come, but with the nature of the adult education which is offered. She concludes her insightful article:

> The issue is not whether individuals have needs nor whether they should be met but how those needs are socially and politically constituted and understood, how they are articulated and whose voice is heard. Adult education responds to the collective voice of individualism, but it has in a large measure failed to identify or to identify with the needs of those who reject the premises on which individualism is based. (p. 64)

In addition to Thompson's and Westwood's books, Inkster's (1985) *The Steam Intellect Societies* is also from a Marxist philosophical perspective. This book is an edited volume about the Industrial Revolution and the resultant educational innovations designed to bring knowledge in science and technology to the average working person. In particular it is a history of mechanics institutes which first appeared in Britain in the 1820s and spread with industrialization to other parts of the world. Chapter authors situate the mechanics institutes within technical training and adult education. The impact of industrialization, or the "steam intellect," in terms of culture and class is discussed in chapters such as "Mechanics Institute and Working Class Culture: Exhibition Movements, 1830–1840's," "Polarised Culture and Steam Intellect: A Case Study of Liverpool and its Region, Circa 1820–1850's," and "Mechanics Institute and the State."

Youngman's *Adult Education and Socialist Pedagogy* (1986) attempts to advance a socialist, Marxist framework for guiding adult education practice worldwide. In more explicit terms than Inskster, Youngman states that capitalism presents obstacles to social justice and educational equality. In addition to chapters on the economic and political context of adult education and on Marxist theory and its relevance to adult learning, Youngman devotes a chapter each to a critique of traditional learning theories and to Freire's pedagogy. He considers, but ultimately rejects Freire's pedagogy as a basis for restructuring adult education. Freire's philosophy and pedagogy, Youngman feels, is too eclectic to be useful, for "if a capitalist corporation and a socialist teacher can both refer to the same source of ideas, then obviously that source is deeply equivocal" (p. 190). What Youngman proposes instead is a socialist pedagogy that has the dual aims of challenging "the ideology and culture of capitalism," and developing "the general knowledge and technical expertise necessary to reorganise production and society in a fully democratic way" (p. 197). To this end he offers nine philosophical principles of a Marxist approach, and six pedagogical principles derived from a Marxist theoretical framework. Youngman's thoughtful critique and clear writing style result in this book being a substantive contribution to the literature representative of a radical Marxist perspective.

Critical Theory

The main architect of critical theory who has influenced adult educators is Jurgen Habermas, a German philosopher. Habermas sought to move beyond a Marxist social analysis and in so doing split with the famous "Frankfurt School" of social theorists (Welton, 1993a; 1993b). As noted in the section on Humanistic Adult Education, Mezirow's theory of perspective transformation was originally influenced by Habermas's notions of technical, practical, and emancipatory forms of knowledge. Other adult educators writing from a critical theory perspective and influenced by Habermas are Griffin, Collins, Welton, Finger, and Wilson.

A sustained attempt to apply critical sociology to adult education can be found in Griffin's *Curriculum Theory in Adult and Lifelong Learning* (1983). Although working in the field of curriculum theory, Griffin's work can easily be identified with the work of philosophers of adult education. Griffin explains how critical sociology rejects the mechanistic and technical approaches to adult education by focusing on issues of knowledge as ideology, cultural reproduction, and the power of social control as these relate specifically to education. Griffin argues against approaches to define adult education in terms of adult characteristics, needs, design, strategies, and structures (as in andragogy). An adequate theory of adult education would look rather at the issues raised in philosophy, sociology, and politics. As aims for adult education, Griffin proposes not the concepts of needs, access, and provision, but an ideology of autonomy, individuality, and equality. Adult educators need to focus, he asserts, less on technique, methodology, and administration, and more on philosophical and political ideas that lie at the heart of the enterprise. Underlying these suggestions is Griffin's concrete proposal to adopt the ideas of Gelpi (1979) who has dealt with the social construction of knowledge in relation to production as the most fruitful basis of a curriculum theory for adult and lifelong learning.

In a later work, *Adult Education as Social Policy*, Griffin (1987) argues that policies of adult education are in some sense social, and hence subject to the influence of ideology and cultural reproduction. He suggests that a better way to understand adult education is through the critical analysis of the political, economic, and social aspects of its structure. Griffin acknowledges that the "analysis of any kind of educational policy will of necessity be a complicated exercise" (p. 133), given the lack of standards and prescriptive nature of adult education.

Collins (1991) has offered a similar argument against forms of adult education based purely on psychology and technical rationality. Like Griffin, he also decries the concentration of adult educators on technique and method at the expense of broader social and political analyses. He sees the field of adult education as controlled by the ideology of technique. Collins softens his critique of the ideology of technique when he comes to discuss the elements of adult education programming by making it clear that he does not propose abandoning technique and concern for personal development but rather its authoritative deployment.

Collins takes the vantage point of the critical social theorists Habermas, Marcuse, Adorno, Bourdieu, and Horkheimer. It is his judgment that Habermas's fresh approach to dialogue as communicative action and praxis as a dialectical process adds an important element to Freirean theory. He is also informed in his analyses by the concepts of Foucault and Gramsci on power, knowledge, and hegemony.

Collins's own theory of adult education, which is based on social learning theory, is "directed at social structures and practices that enhance or obstruct the potential for autonomous learning" (p. xii). In his view, this theory should inform both research and practice in the field of adult education. According to Collins, this approach holds potential for enhancing the vocation, mission, and competence of adult educators. Rather than relying on behaviorist philosophy, adult educators should focus on caring relationships in pedagogical settings. One sees here the combination of critical theory, phenomenological analysis, and humanistic concern.

In addition to critical social theory, Collins finds Freire's work on adult education and community development particularly helpful in program planning. He stresses the importance of attending to values in the evaluation process, and critiques the emphasis on the professionalization of the field at the expense of social action.

Collins points out that many adult educators who have used the work of critical theory have reduced their insights to psychology and have not adequately probed its ethical and political implications for a transforming pedagogy. He calls for political involvement in addition to theoretical work, teaching, and analysis. Educators should be involved in movements for social change. He also cautions against some of the negativism and pessimism among social theorists. Collins presents the best summary of this thought:

> A critical practice of adult education provides a context where
> shared commitments towards a socially more free, just, and rational society will coalesce. If these shared concerns are to

drive a transformative pedagogy, though, conventional notions of professionalization will have to be set aside in favour of a vocation that seeks to work directly with the kind of popular constituencies identified in previous chapters and create opportunities for alternative democratic discourses within formal agencies. Ultimately, a vocation to adult education seeks to realize, as critical practice, a just state of affairs where education is determined through the practical interests of free men and women. (pp. 119–120)

While there are many in the field of adult education intrigued with the precepts and implications of critical theory, several are emerging who suggest a new role for critical theory. Finger, for instance, opened an examination of new social movements (NSMs) as indicative of a "transition from the old social and political movements to new ones . . . herald[ing] a new conception of adult education" (1989, p.15). He suggests that a truly critical perspective places the individual as the central focus with the role of adult education being the fostering of such cultural transformation and self-actualization of the person. Welton (1993b) furthers this dialogue by observing that the new social movements are precursors to a new historic movement and a "concept of social justice attuned to the particular predicament of the marginalized and underprivileged" (p.161). Welton concludes, "From a critical educational perspective, the full developmental potential of nature and human beings cannot unfold if the present values and institutional arrangements persist" (p.163). Finally, Wilson (1993) echoes Collins's concern for the detrimental emphasis on professionalization of adult education. Wilson's argument centers on the issue underlying the predominant concern for professionalization, namely that of control of the discipline itself. He critically suggests that our "social movement heritage met its demise . . . with the emergence of the professionalization movement," an unfortunate direction in light of our goal of "understanding and acting effectively in our educational world" (p.14).

Feminist Theory

Feminist theory is a comprehensive philosophical perspective that seeks to explain the nature of unequal power relations based on gender, race, and class. There is no one model of feminist theory. Rather, it is a body of interrelated principles that seeks to explain women's oppression. The feminist perspective in adult education, known generally as feminist pedagogy, has its roots in the radical philosophy of education, as well as critical theory and humanistic psychology. An underlying assumption of feminist theory and feminist pedagogy is that unequal power relations exist that foster the oppression of women. Feminist pedagogy seeks to address the oppression of women through the context of education. It can be said that all of feminist pedagogy is emancipatory in focus and is concerned with the empowerment of women (Hayes, 1989; Maher, 1987; Tisdell, 1993). However, Tisdell (1993) points out that although feminist pedagogy is emancipatory in focus, not all feminist pedagogy literature deals with the nature of structured power relations or women's collective experience of oppression.

A helpful way to examine feminist pedagogy in adult education is through Maher's (1987) analysis. Maher sees feminist pedagogy as falling into two categories: the liberation models and the gender models. The liberatory models approach education from the perspective of neo-Marxist educational theorists and critical theory. Concerned with the structured nature of power relations and systems of oppression based on gender, race, and class that are reinforced through education, critical or liberation models of feminist pedagogy seek to address structured power relations both in the classroom and outside the classroom in the academy and society. They attempt to recover women's voices, experiences, and viewpoints and use these as a means for self-discovery and resistance. Although heavily influenced by the work of Paulo Freire and neo-Marxist educational theorists, liberatory feminist pedagogy is critical of Freire and Marxist educators because of their lack of attention to oppressions based on gender and race, or the interlocking systems of oppression involving gender, race, and class.

A feminist adult educator writing from this perspective is Hart. In *Working and Educating for Life: Feminist and International Perspectives on Adult Education*, Hart (1992) examines and critiques the nature of work and of worker education in a patriarchal market economy and the underlying assumptions, attitudes, and themes of work and worker education as it is presented in much of the adult education literature. She takes issue with the valuing of commodity production over subsistence production because it is subsistence production that sustains life. Gender and race/ethnicity relations are at the center of Hart's analysis since it is mainly women, people of color, and peasants, both men and women, who do the subsistence work throughout the world. Hart offers a view of the possibilities of what work and worker education might look like if work were primarily conceived of as activity that supports human life rather than being conceived of as primarily activity which leads to profit. Hart uses mothering as an example and a metaphor for life affirming work because mothering and other subsistence work are based on connections and relationships absolutely essential to our survival. She calls for the development of principles and premises of an education "which is similarly productive in the life giving, life-enhancing sense as production for life . . . an education for life must deliberately reestablish the original connection between human work or production and the preservation and improvement of life" (p. 213).

Another adult educator writing from the liberatory feminist perspective is Blundell. Blundell (1992) offers a critique of the curriculum of adult education based on a feminist analysis. According to Blundell, although women constitute a majority of both teachers and students in adult education, no detailed research has focused on gender issues in relation to the curriculum of adult education. Her discussion is structured around the four major discourses within the social and political theory of feminism—liberal, radical, Marxist, and socialist feminism. She argues that adult education often successfully masks its patriarchal bias by not examining the role knowledge plays in legitimizing existing gender relations. Blundell calls for a feminist transformation of adult education curriculum which will "transcend the needs-meeting and ultimately reinforcing ideology in to which adult education currently [is] locked" (p. 214).

The gender models of feminist pedagogy are concerned with those aspects of female identity that come from women's socialization as nurturers. They focus on the individual rather than the structure of power relations in society. These models of feminist pedagogy are emancipatory in the personal psychological sense, but do not necessarily attempt to address the structure of power relations in the larger context of society. According to proponents of this perspective, women's concern for connection, relationships, and responsibility for others makes them more empathetic, sensitive, and more able to express emotions than men. Feminists within this perspective view knowledge as contextual and subjective rather than universal. They affirm a "connected" way of knowing that comes from women's socialization in the role of nurturers, and they critique masculine thought and the universality and objectivity of the scientific method.

Belenky, Clinchy, Goldberger, and Tarule's (1986) book, *Women's Ways of Knowing: The Development of Self, Voice, and Mind*, articulates a gender model of feminist pedagogy that advocates a "connected" approach to education. This approach affirms women's experience, voices, and ways of knowing. According to Belenky et al., the nature of truth and reality and the origins of knowledge shape the way we see the world and ourselves as participants in it. "If a woman is to consider herself a real knower, she must find acceptance for her ideas in the public world" (p. 220). In "connected" education, the teacher tries to create a learning environment in which the members can nurture each other's thoughts to maturity. The goal of connected education is to help women to develop their own authentic voices and to see themselves as independent thinkers and constructors of knowledge.

Also approaching adult education from a gender model, Hayes (1989) questions the effectiveness of traditional instructional practices in light of women's experiences and stresses the need for a feminist approach to teaching that encompasses teacher-learner collaboration, cooperative communication styles, and a holistic approach to learning and theory building. Hayes and Smith (1994) have analyzed the portrayal of women in the major journals in adult education and offer new educational strategies for research, teaching, and learning. They call for research on women and gender in adult education that uses women's experiences and perspectives as a focal point. This women-centered focus will allow adult education scholarship to strive for a more pluralistic understanding of women and men as learners and to move toward a broader understanding of gender as a socially and culturally defined system that shapes and is shaped by adult education.

Both the liberatory model and the gender model of feminist pedagogy have significant implications for adult education. Maher (1987) recommends a synthesis of the two models to create a model of feminist pedagogy that includes both the liberatory model's emphasis on power and the gender model's emphasis on the personal domain.

Such a model could promote both personal agency and public effectiveness. Also advocating a synthesis of the two approaches, Tisdell (1993) has suggested that adult educators who want to adopt feminist emancipatory practices must examine how their practices reinforce or challenge the nature of structured power relations based on gender, race, and class, and must also affirm ways of knowing that do not conform to the traditional model of education based on a rationality that is socially constructed by white males.

Analytic Philosophy of Adult Education

The influence of analytic philosophy among British and American philosophers has diminished greatly in the past 15 years. In the field of philosophy of education, books and articles in this genre have become increasingly rare. In adult education, Lawson (1982) has continued to work within this philosophical tradition. One of the continuing values of his work is that it contains a well-thought-out critique of radical theorists in adult education. While his criticisms are mainly directed at the theoretical assumptions of the new sociology of education in Britain, the logic of his argument extends to radical educators who have made use of critical theory and feminist pedagogy.

Lawson provides keen insights into adult education issues by using the methods of conceptual analysis. He contends that conceptual analysis has an important role even in discussions about practical issues. His collection of essays focuses on the interplay between philosophy and practice.

Lawson attempts to show that the use of concepts in educational discourse is connected with values and assumptions associated with a philosophical tradition. Both he and Peters, whose work he draws on extensively, ascribe to the values and assumptions of classical liberal education. The definition of education used by analytic philosophers stresses intellectual understanding and organized bodies of knowledge. Lawson admits that in other traditions education has a different meaning, one which often includes political action or vocational education.

Since conceptual analysis has come under attack from radical adult educators in Britain, Lawson tries to show the conceptual weakness of radical arguments. Radicals argue that the traditional liberal education is not objective, open, and truthful, but is biased in favor of elites. Their attempt, in Lawson's analysis, is to reconstruct or radicalize adult education by basing it on working class values and having it address working class experience. Thus in their view education should be a cultural and political tool.

Lawson points out how the radical position is based on a relativism which rejects universal values, arguing that "there are values which are so universal that they can be used to judge on issues . . . and they are used by members of many groups" (p. 15). Lawson argues that the principle of rationality is such a universal and it is on this principle that he bases his defense of liberal education and his rejection of the radical argument. A commitment in education to predetermined political goals such as socialism does not, in his view, respect the freedom and rationality needed in the educational process. Lawson prefers to base education on such universal values as rationality and understanding rather than on the values of particular classes in society.

In arguing against radical adult educators, Lawson rejects the new sociology of knowledge upon which their educational philosophy is based. He argues that this sociological theory, which is so insistent in pointing out the ideologies and myths of traditional education, has its own ideology, usually a form of Marxist theory. Thus Lawson argues that when radicals speak of false consciousness, they implicitly presume that they have a true consciousness or valid beliefs about society, social roles, and social relationships. Lawson contends that their analysis is no more correct than the analyses presented by liberal educators.

In rejecting radical arguments, Lawson defends important aspects of liberal education. Against educational deschoolers he defends the autonomy of institutions to educate. He asserts the value of curriculum or subject teaching, made up of public forms of knowledge, to counter the views of educators who see teachers as mere facilitators or coordinators of student learning. Finally, he asserts the objectivity and timelessness of knowledge against excessive democratization of knowledge in which all are involved in making knowledge. Lawson questions all forms of political and community education as not only ideologically dangerous but also as diverting educational resources "away from the more traditional role of general cultural diffusion and personal development through studies on a broad perspective" (p. 31).

In Lawson's conceptual analysis of all issues relating to adult education (e.g., lifelong learning, community education, the right to universal higher education, equal educational opportunity, training, relevance, teaching), the relevant criteria come from the philosophical traditions of British analytical philosophy and its justification of traditional liberal education. That there is no necessary connection between these two traditions is shown in the work of some North American analytical philosophers who espouse both progressive and radical standpoints in education.

Summary

Through this bibliographic essay we have attempted to update the original edition of *Philosophical Foundations of Adult Education*. As we noted in the preface to this second edition, there have been numerous developments in educational philosophy in general, and in adult education in particular, that we have acknowledged in this essay. And, as also indicated in the preface, we decided to use the original six schools or systems of philosophy as an organizing framework for this essay.

Most adult educators have encountered the issue of "political correctness" which is strongly linked to a liberal education perspective. Bloom's *The Closing of the American Mind* (1987) and Hirsch's *Cultural Literacy* (1987) are key publications fueling the debate over what should constitute curriculum in higher education. These works, reviewed in the section on liberal adult education, raise important issues on the nature of liberal lifelong learning.

As we discussed in our original edition, progressive education, which is based in rationalism and pragmatism, has had a pervasive influence in adult education. However, there has been little added to adult education from this perspective in the last 15 years. Rather, the history and meaning of progressive education have come under scrutiny by educational philosophers and social theorists such as Ravitch (1982), Rorty (1988), and Westbrook (1991). Analyses such as theirs about public education still need to be carried out in adult education.

In practice, much of adult education is behaviorist. This is especially true in the area of human resource development, or training in business and industry. Several contributions from the human resource development literature were reviewed in the section on behaviorist adult education. It is behaviorist adult education that has received the most critical attention from philosophers, especially those with humanist or radical orientations.

While much of adult education practice is behaviorist, much of the rhetoric is humanistic in its focus on individual growth and development. There have been several major additions to the literature from this perspective, including Stanage's (1987) work in phenomenology, McKenzie's (1991) notion of adult education as worldview construction, Mezirow's (1990, 1991) writings on transformative learning, and Jarvis's (1992) discussion of paradoxes of learning. These are reviewed in the section on humanistic adult education.

In our original chapter on radical adult education we stated that this orientation "has not had any great impact on the practice of adult education" (p. 170). While we still agree with that assessment, radical writers have had and continue to have an impact in their *critique* of practice and theories in adult education. They are providing us with tools to examine our practice and theory, and with new insights into understanding why things are the way they are. To some extent these critiques are resulting in experimentations with new ways of doing things, with a new openness to alternative perspectives, and with action imperatives on multiple levels. Reviewed in this section are contributions since 1980 from a Marxist perspective, from critical theory, and from feminist theory.

Finally, analytic philosophy, although receding in influence more than the above orientations, is revisited. Lawson's (1982) addition to the literature in this area is discussed, especially as it provides a critique of radical theorizing on adult education.

It is clear that there has been greater activity in some philosophical areas than in others. There have been numerous contributions from adult educators within humanistic and radical categories and from human resource development writers within the behaviorist tradition. Discussions in progressive and liberal areas have been situated more within general and higher education. Hopefully, the update provided in this bibliographic essay will stimulate further philosophical reflection and writing in adult education.

REFERENCES

Adler, M. (1982). *The Paideia Proposal.* New York: Macmillan.

Belenky, M. F., Clinchy, B. M., Goldberger, N. R., & Tarule, J. M. (1986). *Women's Ways of Knowing: The Development of Self, Voice, and Mind.* New York: Basic Books.

Berger, B. (1993). Multiculturalism and the Modern University. *Partisan Review, 60* (4), 526–534.

Bloom, A. (1987). *The Closing of the American Mind.* New York: Simon and Schuster.

Blundell, S. (1992). Gender and the Curriculum of Adult Education. *International Journal of Lifelong Education, 1* (3), 129–216.

Bowles, S., & Gintis, H. (1976). *Schooling in Capitalist America.* New York: Routledge and Kegan Paul.

Brockett, R. G. (Ed.). (1988). *Ethical Issues in Adult Education.* New York: Teachers College Press.

Brookfield, S. (1986). *Understanding and Facilitating Adult Learning.* San Francisco: Jossey-Bass.

Brookfield, S. (1987). *Developing Critical Thinkers.* San Francisco: Jossey-Bass.

Broudy, H. (1981). Between the Yearbooks. In J. Soltis (Ed.), *Philosophy of Education.* Chicago: University of Chicago Press.

Caffarella, R. S. (1993). Self-directed Learning. In S. Merriam (Ed.), *An Update on Adult Learning Theory,* New Directions for Adult and Continuing Education, No. 57. San Francisco: Jossey-Bass.

Candy, P. C. (1991). *Self-direction for Lifelong Learning: A Comprehensive Guide to Theory and Practice.* San Francisco: Jossey-Bass.

Carlson, R. (1989). Malcolm Knowles: Apostle of Andragogy. *Vitae scholasticae, 8*(1), 217–233.

Carnevale, A., Gainer, L., & Villet, J. (1990). *Training in America: The Organization and Strategic Role of Training.* San Francisco: Jossey-Bass.

Clark, M. C., & Wilson, A. L. (1991). Context and Rationality in Mezirow's Theory of Transformational Learning. *Adult Education Quarterly, 41*(2), 75–91.

Collard, S., & Law, M. (1989). The Limits of Perspective Transformation: A Critique of Mezirow's Theory. *Adult Education Quarterly, 39,* (2), 99–107.

Collins, M. (1991). *Adult Education as Vocation: A Critical Role for the Adult Education.* New York: Routledge.

Cremin, L. (1957). *The Transformation of the Schools: Progressivism in American Education, 1876–1957.* New York: Random House.

Cunningham, P. M. (1988). The Adult Educator and Social Responsibility. In R. G. Brockett (Ed.), *Ethical Issues in Adult Education* (pp.133–145). New York: Teachers College Press.

Dewey, J. (1938). *Logic: The Theory of Inquiry*. New York: Henry Holt & Co.

Elias, J. (1993). *Foundations and Practice of Adult Religious Education*. Malabar, FL: Krieger.

Elias, J. (1994). *Paulo Freire: Pedagogue of Liberation*. Malabar, FL: Krieger.

Fass, P. (1989). *Outside In: Minorities and the Transformation of American Education*. New York: Oxford University Press.

Finger, M. (1989). New Social Movements and Their Implications for Adult Education. *Adult Education Quarterly, 40*(1), 15–21.

Foltz, N. (Ed.). (1986). *Handbook of Adult Religious Education*. Birmingham, AL: Religious Education Press.

Freire, P. (1977). *Pedagogy in Process: The Letters to Guineau-Bissau*. New York: Seabury.

Freire, P. (1985). *The Politics of Education*. Granby, MA: Bergin and Garvey.

Freire, P., & Faundez, A. (1989). *Learning to Question: A Pedagogy of Liberation*. New York: Continuum.

Freire, P., & Macedo, D. (1987). *Literacy: Reading the Word and the World*. South Hadley, MA: Bergin and Garvey.

Gates, H. L. (1988). The Master Pieces: On Canon Formation and the Africal-American Tradition. In D. Gless & B. H. Smith (Eds.), *The Politics of Liberal Education*. Durham, NC: Duke University Press.

Gelpi, E. (1979). *A Future for Lifelong Education*. Manchester: Manchester University, Department of Adult Education.

Gilley, J., & Eggland, S. (1989). *Principles of Human Resource Development*. Reading, MA: Addison-Wesley.

Giroux, H. (1988). Liberal Arts Education and the Struggle for Public Life: Dreaming about Democracy. In D. J. Gless & B. H. Smith (Eds.), *The Politics of Liberal Education*. Durham, NC: Duke University Press.

Griffin, C. (1983). *Curriculum Theory in Adult and Lifelong Learning*. New York: Nickols Publishing.

Griffin, C. (1987). *Adult Education as Social Policy*. London: Croom Helm.

Hart, M. U. (1990). Critical Theory and Beyond: Further Perspectives on Emancipatory Education. *Adult Education Quarterly, 40*, 125–138.

Hart, M. U. (1992). *Working and Educating for Life: Feminist and International Perspectives on Adult Education*. London: Routledge.

Hayes, E. R. (1989). *Insights from Women's Experiences for Teaching*. New Directions for Adult and Continuing Education, No. 43. San Francisco: Jossey-Bass.

Hayes, E. R., & Smith, L. (1994). Women in Adult Education: An Analysis of Perspectives in Major Journals. *Adult Education Quarterly, 44*(4), 201–221.

Hiemstra, R. (1988). Translating Personal Values and Philosophy into Practical Action. In R. G. Brockett (Ed.), *Ethical Issues in Adult Education*. New York: Teachers College Press.

Hirsch, E. D. (1987). *Cultural Literacy*. New York: Random House.

Hogan, D. (1985). *Class and Reform: School and Society in Chicago, 1880–1930*. Philadelphia: University of Pennsylvania Press.

Ihde, D. (1977). *Experimental Phenomenology*. New York: G. P. Putnam.

Inkster, I. (Ed.). (1985). *The Steam Intellect Societies: Essays on Culture, Education and Industry Circa 1820–1914*. Derby, England: Saxon Printing.

Jacobs, R. (1987). *Human Performance Technology: A Systems-Based Field for the Training and Development Profession*. Columbus, OH: ERIC Clearing house on Adult, Career, and Vocational Education, Information Series No. 326.

Jarvis, P. (1992). *Paradoxes of Learning: On Becoming an Individual in Society*. San Francisco: Jossey-Bass.

Kaplan, A. (1964). *The Conduct of Inquiry: Methodology for Behavioral Sciences*. New York: Chandler.

Keddie, N. (1980). Adult Education: An Ideology of Individualism. In J. Thompson (Ed.), *Adult Education for a Change*. London: Hutchinson.

Knowles, M. S. (1975). *Self-directed Learning*. New York: Association Press.

Knowles, M. S. (1980). *The Modern Practice of Adult Education: From Pedagogy to Andragogy*. Chicago: Association Press.

Knowles, M. S. (1989). *The Making of an Adult Educator: An Autobiographical Journey*. San Francisco: Jossey-Bass.

Lawson, K. H. (1982). *Analysis and Ideology: Conceptual Essays on the Education of Adults*. Nottingham: University of Nottingham.

Lazerson, M. (1971). *The Origins of the Urban School: Public Education in Massachusetts, 1870–1915*. Cambridge: Harvard University Press.

Maher, F. A. (1987). Toward a Richer Theory of Feminist Pedagogy: A Comparison of "Liberation" and "Gender" Models for Teaching and Learning. *Journal of Education, 169* (3). 91–100.

McKenzie, L. (1982). *The Religious Education of Adults*. Birmingham, AL: Religious Education Press.

McKenzie, L. (1991). *Adult Education and Worldview Construction*. Malabar, FL: Krieger.

McLagan, P. (1983). *Models for Excellence*. Arlington, VA: ASTD Press.

McLagan, P. (1989). *Models for HRD Practice*. Alexandria, VA: ASTD Press.

McLaren, P. (1993). *Paulo Freire: A Critical Encounter*. New York: Routledge.

McLaren, P. (1994). *Politics of Liberation: Paths from Freire*. New York: Routledge.

Merriam, S. B. (Ed.). (1982). *Linking Philosophy and Practice*. San Francisco: Jossey-Bass.

Merriam, S. B., & Caffarella, R. S. (1991). *Learning in Adulthood*. San Francisco: Jossey-Bass.

Mezirow, J. (1989). Transformation Theory and Social Action: A Response to Collard and Law. *Adult Education Quarterly, 39* (3), 169–175.

Mezirow, J. (1991). *Transformative Dimensions of Adult Learning*. San Francisco: Jossey-Bass.

Mezirow, J., & Associates. (1990). *Fostering Critical Reflection in Adulthood: A Guide to Transformative and Emancipatory Learning*. San Francisco: Jossey-Bass.

Nadler, L., & Nadler, Z. (1989). *Developing Human Resources* (3rd ed.). San Francisco: Jossey-Bass.

Podeschi, R. L. (1987). Andragogy: Proofs or Premises? *Lifelong Learning: An Omnibus of Practice*, *11*, (3), 14–16.

Powers, E. (1982). *Philosophies of Education*. Englewood Cliffs, NJ: Prentice Hall.

Pratt, D. D. (1993). Andragogy after Twenty-Five Years. In S. B. Merriam (Ed.), *An Update of Adult Learning Theory*. New Directions for Adult and Continuing Education, No. 57. San Francisco: Jossey-Bass.

Pratt, M. L. (1988). Humanities for the Future: Reflections on Western Culture. In D. J. Gless & B. H. Smith (Eds.), *The Politics of Liberal Education*. Durham, NC: Duke University Press.

Ravitch, D. (1982). *The Troubled Crusade: American Education, 1945–1980*. New York: Basic Books.

Rorty, R. (1988, April 4). That Old Time Philosophy. *New Republic*.

Rothwell, W., & Kazanas, H. C. (1989). *Strategic Human Resource Development*. Englewood Cliffs, NJ: Prentice Hall.

Rothwell, W., & Sredl, H. J. (1992). *The ASTD Reference Guide to Professional Human Resource Development Roles and Competencies* (Vol. I, 2nd ed.). Amherst, MA: HRD Press.

Schlesinger, A. (1992). *The Disunity of America*. New York: Knopf.

Shor, I., & Freire, P. (1987). *A Pedagogy for Liberation: Dialogues on Transforming Education*. South Hadley, MA: Bergin and Garvey.

Smith, B. H. (1992). Cult-Lit: Hirsch, Literacy, and the National Culture. In D. J. Gless & B. H. Smith (Eds.), *The Politics of Liberal Education*. Durham, NC: Duke University Press.

Spiegelberg, H. (1975). *Doing Phenomenology*. The Hague, Netherlands: Martinus Nijhoff.

Stanage, S. (1987). *Adult Education and Phenomenological Research: New Directions for Theory, Practice, and Research*. Malabar, FL.: Krieger.

Stewart, D., & Mickunas, A. (1974). *Exploring Phenomenology*. Chicago: American Library Association.

Thompson, J. (Ed.). (1980). *Adult Education for a Change*. London: Hutchinson.

Thompson, N. (1984). Adult Religious Education Life and Nurture. In M. Taylor (Ed.), *Changing Patterns of Religious Education*. Nashville, TN: Abingdon.

Tisdell, E. J. (1993). Feminism and Adult Learning. In S. B. Merriam (Ed.), *An Update of Adult Learning Theory*. New Directions for Adult and Continuing Education No. 57. San Francisco: Jossey-Bass.

Tough, A. (1971). *The Adult's Learning Projects*. Toronto: Ontario Institute for Studies in Education.

van Manen, M. (1990). *Researching Lived Experience: Human Science for an Action Sensitive Pedagogy*. New York: State University of New York Press.

Vogel, L. (1991). *Teaching and Learning in Communities of Faith*. San Francisco: Jossey-Bass.

Welton, M. (1993a). The Contribution of Critical Theory to Our Understanding of Adult Learning. In S. B. Merriam (Ed.), *An Update on Adult Learning*

Theory. New Directions for Adult and Continuing Education, No. 57. San Francisco: Jossey-Bass.

Welton, M. (1993b). Social Revolutionary Learning: The New Social Movements as Learning Sites. *Adult Education Quarterly, 43*(3), 152–164.

Westbrook, R. (1991). *John Dewey and American Democracy.* Ithaca: Cornell University Press.

Westwood, S. (1980). Adult Education and the Sociology of Education: An Exploration. In J. Thompson (Ed.), *Adult Education for a Change.* London: Hutchinson.

Wilson, A. L. (1993). The Common Concern: Controlling the Professionalization of Adult Education. *Adult Education Quarterly, 44* (1), 1–16.

Youngman, F. (1986). *Adult Education and Socialist Pedagogy.* London: Croom Helm.

AUTHORS

JOHN ELIAS is Professor of Religion and Education at Fordham University, New York. He is also the author of *Foundations and Practice of Adult Religious Education, Studies in Theology and Education, Psychology and Religious Education, Moral Education: Secular and Religious,* and *Paulo Freire: Pedagogue of Liberation.*

SHARAN MERRIAM is Professor of Adult Education at the University of Georgia, Athens, Georgia. She is the author of *Linking Philosophy and Education, Learning in Adulthood, Case Study Methods in Education, Adult Education: Foundations of Practice* and the editor of *Selected Writings on Philosophy and Adult Education.*

NAME INDEX

Adler, Mortimer, 9, 21, 35, 210
Apps, Jerold, 221
Aquinas, St. Thomas, 16, 21, 176
Aristotle, 2, 9, 14–15, 23–24, 112, 176
Augustine, St., 15–16, 30
Ayer, A. J., 179–180

Bacon, Sir Francis, 17, 80
Barro, Stephen M., 90–91
Beck, George, 16
Belenchy, M. F., 233
Bellow, Saul, 212
Benne, Kenneth, 10, 61, 65
Bennett, William, 212
Berger, Birgitte, 213
Bergevin, Paul, 10, 45, 59–60, 65–66, 72–73, 129, 209, 221
Bernstein, Basil, 226
Blakely, Robert, 10, 67
Bloom, Allan, 210–213, 236
Blundell, S., 232
Bowles, Samuel, 214
Brameld, Theodore, 11, 142–143
Brockett, R. G., 208
Brookfield, Stephen, 218, 221–223
Broudy, Harry, 209
Buber, Martin, 224
Bugental, James F. T., 114–115

Caffarella, R., 218
Camus, Albert, 10
Candy, P. C., 218
Carlson, Robert, 214
Carnavale, A., 218
Clark, M. C., 222
Collard, S., 222
Collins, Michael, 215, 228–230
Combs, Arthur W., 129
Comenius, Bishop John, 46, 112
Comte, Auguste, 80
Counts, George, 11, 49–50, 142
Cremin, Lawrence, 17, 51–53, 213
Cunningham, Phyllis M., 208

Darwin, Charles, 46–51, 81
Davidson, John, 20
Davis, James, 36
Dearden, R., 226.
Descartes, Rene, 81
Dewey, John, 1, 10, 15, 17, 47–50, 53–65, 74–75, 129, 187, 207–209, 214, 219–223
Eggland, S., 216
Elias, John L., 65, 209, 225
Erasmus, D., 16, 110, 112

Fass, Paula, 214
Faundrez, Antonio, 225
Ferrer, Francisco, 141

SUBJECT INDEX